the ROAD to EMMAUS

Rembrandt, *Supper at Emmaus*
Courtesy Jacquemart-André Museum, Paris

the
ROAD *to*
EMMAUS

Reading Luke's Gospel

by Jan Wojcik

PURDUE UNIVERSITY PRESS

West Lafayette, Indiana

Book and jacket designed by Russell J. Merzdorf

Library of Congress Cataloging-in-Publication Data

Wojcik, Jan, 1944–
    The road to Emmaus : reading Luke's gospel /
by Jan Wojcik.
        p.   cm.
    Bibliography: p.
    Includes index.
    ISBN 1-55753-000-9 :
    1. Bible. N.T. Luke—Criticism, interpretation,
        etc. 2. Jesus
    Christ—Gnostic interpretations. I. Title.
    BS2595.2.W65 1989
    226'.406—dc19   88-27313

Printed in the United States of America

For **Christine Zavgren**

in gratitude for her gifts of insight.

The Messiah will come as soon as the most un-
bridled individualism of faith becomes
possible...Its symbolic presentation
the resurrection of the mediator in
a single individual.

Franz Kafka, **Parables**

Table of Contents

Acknowledgments

The discussion at the beginning of chapter 3 features the early Christian Father Tertullian. He appears as a man of severe, orthodox views. Yet he reads the Christian gnostic Marcion so closely, if critically, that we can now reconstruct Marcion's ideas, even though all of his original writings have been lost. Indeed, so careful is Tertullian's evocation of what Marcion wrote that today readers of Tertullian can occasionally find themselves agreeing with Marcion even while Tertullian is contending the point.

This book has already been blessed by equally critical, albeit more sympathetic readers. Some came through the anonymous kindness of the editorial process. Some I know by name. Donald Seybold was the first. His observations usually came to down to a single, unsettling question: "What are you trying to say?" Raymond Frontain suggested attempting to describe the gospels as clearly as they were written. Warren Wigutow tested what is said about gnosticism in these pages against what lives on in his soul of ancient, gnostic insight. He also helped considerably with orthodox spelling. Would that these generous readers had had an easier time or a more fruitful consequence to their labors of assistance. Not every author can be the equals of his readers.

This book was also blessed with patrons at the most ineffable and vulnerable point of its existence: precisely before the author found out what he was trying to say. Jacob Adler, head of the English Department at Purdue University, and Leon Gottfried, his successor, provided the author the time, resources, and encouragement such a knotty question needs. Owen Brady, dean of Liberal Studies at Clarkson University, supported research trips to libraries at Yale University and the University of Toronto. He also offered continual encouragement and the funds to hire editorial assistance. James Nolte of the Clarkson University Library found many of the old, obscure books any new book on this topic has for its meat and potatoes. John Serio taught the author how to enter ancient words of wisdom into RAM, and David Bray retrieved them when they got lost in there.

My gratitude extends to the trustees of both Purdue and Clarkson universities. The sabbatical leaves they granted the author revived the spirit of Tertullian in another way. Both universities under their control serve primarily to educate young engineers, scientists, and business people. Yet both allow that the knowledge of ancient scripture and gnostic insight might still have something useful to teach the modern student of orthodox technique.

J. W.
Potsdam, New York
2 February 1989

Introduction

Gnosis, Magic, and Parataxis

> I have special eyes, so I can say
> anything—
> like "invisible trees."
>
> *Max Wojcik*

Two disciples are walking toward the village of Emmaus some "60 stradia" or 18.4 miles from Jerusalem. The precision of the measurement contrasts with the ambiguity in language in the rest of the scene. At first we are told only by indirect discourse that the two talk about the strange events of the past few days. We hear what they say only later in the episode when they share their discussion with a stranger who meets them on the road and asks them about their troubled mood—as if he, the stranger, can only hear as indistinctly as we, the readers. It is as if at this point in the scene, the stranger and the reader approach the walking disciples from the same distance, at the same pace. The stranger and the reader hear what the disciples say at the same time. The two disciples explain that Jesus had been arrested, tried, and executed. Now there are reports that he has risen from the dead and has spoken to several of his woman followers. A key phrase occurs early in the episode as the stranger approaches them and "their eyes were held" (*hoi de ophthalmoi auton ekratounto*) and they were unable to see that the stranger was the very Jesus of whom they were speaking. What has proved to be an unsettling word in the phrase is the passive verb *ekratounto* (were held).

Students of writing know that all passive verbs are troublesome. Some are teasers which separate the act from the agent grammatically for a moment so that the reader learns independently what has happened and who did the deed. The separation is usually slight and momentary; the verb and the agent close together in the sentence, so that the effect is only a subtle hint that the action speaks louder than the agent: "The deed was done—by *him.*" Writers use passive verbs with agents to stress the impersonality of the force

1

applied, or to hedge their bets a bit about how the deeds were done. Editors, sensitive to the reader's right to know, often urge writers to be more actively forthright: "Tell us *she* did it."

Some passive verbs such as *ekratounto* are coy—or sly. They appear without the agent, as if to suggest the deed was done all right, but one cannot say at this time who it was that did the deed, or to suggest the writer is unwilling to tell or that the writer does not know. *Ekratounto* is coy if Luke is suggesting that we decide for ourselves who did the holding—or sly if suggesting no reader will ever know. No matter how many times we read this passage we can never even find out how the deed was done: by a disguise, a mist, or a divine intervention blocking the neurological connection between the eyes and brains of these two men? Was it because of their natural psychological disinclination to see alive a man they knew was dead? Did Jesus apply the blinders, or did God? Still, and perhaps more significantly, the narrator will never say *why* the deed was done. What is the point of blinding these men so that they could not get an answer to their questions about Jesus' resurrection right away?

This book is more or less about how that mysterious passive verb *ekratounto* has been translated and understood over almost 1,800 years of Christian biblical interpretation. Gnostic interpreters felt free to imagine any number of agents who could have done the holding. Orthodox interpreters in reaction have also imagined certain agents but carefully restrict the possibilities. We must account for why both kinds of readers felt impelled to supply an agent to complete the action of the verb and why they insist the text must point out certain meanings.

Second-, third-, and fourth-century writers known as gnostics were perhaps the first to embroider on the word with eerie, fascinating retellings of the Myth of the Risen Savior—sometimes named Jesus—who mysteriously disguised himself to illustrate for his followers how hard it is to be certain about anything in this earthly abode of illusions. Original written documents recording their imagination and thought first came to light forty years ago in a jar near the Egyptian town of Nag Hammadi. Marcion, a second-century Christian critic inclined to gnosticism, did not write a gospel narrative of his own. Instead, in the spirit of gnostic revisionism, he fashioned a new canon by throwing out all the other gospels save Luke's. He then cut Luke's Gospel to the point where the whole Jesus story seemed to center around Jesus' magical power to do what he wished in the abode of illusions. The Emmaus episode survived Marcion's cuts. One question that concerns us here is: What drew these writers to feature something very much like Luke's special narrative description of Jesus as a magical, risen savior?

It is not easy to say, because many of the early gnostic thinkers were silenced. No original copies of Marcion's expurgated Luke survive. Single copies of the gnostic gospels were buried about 400 C.E. probably to escape burning at the hands of zealous orthodox Christians. Only in recent years have scholarly editions of these manuscripts appeared that can take their place beside the enormously greater library of orthodox Christian writings. Only now can careful comparisons be made between them, so that we can assess their affinities as well as their emphatically different ways of interpreting everything. Certain gnostic narratives can now be tentatively read as literary interpretations of Luke's narrative Emmaus scene. They emphasize the mysteriousness. They appear to make the risen savior's magical appearance more inscrutable, less open to suggestion and reflection. The wondering disciples are often left speechless, whereas Luke's two disciples are allowed the final word.

In contrast, the more established and self-confident orthodox critical tradition is full of definitive explanations as to how and why the eyes of the two disciples were held—and who did it. Many of the explanations are ingenious, imaginative, original; and more than a few of them are contradictory. But none of them frankly is completely satisfactory. Not one orthodox interpreter has ever ventured the opinion that perhaps Luke, fascinated by gnostic reticence, purposefully and freely refrained from telling why the disciples' eyes were held. This is surprising, because by the law of averages this explanation must have occurred to someone at some point—if the interpreters themselves were free to ask any questions they wanted of this text. Martin Luther and John Calvin were the first to come close when they speculated that there were certain riddles in the episode that interpretation would never resolve; but they and others in the tradition, beginning with the Christian Fathers and continuing to the scientific exegetes of our day, have displayed only glimmers of insight about how even a presumably sacred writer like Luke could be sly. Why can they not see what is there on the page?

This blindness to insight is an interesting phenomenon in itself. It suggests quite simply that Christian interpreters have not been free to ask any questions they wanted of this text. Perhaps the blindness occurs because after their initial brush with gnosticism, orthodox interpreters have trained themselves to repress seeing anything in the gospels or scriptures that might appear tainted with gnostic impertinence on the topic of Jesus, as Luke's passive verb and other literary effects he uses might appear to be.

It is also possible to build a case for how this passive verb and other literary effects like it *might* be understood. Perhaps the riddle of the passive verb holds a key to interpreting this episode, Luke's Gospel, and the other Christian scriptures. One begins with the premise that many things, even in the orthodox gospels, are intended to remain provocative. "Gnosis," "magic," and "parataxis" refer to the other literary effects Luke uses to fill his narrative with the riddle of the passive verb.

Gnosis is the intuitive apprehension of spiritual truths. The term literally refers to a mind acting like a mind—or the mind "minding" itself. In its usual religious application, the word refers to a certain process of mind where the mind thinks for a while and then makes an intuitive leap at a certainty about God or Truth that it is suddenly sure it can grasp. What it "minds" is its own limits of knowing, but in the quintessential gnostic act the mind transcends its limits with an intuitive leap to a conviction toward which rational thinking apparently tends. There is something inherently progressive and creative about this kind of thinking, something unbounded and free. Thinking yields to conviction without the mind being bound to trace the niceties of every logical step in between. At the same time, there is something inherently conservative about it. If the mind is not bound to logic, then it can discover anything the will wants it to. Often enough this turns out to be something the mind was already prepared to know—and perhaps secretly already knew. The leap from logic to conviction is simply a satisfying return. In this case, a moment of genuine surprise occurs because the mind had not realized that it could actually think for a while and rationally justify what it already intuited. In either case, there is also something passive about the gnostic moment of truth. Another critical component of gnosis is that the leap to conviction is aided and abetted by some force that can literally "hold the mind's eye" until it is ready to be opened to a perception. It is never quite clear where this force comes from, and this explains the proclivity to use unattributed passive verbs in accounting for its intervention. Often it is depicted as coming from God, but it could come from the spirit world indiscriminately, or from someplace else in the mind or soul.

The Emmaus episode and other renditions of the Myth of the Risen Savior in the gnostic scriptures that we consider in these pages provide verbal pictographs of both directions thought takes in the gnostic religious experience, as well as its necessary outside intervention. A disguised master instructs docile disciples who are *already* curious about what the master will teach. The disciples hang on every word the master says, but do not come to understand the full extent of what they are hearing until a magical moment at the end of the instruction when the master throws off the disguise and appears as he really is. The instruction prepares for the revelation; but the revelation provides the teaching an explosive, emotional release that always comes unexpectedly. This experience seems to be the instruction's point. More important than the logic of what is said or understood is the experience of a progressive understanding suddenly exploding into insight. Gnosis could be called another term for "faith." At some point in any religious experience, one stops thinking in order to affirm a truth that is beyond the range of earthbound reason to secure, but "faith" is usually thought of as an act of recognizing for oneself a difficult truth that has been previously accepted by others. In contrast, the gnostic act discovers some truth that is either new or tailored specifically to the individual knower. The term is usually used for a special kind of faith in which the believer is made personally aware of the need to think and the need to stop thinking about what he or she knows, as well as the need to depend on some outside force for the insight.

This definition of gnosis passes over for the moment the distinct varieties of gnostic thought discovered by scholars such as Edwin Yamauchi, Henry Chadwick, and Malcolm L. Peel. It also passes over the broad content of ideas or dogma—its mythological constellations if you will—derived by great gnostic thinkers and described by Hans Jonas in his masterful survey *The Gnostic Religion.* This way of thinking naturally lends itself to particular and colorful notions of disembodied spirits, doubled worlds, and a suspicion for worldly concerns—not just the process of reason itself—which early Christian orthodoxy found easy to ridicule and condemn. That was because, strictly speaking, there were no constraints on what gnostic thinkers could imagine to be the source of the insights that came to them outside the parameters of evidence and reason. The superworldly world could have any kind of God. That God could be imagined in a variety of ways, especially if the thinker did not hold him or herself to the outlines of the images of God to be found in sacred images and idols or in any written scriptures.

Rather, the definition reflects the particular gnosis shared by the literary narratives, whether deemed heretical or orthodox, featured in these pages. Specifically, Luke in his Emmaus episode and throughout his gospel makes use of certain images in such a way as to suggest that he knew some gnostic notions of mind or at least the notions that gnostic narratives manifest.

Consider two other episodes unique to Luke's Gospel, one at the beginning of the story, another at the end. Both provide images of a powerful emotional experience. The experience leads to a rich understanding because in both cases, characters in the scene already know certain important religious teachings.

In the earlier episode, shepherds are out in their fields, keeping watch through the night over their flock. Angelic brilliance shatters the familiar darkness, and the shepherds are afraid at the sudden change. As Jesus does, the angel corrects their original response: "Do not be afraid." The angel proceeds to explain to them the meaning of the change from darkness to light. The messiah has been born. Then, like the disciples on the road to Emmaus, the shepherds almost immediately begin to think rationally about what they have seen and had explained: "Come, we must go straight to Bethlehem and see this thing that has happened, which the Lord has made known to us" (2:15).

In the later episode, two criminals hang adjacent to Jesus' cross. One of them taunts Jesus. The other has the presence of mind, in his great pain and terror, to rationalize why he and the other criminal are being executed. He corrects his fellow: "But this man has done nothing wrong." And he said, "Jesus, remember me when you come to your throne." He answered, "I tell you this: today you shall be with me in Paradise" (23:39–43). Luke creates many literary images of emotional, provocative insights, such as these characters have. They are to be found only in his gospel. I propose that these unique narratives suggest his interest in the gnostic way of thinking.

This hypothesis exploits an interesting ambiguity in current scholarship about gnosticism. On one hand, there is a scholarly consensus that some form of gnosticism quite likely captured the imagination of religious people who lived just before or during the time the gospels were written, although it is very difficult to trace any direct influence of any specific gnostic ideas on specific Christian scriptural texts. Still, Luke and John and Paul might have known these ideas—even in written form. On the other hand, there is a scholarly consensus that the Christian scriptures we have were written before the texts that were found at Nag Hammadi and that certain of these younger texts do betray the influence of their Christian literary forebears. But this strict chronology does not have to restrict the order of our comparisons if we are careful to keep the historical record straight. According to the German scholar Walter Schmithals, this ambiguity of influence creates a "hermeneutical circle" where we can compare orthodox and gnostic texts with each other as if they were parts of a whole body of religious imaginative literature with fascinatingly different perspectives on common concerns about God and mystery and human life, and with ideas of the relation between venerable stories and events they did not anticipate. I argue that Luke adapted gnostic ideas to narrative forms that appropriated their spiritual energy for orthodox ruminations.

This hypothesis is compatible with the modified two-source theory that Father Joseph Fitzmyer defends in his massive commentary on Luke's Gospel in the Anchor Bible Series. According to this theory, Luke and Matthew drew on Mark for the basic narrative structure of their gospels. They also drew on a collection of sayings and stories with which they augmented Mark's spare narrative. It has been named "Q" from the German *Quelle,* or "source." Luke also possessed a unique collection of stories which Fitzmyer calls "L." It contains episodes such as the one on the road to Emmaus and the shepherds in the field at night. The episode of the two criminals executed with Jesus appears in Mark (15:27), but the words they speak with Jesus appear only in Luke. Fitzmyer claims that at this remove in time, it is impossible to say whether Luke drew this sort of material from eyewitness reports to which he alone was privy, or whether he drew it from his own imagination (p. 83; see his discussion of what he calls a "modified Two Source Theory," pp. 61–85).

It is therefore plausible to suppose that Luke did something more than snap already known or new source material into place. He might have modified or composed wholly new stories that would permit him to restructure the order of all of his inherited materials. As he did so, gnostic narratives might have helped Luke to envision how the restructuring of Mark would work. They drew him to choose (or contrive) certain episodes such as the shepherds in the field or certain sayings such as the parables of the Good Samaritan or the Forgiving Father (Fitzmyer's preferred title for the parable of the Prodigal Son) or the story of Jesus' revelation to the disciples on the road to Emmaus. Each comes to a resolution surprising to the characters acting in the story; and surprise is the essence of the gnostic experience.

One striking piece of evidence that Luke is influenced by the gnostics is that for the Emmaus scene he certainly creates a narrative form unlike anything in the venerable scriptures to which his Jesus refers, and there is no other literature to which his narrative refers. A second is that he prepares for the scene throughout his gospel, beginning with his dedication to the revered Theophilus. In his preface Luke promises him a meaningful artifice: "an orderly account that you may understand the certainty of the words in which you have been instructed" (I:4). Note how nicely Luke's words sum up the gnostic learning experience. The new ordering promises its reader Theophilus (literally "a lover of God") new certainty about matters on which he already has some understanding. Origen thought the name was symbolic of the attitude with which the reader should read the gospel. Fitzmyer says more plainly: "Theophilus stands for the Christian readers of Luke's own day and thereafter" (p. 300). We could take a position somewhere between these two. With the name, Luke represents a new kind of reader. Theophilus becomes an idealized, implied reader in imitation of the two initially curious and eventually enthusiastic disciples. At the beginning of the gospel, Theophilus is counseled to concentrate on deconstructing the extraordinary juxtapositions of elements until he "gets" the basic meaning which is apparently implied. The moment of insight comes as refreshened memory ("what oft was thought, but ne'er so well express'd") as if one's deconstructive intuition recreates for the perceiver the magical moment of inspiration behind the creation of the artifice.

Luke found particularly attractive the gnostic license to ignore logical connections and explanations, especially when the mind might intuit what evidence could not strictly support. This way of thinking was especially amenable to considering the question of the relation of Jesus' story to the venerable tradition of scriptural stories that preceded his. How could something new be a part of something old? Narrative gnostic thinking could engage the question. What Luke added was a conviction that gnostic intuition did not exhaust the possibilities of the mind. Its insight was amenable to continuing intellectual reflection. For example, one simple difference between the gnostic experience of the two disciples in the Emmaus episode and that of the characters undergoing comparable events in the gnostic scriptures is that the Emmaus disciples continue to reason again after their explosive experience, with more or less the same curiosity they displayed before the stranger appeared on the road. Now they comment, albeit with enthusiasm, about the appropriateness of the way Jesus taught them: "Was not our heart burning as he spoke to us of the Scriptures?" In the gnostic scriptures, the same sort of revelation would overpower reason more emphatically and sometimes more definitively. In discussing these episodes, however, we should be guided less by what the characters say and do and more by the way the narration renders the scene. Luke's narration, for example, prepares the reader for their oddly mundane and tough-minded—we could say "embedded"—gnosis by its handling of magic and parataxis.

All magic, like the magic in this scene, resembles gnosis to the extent that a spectator (or victim) apprehends without being able to understand how the illusion occurs: "Now you see it; now you don't." In this scene, which occurs only in this gospel, Luke has a disguised Jesus instruct two disciples in spiritual truths as they walk pensively toward the village of Emmaus. This Jesus appears as Jesus and disappears in the same instant in the narrative. Luke handles the magic in the scene through the device of narrative parataxis.

Parataxis is like both gnosis and magic in that something appears in written discourse that literally is not stated. Ordinarily the term refers to the grammatical practice of connecting phrases or statements in a sequence with coordinating conjunctions that do not state the syntactical relation between the elements. The nineteenth-century Christian historian W. T. Brande defines it, commenting on certain biblical narrative techniques, as "[t]he mere ranging of propositions one after another, as the corresponding judgements present themselves to our mind, without marking their dependence on each other by way of consequence or the like" (p. 43). It is a device that can be used for great rhetorical effect when a speaker says one thing and then another and implies a connection between them without stating what it is: "It is written . . . but I say to you." Parataxis is like gnosis in that the auditor or spectator apprehends an unstated thought; it is like magic for the same reason. One "sees" an idea that appears as if it were out of nowhere. But—and this is the key point to understanding Luke's narrative gnosis—one is expected to start thinking about what parataxis provokes.

We find all three elements in this scene. "Their eyes are held" as the two disciples learn with enthusiasm that the rumors they have heard about Jesus are not only true, but the events they report were written down beforehand "in all the Scriptures." But they do not know who teaches them until the stranger magically appears as Jesus and immediately disappears into thin air at the same instant his lesson is through. They exclaim how their heart had been burning as he had taught them his strange and wonderful doctrine. Rhetorical parataxis becomes a narrative device when the narrator plays a trick on the readers. Although the readers know who the stranger is from the beginning, and thus have a superior perspective to the characters in the scene, they cannot, as the characters presumably do, overhear the lesson Jesus gives to his disciples. That is to say, the readers "know one thing," but at the same time they cannot know another; and so where the disciples are blind the readers are deaf. And interpreters of this scene and the others in the gospel under its spell should wonder analytically (and one would hope enthusiastically) about what connections should be made concerning what we see, what we hear, what we read, and what we know. One can argue through an analysis of this scene in the first chapter that there is an implication that such a connection must be made if Jesus' teaching is to be apprehended; if his place in *all* the scriptures is to become clear. Gnosis, magic, and parataxis are various forms of the art of uncanny and provocative coupling.

Any proposal for a new method of reading the Christian scriptures has to engage the question of why it has not been used before. Perhaps it is because the tradition of biblical scholarship has suffered from what Whitehead calls the "fallacy of misplaced concreteness" (p. 72). In order to deny the validity of any gnostic imagination or thought in any document considered to be orthodox, it was necessary to claim that scriptural texts referred to literal facts, or, if they exercised any imaginative license whatsoever, they referred to other palpable scriptural texts that stood in an unbroken continuity with the text at hand. Thus in Luke's Emmaus episode, biblical scholars stress the implication that Jesus' story belonged in the context of the older scriptures. They do not find it equally important that Luke refrained from speculating on precisely *how* it belonged. But the whole story of what goes on in the tradition of Christian biblical interpretation is even more interesting.

Elaine H. Pagels argues in her book on the gnostic gospels that the earliest ecclesiastical authorities used dogmatic interpretations of the Christian scriptures to narrow the scope of religious imagination. They did so to gain power. They declared as orthodox only certain lines of thought that they could comfortably control. For the same reason, they incorporated the Jewish scriptures into the canon of the Christian scriptures. They restricted the context in which the Christian scriptures could be understood to certain definitive texts to which the Christian scriptures themselves referred. This was one way to silence gnosticism's cry of the heart for a clean break with all previously written texts and, in fact, with the idea of textuality itself. Gnosticism wanted to turn away from the idea that texts have a texture which can be worked to a certain point without the text losing its integrity; stories can be varied and narratives can be rearranged with the kinship between model and imitation remaining palpable. This is the general principle behind the Jewish notion of midrash, the patristic notion of allegory, or the modern critical notion of palimpsest—text embroidered on text. To put it figuratively, narrative stories can be told in many different ways in the same way that wheat flour can be made into many different kinds of bread. Where the gnostics wanted to mix the dough of their religious stories each time from scratch, the orthodox critics wanted to bake the scriptures into a firm loaf according to an agreed upon recipe.

There is merit in Pagels's idea. We can extend it by examining the aesthetic dimension of the politicized process of scriptural interpretation she describes so well. Perhaps the early authorities did more than counter gnostic interpretations with dogmatic interpretations of Luke's Gospel. Perhaps they were unable to understand aspects of Luke's writing because he learned how to write in part from gnostic ideas, and these ideas in any form made no sense to the early authorities.

What attracted Luke to this way of writing was precisely its possibilities for raising unresolvable riddles. Perhaps he sensed the tendency in his fellow worshippers to be dogmatic about the new religious ideas that fascinated him. He understood that the question of the relation of Jesus' story to the venerable older scriptures was particularly susceptible to harsh or simplistic answers. With this new narrative style, he could feel confident that no critical reading could ever completely account for his insight about this question in *his* narrative artifice. Its measure was beyond what even the best rational or dispassionate reading could recover. Luke's narrative ineffability is the essence of his art. It is his particular articulation of religious freedom.

To the extent that the hypothesis appears reasonable, perhaps we gain a new, critical understanding of why orthodox readers have rarely read Luke's Gospel as literature. We return to Pagels's thesis about the antignostic tendencies in early orthodox authorities. Now we notice their corresponding distaste for the literary quality of the Christian narratives that they felt they knew well. The early, classically trained Greek Fathers expressed dismay at the grammatical crudities of *koine* gospel Greek, especially the paratactic sentence construction. This led to the concept of the *sermo humiles* of Augustine, according to which the gospel story is written poorly to reinforce the earthliness of its divine wisdom. In our own century, the German critic Dibelius has insisted that all the gospels are too crudely stitched together of rough fragments to be considered literature. He found the narrative arrangement paratactic as well, lacking the connecting rhetoric of *belles-lettres*. Luke's most recent comprehensive commentator, Joseph Fitzmyer, remarks that Luke has always been treated with considerable suspicion in the tradition precisely because of his literary effects—his polished preface and his extraordinarily unique and self-contained episodes such as the parables of the Good Samaritan and the Forgiving Father and the episode on the road to Emmaus. Perhaps, to put it simply, some of what is literary about Luke is also gnostic. And if everything gnostic is anathema to orthodox readers, then they will not readily honor what is literary in Luke.

But at the same time, this prejudice against the literary and gnostic has sometimes faltered. We can qualify Pagels's thesis when we note that even the earliest and most orthodox of Christian interpreters sometimes saw more (or less) in the scriptures than they would admit openly. Repression, blessedly, has its own weak moments, and insights flash free precisely from the point where we least expect to see them. When we look at the orthodox tradition, its *collective* insights suggest that even consciously repressed interpreters can see what they are not supposed to see. Today a few biblical scholars come close to understanding Luke's narrative ambiguity. Literature received as sacred writ provides a fascinating case study of what the special eyes of interpreters allow them to see—and not to see—about what the text says.

These insights inspire some thoughts in my epilogue about how the Christian scriptures can be read as literature. Luke's narrative raises more than one question. It is continuing an exploration into the relationship between different and even apparently antagonistic systems of belief that no believing Christian, Jew, gnostic, or agnostic ever need conclude. Luke, often called the genial physician, learned from the gnostics how to write a healing narrative. The insights it provoked provided punctuations, not conclusions, to an endlessly fascinating dialogue of the reader with the story. Luke's transformation of the gnostics' open-minded curiosity is evidence of gnosticism's useful and lasting contribution to religious thinking.

Chapter One

The Implied Author of the Emmaus Episode

> If every event which occurred could be
> given a name, there would be no need
> for stories.
>
> *John Berger,* Once in Europa

The Magical Encounter

The four canonical gospels describe many miracles, but only one *bona fide* magic trick. It serves as the climax to the episode toward the end of Luke's Gospel in which the resurrected Jesus in disguise meets two disciples on their way to the town of Emmaus and talks with them a while:

And now consider, two of them were going that very day to a village named Emmaus, which is sixty stradia from Jerusalem. And they were talking to each other about all these things that had happened. And it happened while they were conversing and arguing together, that Jesus himself also drew near and went along with them; but their eyes were held, that they should not recognize him. And he said to them, "What words are these that you are exchanging as you walk and are sad?" But one of them, named Cleopas, answered and said to him, "Are you the only stranger in Jerusalem who does not know the things that have happened there in these days?" And he said to them, "What things?" And they said to him, "Concerning Jesus of Nazareth, who was a prophet, mighty in work and word before God and all the people; and how our chief priests and rulers delivered him up to be sentenced to death, and crucified him. But we were hoping that it was he who should redeem Israel. Yes, and besides all this, today is the third day since these things came to pass. And moreover, certain women of our company, who were at the tomb before it was light, astounded us, and not finding his body, they came, saying that they had also seen a vision of angels, who said that he is alive. So some of our company went to the tomb, and found it even as the women had said, but him they did not see." But he said to them, "O foolish ones and slow of heart to believe in all that the prophets have spoken! Did not the Christ have to suffer these things before entering into his glory?" And beginning with Moses and with all the prophets, he interpreted to them in all the Scriptures the things referring to himself. And they drew near to the village to which they were going, and he acted as though he were going on. And they urged him, saying, "Stay with us, for it is getting towards evening, and the day is now far spent." And he went in with them. And it happened that when he reclined at table with them, he took the bread and blessed and broke and began handing it to them. And their eyes were opened, and they recognized him; and he vanished from their sight. And they said to each other, "Was not our heart burning within us while he was speaking on the road and explaining to us the Scriptures?" (Luke 24:13–35 after the translation of Joseph Fitzmyer).

The disguise or whatever power it is that "held their eyes" sets up the magic trick. It occurs when the disguise falls away, the disciples recognize him, and in the same instant, Jesus vanishes from their sight. It is magical because it is inexplicable.

There are many things remarkable about the trick *qua* trick. One is that it does not seem to faze its intended dupes in the least. The two disciples see the trick, or more properly, see that they have been tricked, but say not a word about it in the short scene after it occurs. They speak among themselves only about the mundane interpretation of "Moses and the Prophets" that Jesus led them through, "interpreting to them in all the Scriptures the things referring to himself." If the disciples are intended to serve as guides for the readers (or surrogates), then the narrative might imply that one should ignore its magical element and concentrate on Jesus' mundane reading. For the most part, that is what biblical interpretation has done, beginning with the early Christian Fathers and continuing until this day. According to Elaine Pagels, the earliest interpreters were especially attracted to the mundane in postresurrection narrative episodes such as this one because featuring ordinariness underscored the factual reality of the resurrection itself. Whereas Coleridge described the quality of aesthetic engagement as "the suspension of disbelief," early orthodox interpreters of the resurrection episodes did not have disbelief to suspend. Again, this instinct for the factual continues in modern orthodox interpretations.

But the narrative might imply that one should at least consider what the magic does in the scene. This could be done as an audience would accept the illusion of a magician, be entertained, and at the same time wonder at the meaning of the illusion itself as it comes forward to the eyes of the audience. That is to say that as readers of this text we might suspend our disbelief in the fiction of the text and we might take Jesus' magic disguise as equal in importance to his reference to the older scriptures. The interpreter would then respond to the text as an audience before a magician wonders not about the techniques the magician uses in doing a trick but enjoys experiencing an apparently magical appearance as if it actually did appear out of empty air. *Then* if they think about the trick at all, they might wonder whether this magician, like every magician, is not telling them something true about how unreliable human senses are, how easily we are beguiled, or further, how we are unaware that there are things hidden in the air all around us.

Four Authorities

To appreciate both the mundane and the magical requires attending equally to four different authorities in the scene. One of them, the most obvious, is Jesus. He is an explicit authority, for he tells the explicit disciples in the scene certain things in certain ways. The three others are implicit or implied. They do not take part in its action directly as the major character and the two minor characters do, but they certainly determine how that action is perceived. We begin to consider the implied authorities in order to appreciate how they work as foils for what the explicit authority, Jesus, does and says in the scene.

Probably the most familiar implied authority is the narrator who appears on the scene addressing the reader ("Now consider . . .") and sets the scene. Many narrators like this one are something like magicians. In this episode a hidden voice or *persona* (meaning "masked presence") is invisible to the characters in the scene, and the inner characters cannot hear what the narrator says. No one makes reference to the third-party reporter of his words and actions. Yet the hidden presence can see what the inner characters cannot see—that it is Jesus who is walking with them—and reports it only for the reader's discernment.

Narrators always allow readers to imagine scenes they themselves could never see on their own, or, to use an anachronistic analogy, serve like cameramen recording from a certain distance or perspective on the scene. A narrator always addresses an "implied reader," a shadowy character privy to the scene, to whom the narrator in this case reveals the identity of Jesus before the characters learn of it. The "implied reader" is by now a well-known term of Wayne Booth's referring to an idealized attentive listener. Real readers are, of course, always at arm's length from a text, but they can only get into it if a written surrogate is already on the written scene waiting to be enlivened by the real reader's imagination. All real readers instinctively imagine that a narration is being spoken by a narrator to an implied reader within the scene. This speech constitutes the ordinary magic of any narration. A voice coming from nowhere addresses an invisible listener.

What is special about this episode is that the narrator chooses to play on the ordinary magic of the narrative situation. The narrator hides certain things from the inner characters, and certain other things from the implied readers. The readers are not told which specific texts Jesus cites. It is always the essence of a magic trick first to beguile the senses of the audience in order to lead it to perceive only what the magician wants it to perceive. Only then can the revelation of the trick appear magical, coming precisely from where the audience was not expecting it. In this episode the trick is doubled. There is one for the characters in the scene with Jesus; another for the implied reader privy to the scene by the grace of the narrator's words.

The Real Magician

We have not yet considered the real magician, however. The narrator is the assistant of a hidden authority behind the scenes. Wayne Booth also helps us to identify its presence. According to Booth, every narrative scene implies an author—not a living person but the living person's written persona or in his terms the "author's second self" who governs the consciousness of the work as a whole and is the source of the norms embodied in the work. The relationship between them is never clear. One important reason for this is that a living person is very complex, changing from day to day, whereas an implied author is pinned down by the words that have been expressed. It is impossible to gauge the precise relation one had to the other during the day or the days in which the second was fixed. Furthermore, Booth suggests that an implied author is often far superior in intelligence and moral standards than any living human being could be. Writing a narrative is a form of self-aggrandizement (pp. 87, 105).

The implied author is also not to be mistaken for the narrator. Unlike the narrator, the implied author can tell us nothing. He, or better, it, has no voice, no direct means of communicating. It instructs us silently, through the design of the whole, with all the voices, and through all the means by which it has chosen to let us learn (Chatman, p. 148).

Perhaps we can make this clear by attributing to the implied author those hints the once-living author has left of his own reading and points of view. For example, in his exhaustive commentary on the Emmaus episode,

Luke's definitive modern commentator Father Joseph Fitzmyer points out that only Luke among the four evangelists uses certain Greek words, such as the preposition *enantion* (before) used in the phrase "a prophet mighty in deed and word *before* God" (24:19). Moreover, some of his words and grammatical expressions, such as *pros hesperan* (toward evening) (24:29), are what Fitzmyer calls "Septuagintisms"—vocabulary and phrases that reflect Luke's unique familiarity with the Septuagint Greek version of the Hebrew scriptures. This was a Greek translation of the Hebrew scriptures made about 300 B.C.E. by a legendary group of seventy scholars. "Septuagint" reflects the Latin word for seventy. Fitzmyer believes that most of the supposed semitisms of Luke's Greek actually reflect his mastery of the Septuagint Greek vocabulary and diction: ". . . 90 per cent of his vocabulary is found in the LXX [Septuagint], where it resembles most the vocabulary of Judges, Samuel, Kings, and above all 2 Maccabees" (p. 113). In the passage describing the encounter on the way to Emmaus, for example, there are words believed to betray Aramaic influence such as *ophethe* (he appeared) and *aute te hora* (at that hour), but in these cases, as in almost every other, Fitzmyer is able to refer to counterparts in the Septuagint. In his view, Luke is able to apply traditional biblical images to his image of Jesus as a restless progressive by his deft ability to use venerable language to hint at venerable themes.

The Repertoire of the Implied Author

Fitzmyer detects subtle references to other literary texts in the language Luke uses. There are certain characteristic motifs in the episode that appear in other places in Luke's Gospel. He mentions one character, Cleophas, by name, uses a place name, and emphasizes the revelatory nature of knowledge about Jesus. Similar motifs occur in other episodes in the Acts of the Apostles. Fitzmyer wholeheartedly accepts the almost universal scholarly consensus that the Luke writer wrote Acts. He also compares the gospel to the other synoptic gospel writers Mark and Matthew on the assumption that the distinctive use of similar material reveals authorial intention. Luke appears to feature the theme of "learning on the road" in both the Emmaus episode and throughout the gospel more than these other writers. Jesus is born "on the road," and much of his unique material ("L") features roads, such as the stories of the Good Samaritan and the Forgiving Father. One of Jesus' final acts in the gospel is to meet with two of his disciples on the road to Emmaus. Fitzmyer relates the theme or symbol of the road to Luke's progressive elaboration of preexisting theological ideas. Jesus refers to himself as the "messiah (or christ or 'anointed one') who had to suffer" while he is speaking to his disciples on the road to

Emmaus. Fitzmyer comments that Luke's view of Jesus' career "seems to be rooted in the pre-Lucan tradition which used Isaiah 40:3 to describe John the Baptist's role in the desert, making straight the way of the Lord. . . . Regardless of the specific meaning that *hodos* (way) would have had in John's career, it becomes for Luke a special designation for Jesus' salvific mission" (p. 169).

Apropos of the motif of the road and its corresponding theme of a progressive understanding, Fitzmyer makes a point germane to the thesis that Luke deliberately refrains from defining Jesus' precise relationship to the venerable stories that preceded his own. At the time Luke wrote, the meaning of the term "messiah" was generically used for certain historical persons regarded as anointed agents of Yahweh for the service or protection of his people, Israel (p. 198). But Luke was unique in holding the idea that Jesus was a suffering Messiah. "The idea of a suffering Messiah is found nowhere in the OT or in any Jewish literature prior to or contemporaneous with the NT. This is true despite what Luke says in 24:27,46 about 'Moses,' 'all the prophets,' and 'all the Scriptures.' Nor does any other NT writer speak of Jesus as the suffering Messiah" (p. 200). Luke develops this idea on his own. He seems to be the first interpreter of the Septuagint to apply the Suffering Servant passages in Isaiah (42:1; 43:10; 49:6; 52:13; 53:11) to the messiah, and then the first interpreter of Jesus to apply this new idea to him. These are further hints of the creative mind that works behind the veil of the language of the text.

Fitzmyer, who admires Luke's creativity, even forgives the historical inaccuracies in his early chapters. Scholars have not been able to fix on a single historical time when Augustus was emperor of Rome and Quirinius was governor of Syria, which Luke marks for the birth of Jesus (2:1–2). Fitzmyer is likewise unperturbed by the confusion confronting anyone who attempts to discover precisely where the village of Emmaus was. (His commentary reviews these historical obscurities thoroughly.) He says that Luke was a special kind of historian less interested in secular history and more in salvation history, and that Luke is always "right" in spirit even if not accurate in detail. This is close to Aristotle's distinction between history and poetry, whereby poetry mused on the philosophical implications of the recorded facts of history, but it is rarely evoked by biblical scholars because of their discomfort with the terms "literature" or "poetry" when speaking about the Bible. They will talk about literary or poetic *effects,* but only for the sake of discussing the ornamentation of much more interesting underlying theological ideas. Fitzmyer, on the other hand, with his sense of Luke as a *litterateur* who played with facts to draw out their meaning, might very well be comfortable using the term implied author as Booth describes it. Fitzmyer would only need to accept for the moment the specific term "novel" to stand for any narrative form. Booth writes: "Even the novel in which no narrator is dramatized creates an implicit picture of an author who stands behind the scenes, whether as stage-manager, as puppeteer, or as an indifferent God, silently paring his fingernails. This implied author is always distinct from the 'real man'—whatever we may take him to be—who creates a superior version of himself as he creates his work. . . . This second self is usually a highly refined and selected version, wiser, more sensitive, more perceptive than any real man could be" (p. 92).

It should be clear at this point that the work of biblical exegetes has much to teach literary critics intent on the implied authorities in a biblical narrative. Fitzmyer's massive commentary exhaustively reflects the best current orthodox research, thereby helping any scholar, orthodox or literary, to guard against making mistakes about technical matters of vocabulary, idioms, rhetoric, style, and so on. But it is also important to distinguish between their approaches clearly—to take advantage of the special perspectives a literary analysis has to add. Fitzmyer the exegete values the integrity of the implied author less than Booth does. For example, Fitzmyer writes in a passage cited above about "what *Luke* says in 24:27, 46 about 'Moses and all the prophets' . . ." (emphasis added), when literally what is said about Moses is what the character Jesus says in direct discourse. Jesus tells his disciples about his reading in the scriptures of the need of the messiah to suffer. Fitzmyer, in other words, gives all the lines to the implied author and sees even the main character as his mouthpiece.

Harmonizing Voices

Blurring this distinction endangers the literary integrity of the narrative text because it tends toward a single meaning, and that meaning usually turns out to be sectarian. For example, Fitzmyer singles out the story of the walking trip to Emmaus as a particularly good instance of Luke writing like Luke. As already noted, he recounts many Greek phrases and terms unique to Luke and agrees with other scholars who claim Luke was not merely embellishing Mark or other common sources but was using a tradition unique to him. The detail about a road trip is Lucan. It continues the motif of the road that stands for the progressive journey that a life with Jesus is for Luke. The fact that Luke does not cite specific texts when his Jesus "begins with Moses and the prophets" to tell his disciples how his story has been anticipated is consistent with Luke's "global christological use of the OT" (p. 1558). All this is fine for understanding Luke's special stylistic and thematic concerns. But Fitzmyer is intent on bringing them to focus on what he thinks is the central point of the scene: Jesus' progressive action at table in breaking and blessing the bread. It "not only recalls the

Last Supper (22:19) but becomes the classic Lucan way of referring to the Eucharist" (p. 1559). In other words, Jesus intends his instruction to the disciples to emphasize the communal sacrament which they should use in order to recall continuously his presence among them. Thus Fitzmyer, being a Catholic commentator, shares an interest with many other commentators in the question whether Luke was describing in this way the style of the eucharistic celebration typical in his church or of his time.

Characteristically, Fitzmyer is scholarly and cautious with his interest. He admits that "no one can answer [the] question" of what historical circumstances Luke's eucharistic meal might represent. There is no corroborating evidence about liturgical celebrations in the first century. He provides a sound assessment of the scholarship on this matter. Any similar inquiry most likely would come to the same conclusions. But the fact that he raises the question at all indicates, ironically, that he is more interested in what the once-living author Luke *might have known* than in what the character Jesus and the narrator and implied author are actually doing in tandem *on the page* in this situation. He rates the once-living evangelist a more interesting character than his literary creation, and he assumes he can approach that once-living evangelist if he collapses all of the separate authorities in the narrative scene into the manifestations of a single voice. In doing this, Fitzmyer is a thoroughly modern exegete and a sophisticated disciple of Schleiermacher, whose approach to the Emmaus episode we consider in the third chapter. He is the great eighteenth- and early-nineteenth-century theorist of Christian interpretation. He diverted the interest of interpreters away from investigating the actions of the holy spirit and toward investigating the actions of once-living authors who thought very much like interpreters do. What orthodox interpreters like Fitzmyer retain in the shift of focus, however, is an abiding interest in the single meaning *underlying* all the details of the narration—and they thus still find it attractive to blend and to blur and to harmonize.

Blurring these distinctions is endemic to any truly orthodox interpretation, regardless of its sectarian bias. In his recent, erudite reading of Luke's Gospel, James M. Dawsey is more careful than Fitzmyer to distinguish between the language of the narrator and the language of the major character. According to Dawsey, the narrator in all the descriptive passages appears well educated, formal, aloof, and didactic. He uses the style and diction of a highly sophisticated Hellenistic Jew in order to suggest the voice of someone presiding over a community's worship. Jesus, in contrast, appears self-educated, colloquial, and familiar in his direct speeches and sermons. He uses the style and diction of a prophet pointing to the way of the cross and suffering as the way to personal salvation. In his analysis of the Emmaus episode, Dawsey emphasizes Jesus' admonition to his disciples that the Christ was meant to suffer. Moreover, Dawsey reads the narrative of Luke as if these two voices, the narrator's and Jesus', were in dialogue with each other: "on the one hand, the focus is firmly in the exalted Christ; on the other, on the call to renunciation, to taking up the cross" (p. 152); "the narrator thus stands for the community of believers who must confront the 'suffering Jesus' " (p. 154). But in his final analysis, Dawsey believes that the dialogue should come to a definitive conclusion as quickly as possible. The sophisticated narrator and the community of believers who want to celebrate Jesus with joy must stand corrected by the humbler Jesus. Jesus' message is that they make a personal decision to embrace his cross. Therefore in the end, all gaps close around a resolution, albeit a different one than Fitzmyer has in mind. Instead of centering on the importance of the eucharist, the scene centers on the need for redemptive suffering.

By following Booth, however, we can entertain these distinctions more rigorously as part of an interest in all the voices of a narrative that might have similar perspectives, but not necessarily the same ones. "There is always a distinction," Booth says, "even though the author himself may not have been aware of it as he wrote" (p. 93); and we could say this even of the gospels. The author is implied by the arrangement of the material and the style of the language, but the voice that speaks the narrative comes between that language and the reader who reads the text. This voice is the one that appears to recite the text to the implied reader's inner ear. Booth describes two basic kinds of narrative voices: a "dramatized narrator" seems to be on the scene itself, often identifying itself with the first-person pronoun, singular or plural, as Luke does in the "we" sections of Acts. The gospel narrator, however, is "undramatized or unacknowledged"; it is a voice that appears on the scene and knows the scene and even what some of the characters within the scene are thinking, but this narrator does not take part in the scene. Rather, this narrator serves as the unacknowledged observer.

Booth says the unacknowledged narrator may be more or less distant in point of view from both the implied author and the characters. Luke's narrator is discrete but intimate. His narrator is "privileged" to know a great deal of what both implied author and main character know; thus, in Booth's terms, Luke's narrator is "reliable," in that the voice speaks in accordance with the norms of the work. The narrator simply has a way of speaking that differs in strategy and tone from that of the implied author and main character. Finally, the narrator may be more or less distant from the reader's own norms. And here we begin to talk about perhaps the most interesting aspect of the gospel narrative. Luke's narrator is much closer in aspect to the implied author and main character than it is to the implied reader. The implied author, the narrator, and the main character are teachers, whereas the implied readers are grouped with the minor characters as disciples—on the other side of the desk, if you will. All three teaching authorities conspire to keep the various disciples partially in the dark. Otherwise the magic of this particular scene would not work.

"In any reading experience," Booth says in summary, "there is an implied dialogue among author, narrator, the other characters and the reader." A dialogue continues only if every party continues to entertain differences of perspective. This is to say that any reader of Luke who wanted to to join this dialogue with the best possible preparation would need to make full use of traditional biblical scholarship of Luke, such as Fitzmyer's and Dawsey's, to become intimate with the implied author of the text. Such a reader can truly be omnivorous, reading everything the best scholars have to say about the Christian scriptures—but always with the understanding that what is being explicated is the teaching of one or another of the separate but equal authorities within any given scene. Thus the reader should use this scholarly information only as part of a paratactic play of the mind over all the different perspectives in the narrative scene. The resulting meditation on the parataxis is the gnosis of the text that comes from the invisible spaces in the gaps. This is what the genius of Luke suggests.

For clarity we should perhaps add a term to Booth's schema at this point. The "interpreter" is a term for the kind of reader an implied author addresses, in the same way the implied reader is the term Booth uses for the kind of reader a narrator addresses. The difference between them is the difference between a reader reading for a second time and a reader reading for the first time. The second time around, the reader knows what is going to happen and can thus concentrate on how it happens and how it is related. With this additional term, we take the step from literary criticism to hermeneutics.

An interpreter could ask the question: "Why is it that the implied author writes a scene in which the narrator handles the reader in one way, and the major character Jesus handles the characters in another?" The safest way for an interpreter to answer is to make what is at first virtually a tautological statement: the implied author is teaching the interpreter that there are at least two ways of learning about Jesus—Jesus' way and the narrator's way. It is not a large step from this tautology to the assertion that the implied author is also telling the interpreter that each way seems to define the other way. The major character and the narrator both teach paratactically. Each presents images or ideas in a series without supplying logical conjunctions between them, but their emphasis is different. Jesus implies a connection between his disguise and hidden texts. The narrator implies a connection between the implied reader's apparently superior knowledge and abiding ignorance about what Jesus actually says.

Spoken Parataxis

We can distinguish these two authorities further on roughly the same grounds that we distinguish speakers and writers. In this episode both Jesus and the narrator appear to speak. Jesus speaks to the disciples; the narrator to the implied reader. But actually what each of them says is a different part of a written narrative the implied author arranges. What the narrator "says" is much closer to the way an author writes than what Jesus "says." To understand the difference, we need to understand the difference between spoken and written parataxis.

"Parataxis" is a Greek word meaning literally "to lay side by side." In his *Rhetoric,* Aristotle defines rhetorical or oral parataxis as a series of independent statements that a speaker joins together without connecting words. He gives as an example: "I came to him; I met him; I besought him." There is a famous example from *Caesar's Wars:* "I came; I saw; I conquered." This is an effective device to use in a speech, Aristotle says, because it allows the members of an audience the opportunity to figure the connections out for themselves. They supply their own logic to what the speaker says. They gain the illusion that what they are thinking is what the speaker intended all along.

A good speaker knows how to exploit this illusion. Such a speaker shifts rapidly from topic to topic and changes the mood of the address. It is essential that the speaker string many paratactic statements together, without allowing members of the audience enough time to examine them critically. In this way each member naturally assumes that the connections he or she makes are what the speaker intended to infer, and furthermore, that each member of the audience assumes the other members think alike. They all share the common thoughts that the speaker supplies. We can imagine the power of this device in the hands of a demogogue; and even when the intention of the speaker is benign, it would seem that the point of the device is to curtail thinking for a direct emotional affirmation of what the speaker says.

Obviously there are no real speakers in the Emmaus scene or in any other written text. There can only be the illusion of one, created by hints that a character speaks according to certain rules of oral rhetoric. Yet in the Emmaus scene there are several hints that Jesus uses paratactic rhetoric for emotional effect. One hint is that at the moment the two disciples finish telling Jesus why they are troubled, Jesus quickly changes the mood. He admonishes them. He accuses them of being "dull of mind and slow to believe." The shift of mood suggests that the original mood was not appropriate. The disciples are not deserving of consolation but correction. Jesus tells them things are actually better than they had hoped, or as good as they could have imagined. Jesus shifts the mood again at the end when the tranquil preparation for a meal explodes into his magical disappearance. A second hint is that Jesus' rhetorical delivery makes use of a special dramatic gesture. As we have already noted, he speaks to them in a disguise that he magically reveals at the moment he disappears. He implies a connection between his teaching in disguise and his pointing out the "disguised" texts. A third hint is the disciples' response. Remarkably, the disciple who speaks for both of them uses the genitive of the first person plural pronoun in saying "Was not the heart *of us* (*haemon*) burning while he spoke to us on the way, and interpreted to us the Scriptures?" (24:32); but the disciple uses the singular form of the word for *heart* (*chardia*), as if to suggest the two of them possessed a single, profound understanding. They respond just as Aristotle predicted an audience would to a skillful use of parataxis. They imagine their understanding to be identical.

Beyond these hints, of course, the text is mute. Luke refrains from reporting the actual interpretation Jesus makes of all the scriptures, and at this point in the narrative there are no hints about how Jesus himself would have read the stories that preceded his. But before moving on to consider the narrator's parallel strategy in setting the scene this way, we can consider a few more implications to be gleaned from the minimal details the scene offers about the way the character Jesus speaks, acts, and thinks.

We consider the question of whether, on the basis of these details, we can really say that Jesus' language and dramatic gesture in the scene constitute a paratactic *rhetoric*. In other words, can we infer that Jesus spoke and acted elliptically and deliberately for a certain calculated effect? We pursue the question because of what the answers might point up about the narrator's more obvious rhetorical effects that work in tandem with Jesus'. We are working toward a distinction between oral and written parataxis, between a character's and a narrator's teaching.

We continue the exploration by returning to Dawsey's notion that Jesus spoke Aramaic, a language whose idioms and style encouraged paratactic rhetoric. According to Matthew Black, on whom Dawsey relies for his study of Jesus' speech patterns, the Aramaic language that Jesus probably spoke favored the frequent use of asyndeton. This is the rhetorical mannerism, related to parataxis, of leaving out the particles that usually connect sentences to each other. The particles are something between punctuation and conjunctions; they indicate with words like "and" and "but" or with the semicolon that one sentence depends on another. These particles are very common in normal Greek prose. Black points out that the Greek used in the narrative sections of the gospels supplies particles between the sentences in the normal style. However, the Greek used to record Jesus' direct discourse frequently leaves them out. This suggests first that Jesus spoke Aramaic; second that many of his speeches were first recorded in Aramaic sources; and third that the evangelists who wrote in Greek tried to capture Jesus' speech patterns with rough, literal Greek translations of Aramaic sources. Black's focus is somewhat different from Fitzmyer's, who claimed that he could account for most of what he considered Luke's so-called semitisms in the Septuagint Greek text Luke used for his major source. Black considers how the particular speeches attributed to Jesus in the gospels differ from the rhetoric of the other narrative sections. He finds that Jesus speaks more elliptically than the narrator or other characters. He comes to the general conclusion that Jesus' direct discourse in the narrative reflects original *verbatim* sources.

Black (like Fitzmyer and Dawsey) does not consider the asyndeton that characterizes Jesus' speech beyond the sentence level. But because he uses the term "spirit" in describing Jesus' tendency to speak this way, we could speak of a certain cast of mind that a particular language might encourage. Perhaps the Jesus we find in the gospel narratives tends to think asyndetonically when he considers the connection between the scriptures he knows and his own interpretations of what they mean. Recall his famous dictum that Luke cites several times: "It is written. . . . but I say to you." In this saying, he clearly leaves out the logical links in moving from text to meaning, as if to suggest that one moves from one to the other by insight, not reasoning.

What Black says about the use of parataxis in the gospels bears out this extension of his idea. Usually parataxis takes the form of sentences loosely connected by the conjunction *kai* (and). The logical connection is thus left completely to speculation. Again Black cautions about attributing the use of this construction too precisely: "Parataxis is much more frequent in Aramaic than it is in Greek. But it does occur in Greek, especially when the Greek has few literary pretensions. The Gospels are written in a common Greek called *koine,* or literally common. It could also be translated as colloquial. Like any colloquial speech it is less formal than deliberate or literary language. It can tend to drop the particles and connecting words that spell out the logic of an idea. It can also be elliptical, inferential, the language used among people who understand each other well. In other words, it is difficult there to decide whether parataxis in the Greek gospels reflects an Aramaic original, or a sympathetic Greek translation, or simply loose writing" (p. 48). For Black parataxis nonetheless constitutes a certain limit and opportunity in the text. Frequently the narrator and the central character Jesus use paratactical sentences. The lack of connections in these sentences allows them both to say a few things and to imply more.

Now the question is whether this way of speaking is inherently clumsy. Does its use in Jesus' speeches reflect his lack of a formal education? Does parataxis inhibit what he can say? Even if he should wish to, is it possible he lacks the skill to make subtle distinctions and to connect idea to idea in tight logical sequence? If the answers were yes, then it would be unfair and wrong to read into what he says more than he literally says. We could not assume the parataxis in his speech was an invitation for the listeners to think for themselves. It would simply be evidence that the speaker himself could not think very well. These questions cannot be answered for sure. We would need to be present while the speaker Jesus speaks to catch his innuendo. Lacking firsthand information, we rely on written reports of what Jesus said, such as Luke's Gospel. But here we cannot be absolutely certain whether any given instance of parataxis reflects Jesus' speaking style, or simply the limits of the Greek style Luke used.

Jesus as Narrator

There is circumstantial evidence that Jesus might have spoken and thought this way deliberately to convey the importance of something like a gnostic insight to his disciples. When we look over the entire Gospel of Luke, we can see that when Jesus becomes a narrator himself and puts his teaching in the form of parables, he tells stories not unlike the story Luke's narrator tells about him in the Emmaus episode. We should find this reciprocity suggestive. Consider, for example, the parables of the Good Samaritan and the Forgiving Father. They are unique to Luke, and scholars have attributed them to his own special source, or "L." Each parable shows Jesus to be a master of paratactic suggestion. At the same time, they show him to both honor the venerable scriptures and to feature the importance of something very much like gnostic insight in the process of understanding. Thus, they rehearse critical narrative and rhetorical aspects of the Emmaus scene.

Jesus tells the parable about the good Samaritan (10:29–37) in response to persistent questions from a lawyer who wants to know, "What must I do to gain eternal life?" Jesus' first response is to ask the lawyer to tell him what is written in the law. The lawyer answers with an amalgam of Deuteronomy and Leviticus, saying that one must love God wholeheartedly and one's neighbor as oneself. Jesus answers by saying, in effect, that the lawyer is right, and that nothing else needs to be added to what the venerable scripture says. When the lawyer presses Jesus for an elaboration of who his neighbor is, he asks for an interpretation of the one word in the citation he has given whose meaning is not clear. "Neighbor" has an ambiguous range. It can refer to people outside one's family and circle of friends, or to people who live in simple proximity. Jesus responds with paratactic dispatch.

He begins a story without any introduction, only implying that the story will provide an answer to the question. Like the Emmaus story, it centers on a fallen man, this one beaten by robbers and left for dead. Like the

Emmaus story, two walk by on a journey, although each of them is going his separate way. Jesus does not rationalize their motives for passing the beaten man by. It is as if their motives were clear to all who listened, or if they were not, that they were beneath comment, even contempt. Perhaps there is a hint here that a priest and a Levite disdained touching a body that might be dead for fear of ritual defilement. "This affected those of the priestly and levitical status more seriously than other Jews" (Fitzmyer, p. 883). If this is indeed the way they thought, in accordance with what had been written in the Law or commentaries on the Law, the Samaritan acts at first, it appears, without thinking at all. "He was moved with compassion," Jesus says, and binds up the beaten man's wounds. Afterward he does calculate with the innkeeper for the man's care, and so his good deed extends to the arrangements required to make it complete. But like the disciples on the road to Emmaus, his gnosis of who he is, who the beaten man is, and thus what a neighbor is, derives from his acting upon what was initially a spontaneous, personal intuition.

Jesus does not draw a moral from his story directly. Instead he asks the lawyer to interpret who in the story was the neighbor to the beaten man. Of course there can be no other answer than the one the lawyer gives: "the one who showed him kindness." But it appears to be important that the lawyer give the answer himself, based on his own intuitive interpretation. That is the story's point. Only thus will one know who one's neighbor is. Only thus will one identify those whose needs one will care for. Jesus responds paratactically again. He says, "Go and do the same yourself." This is not strictly the answer the lawyer sought. The lawyer had asked for a legalistic definition, in accordance with the Law, of what a neighbor is. Instead he receives a moral exhortation to act like one. The unspoken implication of Jesus' parataxis is that this is precisely the sort of answer such questions properly deserve. He implies they are the only answers that the Law really requires. As in the Emmaus scene, his teaching is that the venerable scriptures supply the context for imaginative interpretations. Such interpretations, like the Samaritan's discovery of a fallen neighbor, make good on the best sort of intuitions.

Jesus apparently tells the story of the Forgiving Father in response to similar hostile intent. In this case, it is some Pharisees and Scribes who note: "This man welcomes sinners and eats with them" (15:2). The links between their statement and Jesus' response are not as clear as they are in the case of the lawyer's question. Luke's implied author arranges four parables to follow the statement paratactically, each one introduced with indefinite phrases: "But he spoke to them"; "Or what woman"; "And he said"; "And he also said." These phrases do not state that Jesus spoke each parable in direct response to the hostile questions, or even all at one time. Unlike the episode with the lawyer, there is no direct follow-up after the stories are told. After the four stories, the Pharisees change the subject and sneer at Jesus on other grounds (16:14). The implied author's arrangement of scenes implies only that Jesus had among his repertoire a number of stories appropriate for a response to the hostile innuendo.

The third response, the parable of the Forgiving Father, actually seems the most appropriate. It weaves the theme of sinning and eating into a captivating story of forgiveness. This time the venerable scriptures are present only by suggestion. Certain details are reminiscent of the stories of Cain and Abel, Ishmael and Isaac, Esau and Jacob. Once again a father has two sons, the younger of whom the father appears to favor over the elder. At least this is the opinion of the elder son, who can only point incredulously to the long record of faithful service he has shown his father: "Look, I have been serving you so many years, and I have never disregarded a single command of yours; yet you never gave me even a goat that I might make merry with my friends. Now that son of yours has come back, who has devoured your estate with prostitutes, and you have slaughtered for him the fatted calf!" (15:29–31).

As in the parable of the Good Samaritan and in the Emmaus scene, the focus of the story falls on ways of knowing. The father replies to his petulant son paratactically, not really answering the point of his accusation. Instead he says his joy at his son's return subordinates all calculation: "Son you are always with me, and all that I own is yours. But we must be happy and rejoice. For this brother of yours was dead and has come to life; he was lost, and is found" (15:31–32). In this way the father shows himself to be emotionally and spiritually close to his younger son, who, as Jesus says in an intriguing phrase, "comes to himself" on the pig farm. At that instant the younger son discovered where he really belonged. At that instant he began to calculate how much better it would be to be one of his father's servants than one of his father's lost sons. Like the disciples on the way to Emmaus, the good Samaritan, and his own forgiving father, the prodigal son calculates only in the aftermath of his explosive moment of gnosis.

We learn something about Luke's narrative art and the amorphous nature of what we are calling gnosis when we discover that the Roman Stoic philosopher Epictetus, a rough contemporary of Plutarch, Tacitus, and Luke, uses the same Greek words. He describes a young man who, the philosopher imagines, "comes to himself" (*hotan eis sauton elthaes*) because of his teaching and discovers the vanity of his fashionable haircut and clothing. W. A. Oldfather, Epictetus's modern translator, makes note of the linguistic resemblances but decides they "are only accidental, because Epictetus was speaking the common language of ethical exhortation in which the evangelists and apostles wrote" (p. xxvi). If this is so, then Luke had an ear for picking up phrases and ideas from secular, as well as religious or scriptural sources, and projecting them effortlessly into the teaching of his main character. Or it could mean that he found such phrases to sum up succinctly the essence of what Jesus might have said in different words from the sources about his life and teaching that Luke found at hand. In either case, he was able to integrate a stoic or gnostic moment of insight into a dramatic situation set in Palestine, in which Jesus makes allusions to the religious controversies of his day and to the venerable scriptures that various antagonistic Jewish sects revered in common.

Two other episodes, one comic, the other tragic, show Jesus instigating an experience very much like that of the younger son "coming to himself." They suggest that Jesus considers such experiences essential to the kind of understanding he cultivates in his followers. These episodes demonstrate affinities between Jesus' narrative style and speaking style. Both make use of parataxis to feature a spontaneous experience that promises to have long-term consequences—the special kind of gnosis that Luke's Jesus features.

The comic episode is unique to Luke's Gospel. Jesus is passing through Jericho on his way to Jerusalem for the last time:

> There was a man there named Zacchaeus who was a chief tax-collector and quite wealthy. He was eager to see who Jesus was, but because of the crowd he could not, for he was short of stature. So he ran on ahead and climbed a sycamore tree in order to catch sight of Jesus as he would pass by. When Jesus came to the place, he looked up and said to him, "Zacchaeus, hurry and come down, for I must stay at your house today." He hastened to get down and was very happy to welcome him. But all those who saw this grumbled at Jesus and said, "He has gone to lodge with a sinner." Zacchaeus, however, just stood there and said to the Lord, "Look Sir, I give away half of what I own to the poor. If I have extorted anything from anyone, I pay it back four times over." Jesus said to him, "Salvation has come to this house to-day. For this man too is a son of Abraham! For the Son of Man has come to seek out and to save what was lost" (19:1–10).

The key figure this time is rich *and* experiences a change of heart, if we follow A. Plummer and other scholars. They take the ambiguous present tense "I give away" (*didomi*) and "I pay back" (*apodidomi*) to be a heart-felt promise to perform a future repentant act, rather than a self-righteous protest that Zacchaeus has always been generous and fair. Zacchaeus has his experience after he has seen Jesus and heard the grumblings directed at Jesus for visiting a sinner. This time we do not get a description of any emotional surge, as we do when the good Samaritan is "moved with compassion" and the prodigal son "comes to himself," or as the two disciples do when they say they feel their "heart burning," or as Peter does in the next episode we consider, when some witnesses say he "wept bitterly" after realizing what he had done. Zacchaeus's change of heart appears to be more drawn out. Jesus' friendly gesture and the unfriendly grumblings were only the immediate causes of what Zacchaeus had already primed himself to do when he put aside his dignity to climb a tree. Jesus uses a paratactic style this time in order to ignore the grumblings directed at him and directly addresses and approves Zacchaeus's spontaneously generous offer. Here is another incongruous good Samaritan, a "sinner" whose virtue shames the arbiters of virtue. Jesus declares he is also "a son of Abraham," and thereby does virtually the same thing he does on the road to Emmaus. He declares that the connections between what was written and what is happening now can be closer than one might think.

In another episode, the connection is between what was said and what happens. The moment of insight occurs in the courtyard after Jesus has been arrested and Peter is accused of being one of his disciples (22:54–62). In this case, the narrator tells the story, and Jesus appears for only the space of a single line, without saying a word. Peter's gnosis occurs when "the Lord turned and looked at Peter. Then Peter remembered the Lord's saying . . ." Like the disciples on the road to Emmaus, Peter already knew the words that would explain what had happened to Jesus and to him. He simply did not know what they meant until Jesus again appears and disappears from his view: "And he went outside and wept bitterly" (22:62). At this moment, the implied author dramatically shifts the scene to a close-up of Jesus being taunted and beaten by his enemies. The parataxis suggests he receives blows simultaneously from within and from without. What makes this moment more closely resemble what we have already described as the gnosis is that here an outside presence, Jesus, apparently "holds Peter's eyes" until a climactic moment when, with a look, he suddenly conveys to Peter a complete understanding of what he had previously been told. The good Samaritan and the prodigal son come to their understanding on their own.

This scene provides particularly strong evidence of Jesus' deliberately paratactic and gnostic teaching style. Peter is the only character in Luke's Gospel whom Jesus singles out for systematic instruction. In many ways, he is the ideal student. He is always attentive, always eager to please and to understand. Yet his education is difficult despite his being a particularly promising pupil at first.

Early in his account of Jesus' career, Luke transposes many details onto a simple scene from Mark. Mark has Jesus walking by the Sea of Galilee and beckoning to Simon (Peter) and Andrew, who are fishing with a net. "Jesus said to them, 'Come with me, and I will make you fishers of men' " (Mark 1:16–18). He says more or less the same thing at the end of the episode in Luke. But in Luke's version, a strong emotional response on the part of one individual yields an emphatic understanding. Luke's Jesus asks Simon for the use of his boat as a preaching platform because the crowds are pressing him by the shore. When he has finished speaking, he asks Simon to cast out his nets for a catch. Simon protests that they have been fishing all night without luck. But he will try again. He does, and the catch is almost large enough to sink the boat. "When Simon saw what had happened, he fell at Jesus' knees and said, 'Go, Lord, leave me, sinner that I am.' " Jesus then corrects the impression Peter seems to have that Jesus performed this miracle to draw attention to his power. "Do not be afraid," he says, echoing the words of the Angel to the shepherds. Then, paratactically, without elaborating on the difference between Peter's response and the true intent of the story, Jesus interprets. The wonderful catch of fish symbolizes the wonderful success Peter and his crew will have proclaiming Jesus' message.

Sometime later, Peter meets with Jesus' approval when he asks his disciples, "Who do the people say I am?" and, after the disciples recount various popular opinions, Peter gives his opinion that Jesus is "God's Messiah." Jesus does not exactly assent. He simply tells the disciples not to tell this to anyone. Then he uses another title for himself, "The Son of Man," and goes on to predict that he will suffer at the hands of the authorities, be put to death, and rise on the third day. It is interesting to note that, as Fitzmyer points out, Luke has his Jesus define himself as a suffering messiah, as he will try again to explain to the disciples he meets on the road to Emmaus. It is also interesting to note that this time Luke deletes a significant detail from Mark's version of the episode. In Mark, Peter protests that he and the disciples will never allow Jesus to suffer. Jesus then admonishes Peter for thinking like a man rather than like God (Mark 8:33). It is almost as if, in Luke, Peter appears to be progressing in his correct understanding of who Jesus is. He is coming to understand that it is essential that the messiah, or the Son of Man, has to suffer before he can be apotheosized. In ideal gnostic fashion, Peter appears to be thinking rationally about the first overwhelming experience he had of Jesus' power. In that case, a sea empty of fish became a sea full of fish. Perhaps Jesus meant the event to be as much a symbol of proselytizing as a symbol of mysterious abundance appearing suddenly out of nowhere, like life from a tomb.

Peter's understanding of who Jesus is and how he must suffer before being glorified is, however, incomplete. In the very next episode, Jesus arranges another overpowering experience for Peter like that of the miraculous catch. This time he takes Peter, James, and John up into the hills to pray. He allows them to see a transfiguration that presages, perhaps, the glory of his resurrection from the dead. Luke adds significant details to Mark's version of the scene of Jesus' transfiguration in order to suggest that Peter again cannot immediately come to grips with the meaning of a power-

ful insight. In Mark, Peter and his companions see Jesus transfigured immediately upon reaching the top of the mountain where Jesus leads them
(Mark 9:2–8). Luke has Peter and his companions awakening from a deep
sleep when they behold Jesus transformed. They come from a deep darkness to see a bright light. They come from farther back in their consciousness to see what they come to see. Mark then has Peter suggesting to Jesus
that they make three shelters for Jesus, Moses, and Elijah. His narrator
adds the parenthetical remark: "(For he did not know what to say; they
were so terrified.)" Luke's narrator personalizes and intensifies Peter's
dumbfoundedness at the sight: "but he spoke without knowing what he was
saying." Once again, Peter fails to grasp the significance of the sign in the
scene. His responses are still wholly emotional and thus inappropriate. In
this scene the correction occurs while "the words were still on his lips." A
cloud casts a shadow over them and a voice informs them that Jesus "is my
Son, my Chosen; listen to him" (Luke 9:28–36).

Peter does better when Jesus tells the parable about the master returning
from a wedding feast. It concludes with the moral: "Hold yourselves ready,
then, because the Son of Man will come at the time you least expect him."
The mention of the same title and another reference to the future appears
to jog Peter's memory: "Peter said, 'Lord, do you intend this parable
specially for us, or is it for everyone?'" Jesus this time does something
new. He uses what could be called a Socratic method, answering Peter's
question with another question: "Well, who is the trusty and sensible man
whom his master will appoint as his steward, to manage his servants and
issue their rations at the proper time?" (12:41–46). This implies at least two
things. One, Peter has to answer the question for himself; two, Peter is
perhaps to understand that he himself is both servant and steward. It is he
who will bear a special responsibility to see that the others remain ready. It
is for this reason that Jesus singles him out for instruction. Significantly,
that instruction is not in codes or facts but in a manner of rationalizing
one's most unsettling insights.

Peter appears to come to the edge of a complete understanding only with
the final lesson Jesus teaches him. It is the most elaborate lesson, with two
parts. This time, Jesus first reminds Peter and the others of his prediction
that he will suffer and die. He elicits Peter's brave promise: "I am ready to
go with you to prison and death." He corrects Peter and counters with the
prediction that "the cock will not crow tonight until you have three times
over denied that you know me" (22:31–35). It is important for the point I
am making here that Jesus prefaces his prediction of Peter's failure with a
prediction of Peter's recovery. He uses a similar phrase to the one he uses
in the parable of the Forgiving Father in referring to the prodigal son's
moment of decision. Jesus tells Peter: "*when you have come back to yourself,* you must lend strength to your brothers." The words are not precisely

the same as the ones used in the parable. The meaning of the key term in this phrase, *epistrepsas* (to return, to turn back), is obscure. Fitzmyer describes various theories about its meaning and favors the most literal, "to be converted." Thus Jesus would be referring to the moment "[w]hen Simon has repented of his denial of Jesus, or when he has turned back from his (period of infidelity)" (p. 1425). Fitzmyer thus interprets the verb to refer to an essentially moral action. But we could compare what Jesus says here to what he says in the parable. In this way we could read both phrases to refer to a method of moral reasoning as well. Peter learns the proper moral lesson only by going back over his original, unsettling experience and trying to decide what it has to mean. This is gnostic learning. It is part of Jesus' gnostic teaching style to leave large, paratactic gaps between what he says and what his disciple will eventually come to learn it means.

At this point, Jesus appears confident that Peter, like the prodigal son, has learned enough now to be able to recover from his inevitable, initial failure to understand. The gnostic way of knowledge demands as much. The original insight will always be befuddling, and sometimes painfully so.

For the denouement of Peter's gnostic education, Luke once again elaborates on Mark to emphasize Peter's personal response. The detail of Jesus turning to Peter at the moment of his self-discovery appears only in Luke's version of the denial scene. Fitzmyer speculates that this is "the type of detail that Luke would like to include," without elaborating why (p. 1457). We could say it is because it provides another fascinating depiction of something like gnosis that captivated Luke's narrative imagination. In this episode, as in the Emmaus episode, Luke follows the causality favored in gnostic narratives where, unexpectedly, a powerful personality suddenly appears to instigate an unexpected insight. Furthermore, the power of parataxis to evoke an image of gnosis is demonstrated when his implied author arranges the scenes, his narrator notes Peter's reaction and the enemies' taunts, and his main character turns wordlessly toward another. While we can never know for certain whether the living Jesus thought and taught paratactically with deliberate effect, we can at least say that *Luke's* Jesus did. That was the only way Luke himself could depict Jesus narratively.

Parallelism "in all the Scriptures"

There is some additional circumstantial information we can gather about where and why Luke's Jesus learned to think and teach this way. It reposes "in all the Scriptures" that Jesus reviews with the two disciples he meets on the road to Emmaus. When we search the Hebrew scripture, we find it replete with narrative techniques that appear to encourage paratactic rhetoric. In other words, Jesus' elliptical speech patterns and Luke's "Septuagintisms" might mean that both men were educated in a highly elliptical literature, and so their use of asyndeton and parataxis might be the very opposite of a crude and halting manner of expression. Perhaps both grasped the genius of biblical literary parallelism that recent scholars have recovered.

We can begin searching the venerable scriptures, as Jesus does, with "Moses." This title refers to the first five books of the Hebrew Bible, the Pentateuch, frequently attributed to Moses. We view these texts from the perspective that several modern Jewish literary scholars provide. They reread their scriptural heritage for evidence of its great literary skill as well as for its great religious imagination. In their view, the writers of the Hebrew Bible had a penchant for parallelism, a close rhetorical kin of parataxis, as we shall see.

As we entertain their view, I single out what they say about the theme of brotherhood in the Hebrew Bible. This is important for our concerns for several reasons. For one, parallelism is a literary device inextricably tied to this theme. With it Hebrew writers suggested that there were close similarities in the life stories of heroes related by close ties of kinship. For example, we find in the Pentateuch similarities in the stories of Abel, Isaac, and Jacob, in that each is the younger of two brothers and more favored by God. The story of Joseph in the Pentateuch and David in the Books of Samuel vary the type of the younger son somewhat. These characters are the youngest sons in large families whom God once again singles out for special favor. Often such characters are several different types at once. Isaac, Jacob, and Joseph, like Samson and Samuel, are born of mothers who have been painfully barren for a long time, and are born only after their fathers had prayed to God for their wives' fertility. Jacob, Joseph, and David wander far from their original home and suffer many trials before winning a high position. Jacob appears to intuit this historical and narrative pattern when he inadvertently at first, but then adamantly, blesses Ephraim instead of Manasseh when blessing the two sons of Joseph (Genesis 48:9–22). In Joseph's and David's stories, the parallels with the earlier stories are looser; their events are elaborate and often dramatic. But again the reader comes to an image with other images in mind and finds a frame of reference thereby. Younger brothers have a special place in this family of stories; great things are expected of them.

For another reason, this theme appears to interest Luke's Jesus, who in the postresurrection scenes appears preoccupied with the kinship of the older stories with his own. Perhaps he learned a rhetorical style from his close reading. For a third reason, the venerable literary device and its attendant theme appear to inspire Luke to improvise on both. We can appreciate his artistic feat more after we consider what Robert Alter, Meir

Sternberg, and James Kugel say about the provocative inexactitude of Hebrew biblical parallels.

Alter and Sternberg concur that the inexact repetitions have a fundamental religious purpose: God acts consistently with his chosen people, but never in precisely the same way, because the story of each hero differs with his or her time. For example, we find that the first commentary on the parallels in Genesis occurs in Genesis itself when God reminds Jacob that "I am the Lord, the God of your father Abraham and the God of Isaac" (Genesis 28:13). Here God is suggesting that these family members are each characters in the ongoing family history of its relationship with God. But when he repeats this formula to Moses and adds Jacob's name to the list, suggesting that now Moses' story belongs to the same narrative, God tailors the announcement to suit Moses' primary concern. He reiterates the promise of the promised land: "I will lead you to the land which I swore with uplifted hand to give to Abraham, to Isaac and to Jacob" (Exodus 6:8). Alter and Sternberg note that the ongoing narrative development impinges, in turn, on the words and actions of God. As the story of each character changes, so does the promise in order to adapt the blessing to particular circumstances and needs. In other words, the need of stories to be different is the principle according to which God accommodates his protection to each individual character. Characters are free to be individuals. In the Hebrew Bible, the type of the godly man is not cast in the concrete repetitions of myth.

Alter and Sternberg both cite the long tradition of Jewish exegesis that stands behind their modern and sensitive reassessments of the parallels in Hebrew narrative. They both claim their work belongs in this reverential context as its modern, literary extension. They point out that the earliest rabbinic commentaries in the exegetical Haggadah extend God's way of reading all history to a way of reading biblical narrative. One narrative, one character continually reminds the commentator of another, and every recollection prompts an underlying theme which changes from day to day and from reading to reading. For example, the legendary Rabbi Shemoth, when reading the first line in Exodus, "Now these are the names of the sons of Israel who came into Egypt with Jacob," is reminded of the proverb "He that spares his rod, hates his son" and then calls to mind the disasters that occurred when fathers spared the rod. He recalls David's mistake in refusing to rein in his older son Absalom after he killed his younger brother Amnon. In Rabbi Shemoth's hands, the method of interpretation is appropriate to a text apparently built to invite such readings (1:1).

What Rabbi Shemoth does is typical of rabbinic readings, in his day and today. It is not, strictly speaking, the sort of response Alter and Sternberg make to biblical parallelism. They would honor the integrity of each individual story and not jump from text to text on the strength of brief verbal associations. They would notice that the pattern of the younger brother-older brother story underlies the entire David-Amnon-Absalom story. Like Cain, Absalom kills his younger brother and thus dooms himself to becoming an irreconcilable outcast. There are additional and perhaps more subtle moral lessons to be learned when one becomes attuned to the continual, cryptic reference all biblical stories make to each other. But there is something similar in the rabbinic and literary critical approach. Both range over an entire canon for context. Both respond to the Bible's special genius for juxtapositions of this kind, both immediate and remote. Indeed, parallels make a family of these texts when one narrative invites the reader to compare it with another in the same family, as if the independent narratives were themselves adjacent to one another.

We find the same literary structure when we turn from the prose to biblical poetry of the sort used in the psalms, some of the wisdom books, and the prophets whom Luke says Jesus also cites. Here again, we can consider both the form of the poetry and the theme of brotherhood and the special way both work together. In a recent study of biblical Hebrew poetry, James Kugel provides a subtle analysis of what he also calls the biblical poetic technique of parallelism. The poet brings together images or ideas that share certain characteristics as if suggesting that the reader can learn about each from what they have in common. For example, consider the first two lines of Psalm 133:

> How good it is and how pleasant,
> for brothers to live together!
> It is fragrant as oil poured upon the head
> and falling over the beard.

The first image is vague, unspecified. The listener or reader imagines any group of brothers in a happy scene that would be typical of their general bonhomie. The second image is much more focused. One could imagine a cruet pouring scented oil on a particular pate in such excess that the oil poured off through the beard and onto the shoulders and floor. The second image is also more culturally specific. Our society has a stock of images of men pouring champagne over their heads after championship athletic victories, and we read in Homer of Greek men being rubbed with olive oil after their baths. Thus we can imagine how another ancient culture of men might have expressed an excess of joy by pouring expensive essences on each other's heads. The point that Kugel makes in analyzing this song and other verses in both the prophets and the wisdom books is that the images work precisely because the paralleled images do not compare exactly. This is what makes them provocative. The mind notices what is the same, what is different, and catches the implication. (Here: brothers together are as smooth as oil and expansive with each in a happy moment of excess.) Kugel takes great pains to qualify the prevalent and simplistic notions about this sort of parallelism. It is not that "a" (the first image in the pair) equals "b" (the second image) so much as that "a" is "a" and, what's more, "a" is like "b." It could even be said that there is a benevolent internecine struggle between the images, each one different, each one struggling, as it were, to wrest the central meaning of the moment from one set of correspondences to another. It is like the struggle of brothers. For example, in the next line the paired images of the happy brothers and the oil over the hair are joined with a reference to sacred literary history:

> Aarons' beard, when the oil runs down
> over the collar of his vestments.

The context of the joy becomes historical and religious. Aaron is being anointed while dressed as a priest. The good-humored bonhomie of the brothers receives a historical and religious context, and the addition sobers whatever impression of abandon and excess the listener or reader might have entertained for the first moment of the lyric. Here the familial and the religious aspects of this culture jostle. The next image of anointing takes the action out-of-doors and naturalizes it:

> It is like the dew of Hermon falling
> upon the hills of Zion.

The next one shifts the center of the song from people at ease with each other, their rituals, and their chosen place to put the focus strictly on the action of something liquid flowing down; these images of the oil pouring and the dew falling prepare us to understand how sweetly and persistently the blessing of God falls:

> There the Lord bestows his blessing,
> life for evermore.

Kugel continually draws attention to the subtle but palpable dramatic shifts from image to image. They resist reduction into a central theme. The pivot point shifts from moment to moment as the parallels represent a restless lyric mind, never settled with an exact image of what it wants to express. Kugel's version of Hebrew biblical parallelism is much closer to what we

have been calling narrative parataxis in Luke than earlier, simpler ideas
that the parallels reinforced each other. Here they remain independent, in
a dialogue, as it were, of mental images.

In a recent study, I suggested that the poetry of biblical prophets works
very much like the poetry of the psalmists, except that the gaps between
the rhetorical units are wider and more disconcerting. Consider a passage
in Isaiah, popularly known as his messianic prophecy and often thought to
refer to Jesus. Many interpreters have referred to this section of Isaiah in
supplying texts to Jesus' teaching in the Emmaus episode. In one couplet,
the prophet speaks with the voice of God, referring to a special servant:

> Behold, my servant shall prosper,
> he shall be lifted up, exalted to the heights.

In the next stanzas, the speaker continues to be God, but the topic shifts to
the terrible state to which his people have fallen:

> Time was when many were aghast at you, my people;
> so now many nations recoil at sight of him,
> and kings curl their lips in disgust.
> For they see what they had never been told
>   and things unheard before fill their
>   thoughts.

Within the stanza there is a shift from a second-person address (you) to a
third-person address (him) as well as a shift of focus from the downtrodden people to the astonished onlookers. In the next lines, there is another
shift. Now the speaker seems to be either the downtrodden people *or* the
onlookers:

> Who could have believed what we have heard,
> and to whom has the power of the Lord been
> revealed?

These jagged juxtapositions could be likened to a shifting kaleidoscope.
Now it is not only impossible to follow a logical sequence of ideas, it is also
impossible to determine any thought at all. We are given an image of a
mind under enormous stress. Every image and momentary impression is
driven away by the next.

In discussing this fundamental literary structure that underlies both the
prose and the poetry, Alter, Sternberg, and Kugel alike stress the indepen-

dence of each party to the pairing. The narrator or poet invites the listener or the reader to carry out the inference of the comparable contrasts. Sternberg even uses the term parataxis occasionally to discuss how these juxtapositions work. But usually, like Alter, he uses the term parallel. In the end, the two of them, like the rabbis, are really interested in the coherence and harmony of the scriptures. Sternberg in particular is clear in his belief that the narrative gaps in stories or between stories postpone closure only temporarily. Like Fitzmyer and Dawsey reading the Christian scriptures, Sternberg reading the Hebrew scriptures is convinced that uncertainty is not invincible; there is "an overall complex pattern" (p. 228). Eventually a reader reading widely and deeply, connecting fragment to fragment, text to text, sees the entire meaning, even if in the case of the David story, the point is that David's story was "intended" to remain morally ambiguous. Authorial intention is all.

But there is an interesting ambiguity in the thinking of these two modern Jewish critics about the nature of biblical parallelism; it reflects the ambiguity in biblical parallelism itself. Parallels both invite the mind to look for an underlying pattern and insist that each party to the comparison remain distinct. And it is important for the kind of reading of the Christian scriptures being recommended here that we understand a special point about the use of parallels in the older scriptures. Sternberg and Alter both distinguish their description of the inexact, endlessly fascinating parallels in the Hebrew Bible from the interpretations made of those parallels by the earliest Christian exegetes of both the Old and New Testaments. The Fathers certainly knew about both biblical narrative repetitions under the headings of biblical "types" and "foreshadowing," for which they devised what has been called the "allegorical" or the "anagogic" methods of reading. The Fathers thought that the sententious passages in the New Testament (the Emmaus episode among them) that drew attention to the timeless parallels in the Old were signs that the canonical scriptures were divinely inspired to possess a single overall theme, the progressive revelation of the meaning of the life of Jesus.

Nowadays Christian biblical scholars believe that repetition results from more mundane causes, such as the understandable interest a later author like Luke might have in deliberately echoing the details and themes in the narratives of earlier authors. This is correct. Furthermore, it is important that Hebrew biblical parallels be understood as Sternberg and Alter do in order to understand the way that reading them might have inspired Luke or any other writer.

At this point, we return to the question of Jesus' rhetorical intent at the moment in the Emmaus scene when he speaks to the two disciples. We can now answer: From the few details in the scene, Jesus as a character appears to have developed a paratactic bent to his speech. He is likely to have learned to speak this way from reading a venerable literature with a genius for provocative parallelism. This is an archaic form of composition in which logical connections are not consciously made. But from what we read in the venerable scriptures, it is not necessarily a primitive or crude style of composing. It simply operates within certain parameters; and when it is used deliberately, it can be used for great emotional effect, as Jesus appears to use it in this episode.

Jesus' narrative style as depicted in Luke and its correspondence with the Hebrew Bible's narrative style provide us with only circumstantial evidence of what the historical Jesus' speaking style might have been. But on the basis of this evidence, we can say with confidence that the style Jesus uses in the narrative is deliberate. It is used with conscious effect. Luke portrays a Jesus who could use the simple tools of a direct, idiomatic speech with great power.

Written Parataxis

However little we can say for certain about what Jesus says or how he might say it, we can say more about the narrator's rhetoric in the episode. What the narrator "says" is written for every reader to see. From this evidence we are reasonably assured that the Luke who created the character Jesus out of the stuff of the once-living man was aware of poetic and narrative parallelism in the older scripture. As Fitzmyer shows us, Luke often echoes the venerable scripture in his vocabulary and style. Luke probably saw the parallels in them working more as Alter, Sternberg, and Kugel see them, and less like the Fathers after him would see them. Luke probably saw that reading two parallel texts together does not necessarily require the reader to dissolve the differences between them. Rather, the reader can allow each image or story to comment on its kin. Neither need lose its independence of meaning or place.

When the narrator reports that Jesus refers to the meaning of his story to be found "in all the Scriptures," but does not report for us the precise connection, the implied author improvises on the genius of the literary parallelism to be found in the Septuagint translation he read of the Hebrew Bible. The implied author preserves the autonomy of Jesus and his predecessors. His parataxis differs from the timeless parallels that Sternberg especially celebrates in the Hebrew scriptures. It also differs from what are generally understood to be the progressive parallels that the Fathers found throughout both testaments. They thought that all parallels contributed to a pattern of events culminating in what was to them the climactic story of Jesus. Alternatively, according to Harold Bloom, the venerable Septuagint Bible was, for Luke, a "strong text." This means that it resisted tampering. It was so strong that any attempt to alter its meaning or to add to its canon (as Jesus apparently does with his disciples) was an act audacious enough to strike Luke's written narrative dumb. This is why the readers do not get to hear what Jesus says to his disciples about "all the Scriptures."

Spoken versus Written Parataxis

At this point, we can entertain the difference between the way Jesus appears to teach and the way the narrator and the implied author do teach. It is the difference between once-spoken and forever-written parataxis. As Aristotle says, when parataxis is used in an oral speech it is critical that the members of the audience do *not* get the opportunity to discuss their different ways of connecting statements or spelling out connotations. This kind of analysis might lead them to discover that each one was responding differently. This discovery might destroy the illusion that they each thought like the speaker and so dissipate the sympathetic mood the speaker wishes to exploit. Scriptural homilies exploit this mood. So does Jesus when he can get his Emmaus auditors burning with enthusiasm or when he allows his hostile questioners to interpret his parables for themselves. When parataxis is used in a written narrative, however, its effects are cooler. In the written narrative, different statements (or strategies or effects) remain unconnected on the page. They remain so as long as the text is read, and each reader is vouched the time and the means to compare one possible connection with another. Like the implied readers and the disciples, each interpreter sees the matter differently.

This insight is as old as Plato's *Phaedrus*. In this story, Phaedrus has been equally beguiled by all three speeches Socrates has made on the same topic of love, although he admits that each speech seems more persuasive than the one before it. This would seem to imply, dramatically, that every speech is equally persuasive in the heat of its realization, and that critical judgment is only possible if the listener has the time to compare the record of one to another.

Perhaps the give-and-take between Jesus' teaching and the narrator's teaching in the Emmaus episode has something to do with the gaps and connections we all sense between spoken and written language. Luke acknowledges in the preface to his gospel that he distinguishes the "reports" of eyewitnesses from the *logon* of his "connected account." He reminds us of this distinction throughout the gospel, most resoundingly in the penultimate scene on the road to Emmaus. We need the reminders. Almost every literary narrative resembles Luke's episode in its being, in Robert Kellogg's terms, "a compound of oral and written discourse." This means simply that characters appear to speak and narrators appear to summarize in what the readers take to be oral speech. But actually everything they say is written down. Because of the easy illusion that writing is speaking and speaking writing, we find it easy to write that an author "says" something. At the same time, we would find it awkward to say that a speaker "writes" upon the air as he or she speaks. This convention that a writer can say something indicates how easy it is to blur distinctions: "This refusal of our language to insist upon a distinction between speaking and writing may reflect an implicit cultural ideal of inseparability between them" (p. 55). Deep down we wish that both oral speech and written discourse would adopt the virtues of each. Oral speech would be premeditative and thoughtful while still being spontaneous; written speech would be direct and sincere while still being composed. Yet, Kellogg warns us, blurring the two modes can be dangerous. It often leads to what the disciples of Jacques Derrida have labeled the logocentric fallacy. A reader imagines that a written text is a slice of once-living speech, and one assumes that the language is directly from the heart. Derrida reminds us of the contrary. Every oral speech also reflects the written language of a culture.

This is what Luke knew when he had Jesus speak according to the style in which the venerable scriptures were written. But in this case, the implied author does more. He insists on the necessary distinction between oral and written speech. He only gives the reader a taste of the style, not the substance, of what Jesus has to say. When he curtails Jesus' oral speech and provides only a summary of what he says, the maneuver invites the interpreter to decipher what the implied author intends. Because there is no resolution to the riddle, interpretation of what Jesus meant to say need never end. For any reader who takes Luke literally and seriously, there is no danger of jumping to a hasty conclusion.

Teaching in Tandem

It is only after we appreciate the difference between Jesus' oral teaching and the narrator's written teaching that we can cautiously begin to consider the way they work in tandem. However different their methods, the narrator is a colleague of the main character Jesus in the story. The narrator teaches his audience (the readers) while Jesus teaches his disciples (the other characters) in the story with him. We now consider what kind of colleague the narrator is.

Stanislaw Eile writes that the form of any narrative represents the author's attitude about the narrative's relation to the world. An omniscient, neutral observer, for example, gives the impression that what happens really happened; there is nothing subjective about the report. This effect works better when the style of narration fits in with other apparent representations of objective reality—such as probable character and situations, characters that fit with their situations, "followability" of the story line, etc. What Eile calls the "auctorial" narrative invites the reader to take matters at face value and not to seek hidden meanings. When such a narrator announces a particular point for the story about to be told, the narrative becomes a kind of lecture illustrating a point. Some verisimilitude is sacrificed, but if the voice appears authentic, the story will still seem true. The narrator is the ultimate authority, possessed of a universal wisdom. A second kind of narrator is one who is identified with the story itself, either as a participant or a presence occupying more or less the same universe as the characters in the story. "His interpretations and value judgments cannot pretend to absolute credibility" (p. 121) because he is implicated in the worldview he is describing. It appears that the genius of Luke combines these two narrative views as a way of authenticating the text in two ways. His narrator represents the implied author's overview and is thus an auctorial narrator intimate with the whole scope of the story; at the same time, the narrator appears close to the characters within the story and able to draw nigh to their intimate conversations. The easy passage the narrator makes back and forth between these various perspectives suggests that all three are somewhat close in point of view; therefore the implied author, narrator, and main character have access to each other's perspectives, and perhaps even creative power. This implies that the intimacy of the narrator with both the implied author and the main character Jesus makes possible the intimacy of all three; and thus, in a narrative sense, Jesus is an extraordinary character who is very close to sharing the perspectives of his own narrator and, beyond that, his own implied author. Their norms are the same. Each appears in the narrative to enforce the others' views. Jesus the character is very close to being his own narrator and his own implied author. We detect the shades of a literary trinity. If the narrator and Jesus share a perspective, and the narrator chooses not to cite texts, perhaps it is Jesus who does not want the readers told the definitive texts of reference. They need to find them for themselves. He treats the readers as he does the lawyer whom he tantalizes with the parable of the Good Samaritan.

By permitting the reader to experience this richness of literary relations, the Emmaus episode compensates readers for their late arrival on the scene. We can never hear the main character Jesus speaking, but we can read the report of a writer who understood what Jesus wanted to say. This is as close as we can get. Luke implies in his preface that had we got closer, close enough even to be "eyewitnesses" to what Jesus did and said, we would still need "a connected account" in order to put together what Jesus meant. Interpretation is every bit as important as the original statement. In Booth's terms, Luke's narrator is fully "reliable," which means that the reader is meant to trust what the narrator says. So is the implied author. The living author lived in a historical time and place not far removed from

Jesus'; the implied author sets a literary scene to represent that long-past world. This written realm is as close as we readers are ever going to get to that historical world. But it is in certain respects superior. It has been organized according to a theme, a *logos,* or a meaning. The language that makes up that world derives from the same Septuagint that Jesus presumably helps his disciples to understand anew. The message we hear from all three teachers in the scene is that we need to read further.

A New Narrative Theology

This way of reading a gospel narrative episode is not entirely unknown to modern biblical scholars. It more or less resembles the practice of deriving what Gabriel Fackre calls the "narrative theology" of the Bible. One assumes that the Bible is literature before it is anything else, in the same way, perhaps, as beautiful ceramics are clay. This is to say, whatever religious literature might say about God and human beings in a story together, the narrator in the story plays a "plotting role," and this narrative plot is as close as any reader ever gets to the actual intention of the once-living author or to the history of the times that that author might have been hoping to represent. "Narrative . . . becomes [therefore] the decisive image for understanding and interpreting faith. Depiction of reality, ultimate and penultimate, in terms of plot, coherence, movement and climax is at the center of all forms of this talk about God" (p. 343). When a reader reads a biblical text or any religious text as a narrative, Fackre says, then the medium becomes a part of the message. The religious story, like any narrative story, both discloses secrets to the reader and jars and jolts the reader with new perspectives that are frequently (when most successful) disorienting. A narrative is a bundle of surprises so wrapped that it is surprising every time it is read, even by the same reader returning again and again to the same narrative story. There is something profoundly unorthodox about every narrative, biblical ones included, because they are designed so that they never yield a definitive statement or answer, or even question. The text appears to say something different every time it is read, in the same way that a work of sculpture appears differently as one walks about its mass and finds the perspective and the background shifting as one moves. Every narrative is language shaped and textured—*rough* surfaces.

But once again, they are not the same. A consistently paratactic reading is not precisely what Fackre has in mind. Like Fitzmyer and Dawsey, he insists that all legitimate criticism of scripture leads to an affirmation of faith, as he says above. The remainder of this book explores the difference between a reading that ends in affirmation and a reading that stays and plays with the endless implications of narrative parataxis. Faith is too hasty for this second kind of reading.

Luke makes it hard to decide just what one is supposed to believe about Jesus. How independent is his story from the venerable stories that went before? When Luke leaves this question hanging, he manages brilliantly to preserve a central theme in the venerable stories as Alter and Sternberg present them. There is an enduring affection for the older, rejected brother in many of the stories of the triumph of the younger brother. Beginning with the early story of Cain and Abel and continuing with the paired fortunes of Ishmael and Isaac, Jacob and Esau, Perez and Zerah, Manasseh and Ephraim, we read of the struggles between the two brothers. The younger one is more favored. The older one becomes angry when blessings pass him by. The younger brother always triumphs, but the older brother manages to survive and even prosper. If the Lord's blessing does not extend to the older brother, at least he enjoys continuing care. Cain wins God's uneasy forgiveness. Jacob is reconciled with Esau at their father's grave. An angel tells Hagar not to be afraid when she is exiled with her son Ishmael, Isaac's older brother: "God has heard the child crying where you laid him. Get to your feet, lift the child up and hold him in your arms, because I will make of him a great nation" (Genesis 20:18). When Joseph finally reveals himself to his astonished brothers, he tells them not to be afraid of their history of estrangement. It was prologue to a present atonement: "God sent me ahead of you to ensure that you will have descendants on earth, and to preserve you all, a great band of survivors" (Genesis 46:7–8). In this spirit, Luke's character Jesus has the Forgiving Father tell his less favored elder son: "All I own is yours . . ." Luke's narrator only hints that there are parallels between episodes in the older scriptures and episodes in Jesus' life. The brothers remain a part of the same family as their separate stories remain a part of the same canon; the younger ones can never escape the influence of their elders. What Luke's Jesus comes to believe is that only gnosis—like the instinct for familial love—can understand how a new character can still belong to an older tradition of stories.

This leads to the supposition that Luke in his gospel counters Paul's and Matthew's rejection of Jewish culture. It seems as though Luke's Gospel might have been written after the Pauline epistles to counter them with a kinder and more ambivalent vision. Wolfgang Iser makes the point that fiction evokes history often to criticize it; fiction asks the questions that a particular culture cannot bring itself to ask otherwise. This implies that fiction criticizes as much as it represents. This prompts the idea that perhaps the "history" of the gospels is precisely what they were intended to counter or resist. Luke's narrative *opposes* the developing Christian thought of the day with a more kindly, a more open and gnostic vision that not every story or image from the past needs to be eclipsed by the new light. More specifically, perhaps Luke's Gospel was intended to be anti-Pauline. Its complex images of a humane, generous Jesus countered Paul's abstract, codified Jesus. The least fruitful way to read this text then would be to place it with Paul's epistles, the very influence of which Luke may have been trying to resist.

Similarly, on literary-critical grounds, I do not accept the current biblical scholarly consensus that Luke's Gospel and the Acts of the Apostles should be read together as if they were contiguous and continuous. Each narrative uses different narrative strategies to suggest very different religious points of view, most specifically the question of the relationship between Jesus' story and the stories in "all the Scriptures" that preceded his. The Paul in Acts, whether he is a character of Luke's or not, comes to a much more definitive and explicit answer to this question than the Jesus in the gospel ever does. In other words, just as we need to keep authorities within each scene distinct for any fully literary interpretation of this episode, we need to keep even canonically related narratives distinct. This is the only way the precise relationship between them can be given its due; and this in turn is the only way the fullest religious interpretation can be given its due.

In summary, when we attend to the implied author of the Emmaus episode, we fall under the spell of a master magician. We experience more than a magic trick vicariously through our reading about the trick Jesus plays on his disciples. As we take in the original words of the story, we are already taking in the language and the atmosphere of the venerable scriptures the implied author reveres. We are being prepared for the trick the narrator will play on us, the implied readers, when we do not get to hear what specific texts Jesus had in mind. We are being prepared to understand that the trick is not meant to frustrate us. It should provoke us into exploring the family tree of stories of which this is a small branching fork pointing backwards toward the source.

In this chapter, I have suggested that Luke learned from the stories in the venerable scriptures about how to tell the story of the struggles between younger and older brothers. His younger brother is Jesus. Luke's version of this story does not cut Jesus off from his older kin, even after he receives the special blessing of the resurrection. In the next chapter, we consider what other literature might have helped give Luke the magic touch he brings to his reiteration of this ancient theme. From the gnostic narrators Luke learned how to fashion a narrative that *resists* a definitive reading.

Chapter Two
Strong New Readings

If ever the search for a tranquil belief
  should end,
The future might stop emerging out of
  the past.

Wallace Stevens, Ideas of Order

There is a tendency to overlook the
power of Christianity to create new
concepts and forms of expression.

Fr. D. E. Schleiermacher, The
Hermeneutics

The Cantonnage

We have considered what Luke could have learned about writing from the venerable scriptures that he has Jesus cite; we now consider what Luke could have learned from the gnostic teachers. Basically he learned how to handle miraculous appearances in a new, understated way. Gnostic narratives frequently present a savior appearing and disappearing, as Jesus does before the two disciples he meets on the road to Emmaus. The miracle, however, does not dazzle or mystify its audience, as do the miracles of the venerable scriptures that Luke knew. The gnostic miracle does not emphasize the power of the miracle maker. The effect of the miracle is domesticated, diminished to the incandescence of a surprising insight.

For example, in *Eugnostos the Blessed,* one of the narratives in the recently discovered gnostic library, an anonymous first-person narrator announces in the first few lines that "the Savior appeared not in his first form, but in the invisible spirit. And his form was like a great angel of light. And his likeness I must not describe." The gnostic narrator does not dwell on spectacular effects. In fact, the narrator does not even inform the reader what the changed appearance looks like. It could be called a "blind description," one that says something happened but makes no attempt to explain what it looked like, as if the reader were blind from birth, so that a verbal picture would be superfluous. This narrative tactic deliberately puts the reader at a disadvantage vis à vis the narrator in the scene, and the narrator will not yield. It is part of the narrative effect to suggest that there is more here than can meet the readers' eyes.

We find the same tactic in the Emmaus scene, of course, where the narrator does not say what holds the disciples' eyes and makes Jesus look like an ordinary man. But perhaps a better transformation for comparison would be the one that occurs when Jesus takes three disciples, Peter, James, and John, with him to a mountain to pray:

> While he was at prayer, the appearance of his face suddenly became different, and his garments white and dazzling. Then two men were seen conversing with him. They were Moses and Elijah, who appeared in glory and were speaking of his departure, the one that he was to complete in Jerusalem. But Peter and his companions had been drowsy with sleep; rousing themselves, they saw his glory and the two men who stood beside him. As these gradually withdrew from him, Peter said to Jesus, "Master, it is good that we are here. Let us put up three huts, one for you, one for Moses, and one for Elijah." But he did not know what he was saying. While he was saying this, a cloud formed and cast its shadow over them; and as they passed into the cloud, they became afraid. Then a voice from the cloud spoke out, "This is my son, my Chosen One! Listen to him!" Once that voice had spoken, Jesus was to be found alone. And they kept silent, telling no one in those days what they had seen. (Luke 9:29–36)

Fitzmyer follows the general scholarly consensus that Luke adapted the scene from Mark's Gospel, changing several significant elements. Whereas Mark's narrator says Jesus was "transfigured," using the word *metemorphothe* to indicate a major change in his nature, not only his appearance, Luke's narrator says only that "the appearance of his face suddenly became different." Thus it is somewhat of a misnomer to refer to Luke's version as a "Transfiguration scene." The emphasis falls more on the magical appearance of three characters from the venerable scriptures—Moses, Elijah, and a God who speaks from on high. The appearance of Moses and Elijah implies, first of all, that they are Jesus' equals in the ongoing tradition of biblical narrative stories. Along these lines, only in Luke do the three share an ineffable "glory" (*doxa*). Fitzmyer says that the term refers only to "an inner quality" rather than to any extraordinary physical manifestation. It is also significant that Luke's narrator identifies the topic of the conversation Jesus has with Elijah and Moses. They talk about his "departure" (*exodos*), a word that recalls the tradition of departures in the venerable scriptures from which Elijah and Moses emerge. Their subsequent disappearance, along with God's identification of Jesus as his "Chosen One" implies that Jesus has somehow preempted their traditional leadership roles. He is another younger brother like that of the parable of the Forgiving Father, which Jesus will tell later on in the narrative. A better name for Luke's version might be the "Succession scene"—where a new character takes over in his turn the protagonist's role. Jesus does not so much replace Moses and Elijah as take their place. This is another instance of Luke's narrative coyness about Jesus' place in the venerable tradition.

Fitzmyer favors the interpretation that these and other changes that Luke makes anticipate the appearance of the risen Christ as he will appear later in the gospel narrative. Jesus departs from death, from the earth, and from traditional patterns set down in the venerable scriptures. As he does, it is important for Luke to stress that Jesus is the same man before and after the extraordinary event of his resurrection. This is not necessarily an inimitable miracle. Luke, in other words, foreshadows his own narrative conclusion with many significant anticipations.

We can certainly find elements in this scene that recur "differently" in the postresurrection Emmaus scene. There only Jesus' appearance has changed, not his nature. There disciples, like Peter, see more than they can understand and experience a sudden change in both their perception and their understanding. Jesus meets them on the first leg of his new *exodos* that he first discusses with his venerable predecessors. Indeed, an element in the Emmaus scene might satisfy the one problem Fitzmyer has with his favored interpretation of the changes: "What would Moses and Elijah be doing in a post-resurrection appearance story?" (p. 796). The answer could be that at least Moses' appearance on the mountain early in the gospel anticipates his appearance in a reference to "Moses and the prophets" that Jesus reportedly interprets for his disciples. This is a "different" appearance surely. But it is typical of Luke's ability to render even his own adaptations of traditional materials into many different narrative forms.

This kind of cross-referencing can also work the other way, of course. When we read backwards from Luke's unique Emmaus scene to the unique elements in Luke's Succession scene, we find that Jesus is an active teacher only in the Emmaus scene. In the Succession scene, Jesus is mute, with the narrator and God speaking the major lines. Perhaps this is because Jesus himself learns more about his particular role and how to describe it from this episode and others he will have before the grand denouement of his story. But in both scenes, Luke's narrator actively manipulates the readers' point of view in order to suggest what the narrator of *Eugnostos the Blessed* says explicitly. There is more happening in these scenes of Jesus' changing, and more implied, than any narrator dares to describe. We can examine other evidence that certain gnostic writings might have inspired Luke to develop the sly coyness of his narrative adaptations.

We are fortunate to be able to consider what Luke might have learned from the gnostics. Only in recent years have the gnostic texts come to light that reflect the thought that might have helped Luke learn how to write. I introduce a comparison of what the gnostics and Luke wrote with some remarks about how the comparison must be made. We cannot be certain that Luke actually read the same gnostic narratives we now possess, although he might have. However, we can rationally presume that he was acquainted with the earlier, possibly oral teaching that these narratives later came to reflect. Furthermore, he was stimulated by that teaching. It inspired him to devise a new way to write a narrative scene.

The written narratives I refer to are the texts in the gnostic library. They were discovered in 1945 in a buried jar near the present-day Middle Eastern village of Nag Hammadi. Although their dating is inexact, internal evidence suggests that they were written in Luke's age, and they were probably buried about 400 C.E. to save them from destruction by orthodox Christians who had already branded them heretical. In fact, many of the texts were known before the discovery at Nag Hammadi only through disparaging description or remarks by second- and third-century orthodox commentators and theologians. It was the genius of Hans Jonas to be able to reconstruct the gnostic worldview primarily through secondary sources. Only in the last decade have scholarly editions been made available that allow close comparisons with orthodox Christian texts.

As we shall see, scholars have been rightfully very tentative in speculating about the relationship between gnostic and orthodox narratives of any kind. The historical record of their relations is not clear. To a certain degree, this lack of clarity allows some speculative scholarly freedom. There are no facts forbidding close comparisons between these two texts, as if they were close relatives of the same family of narratives. The spirit in which these comparisons are done is critical.

We begin our firsthand examination of these texts by fingering, as it were, the cantonnage, or covers. They provide an interesting, material introduction to the contents. The original codices were bound in soft leather stiffened with layers of scrap papyri. When the bindings were undone and the papyri pulled apart, legible writing in Greek and Coptic was discovered to be covering many of the papyri. The writings on these scraps are fascinating because their concerns are unabashedly domestic. They list business transactions, deeds, and ordinary legal proceedings; there are letters between friends, businessmen, and monks. It is as if the ordinary mundane world surrounding the religious movements of the day crowded in on the religious texts themselves, getting as close as the covers to the scripture. Occasionally the writers reveal themselves as Christians, but in very undogmatic, idiomatic ways. A scrap entitled Letter Number 68, a fragment of a fourth-century letter from Harpocration to Sansnos, asks the latter to be patient in a matter concerning some rents due "as behooves your charity in Christ (*tae en Chraesto sou agapae*). Letter 69, from Sansnos to Aphrodisios, discussing the management of a farm, begins with a greeting "in the Lord . . ." (*en Kurio*), a routine greeting used in several other letters as well, none of which discusses any religious matters in length or detail. Piety among the truly religious often becomes conventional. Even the letters whose senders or receivers appear to be monks or priests, especially the Coptic letters, are concerned primarily with matters of business or sustenance. If the letters and other texts of the cantonnage can be taken as typical of the concerns of the day, the literal context they supply to the gnostic gospels serves to localize and soften the language of the scripture within. Although these scriptures might evoke the cosmos and seem addressed to the ends of the earth, they were written to be read by people with the ordinary concerns of getting along in the world. They excited strong religious sentiments in the minds of worshippers whose bodies could move about comfortably in the business of daily life.

The material cantonnage, therefore, provides a special context in which to place these texts. They were written in an ordinary world to stimulate the thinking of ordinary people. The image we receive of Sansnos is very different from the portraits of gnostic villains we often discover in the writings of early orthodox ecclesiastics. In fact, until the discoveries at Nag Hammadi, orthodox polemics against gnostic writing served as a kind of prejudicial cantonnage. The polemics, by their nature, tended to warn any potential reader of the gnostic scriptures of the great differences between orthodox and gnostic perspectives. But these differences appear great only when one is putting a very fine point on the subtleties of dogma. For the more dispassionate reader, the differences between these texts might appear as interesting as the different points of view in various Christian writings today. A believer might well be stimulated, then as now, by reading about another form of religious belief *without* finding his or her faith shaken in the process. Such a reader might reconstruct the mood in which Luke is likely to have read similar documents or listened to thinkers with ideas similar to those expressed in these documents. There was much to learn here about how to imagine religiously.

The Hermeneutical Circle

Today such a comparative reading of orthodox and gnostic scriptures takes advantage of the historical accidents that hid the gnostic scriptures. They have traveled through time with little baggage. George Aichele has called the discovery of these codices "a hermeneutical dream" because they contain texts that exist in and of themselves, with no past, and having almost no historical consequences. For one thing, it is significant that the gnostic gospels at Nag Hammadi come down to us in only single copies. They have not been passed from hand to hand or received an overload of interpretation as the canonical gospels have. For another thing, the gnostic gospels are thought to be Coptic translations of Greek originals. Judging from the quality of the occasional passage for which the Greek original still exists, the translations were poor. Thus one finds the texts opaque. It is very hard to penetrate through to an underlying intention. What the original authors thought lies as remote from the surface meaning of the text as the original language in which it was probably composed. All that is left of that intention are its literal traces in the narrative arrangement.

The orthodox gospels initially appear to be a different story, of course. They were written in Greek, and we possess early copies of the Greek originals. And there is an apparent continuity between the first disciples who appear as characters within their pages and the earliest leaders of the church. Therefore church history, and indeed, even the church itself seem to provide, from the beginning, an avenue through which to explore the pretextual situation. The orthodox gospels seem to have a past, and they certainly have had consequences.

Yet a comparison of orthodox and gnostic scriptures can still be made as among peers. The real differences between them are not all that great. The orthodox gospel texts also had a source in another language besides that in which they have come down to us. According to Matthew Black and other scholars, Jesus and his disciples most certainly spoke Aramaic, and the earliest oral traditions about what he said and did presumably were Aramaic as well; this oral original also lies behind the veil of written translation. Therefore, granting that these texts have inspired eighteen hundred years of close reading, we can probably rest assured that there will never be any serious agreement about the original authors' intentions, or indeed, who they even were beyond their names. To date the study of the history of the early church has yielded only ambiguous evidence in this regard. There is no harm, in the interim, in reading closely the original texts we do possess of both scriptures. A comparative analysis might provide corroboration someday for any harder evidence that scholars might find about the intentions behind each kind of scripture and the precise historical relations of their being written down.

Today, historians of early Christianity are particularly interested in the relationship between gnostic writings and orthodox Christian scriptures; but as of this moment, they are uncertain about what the actual influence of one upon the other might have been. In a recent comprehensive review, Edwin Yamauchi describes current scholarly opinion that there are no gnostic texts that date with any certainty from the pre-Christian era. Therefore it is improper to assume that there was any direct influence of written gnostic texts on the writing of any Christian scripture. Also, as of now, no common source has been discovered upon which both gnostic and orthodox narrative writers might have drawn. Yamauchi agrees with C. M. Tuckett and other scholars that if there was any direct influence at all, it probably went the other way; there is considerable evidence that the gospels directly influenced gnostic narratives.

At the same time, a number of scholars maintain, in Yamauchi's words, that "Gnosticism is an essential element in the hermeneutical circle [required] to understand the New Testament" (p. 23). That is to say, gnostic ideas probably had a currency at the time that the orthodox scriptures were written, and that their writers were likely to have been aware of them in one way or another. Luke did not have to be familiar with gnostic texts to be familiar with gnostic ideas. We could say with Walter Schmithals that the question of the inter-influence of gnostic and orthodox scriptures presents an interesting "hermeneutical circle." We can assume that Luke probably learned from the gnostics and the gnostic narrative writers (at least) probably learned from Luke, without being able to be certain about the precise chronology of their borrowings.

The hermeneutical circle is a term for a style of reading made popular by the late-eighteenth-century and early-nineteenth-century theorist of interpretation, Friedrich Schleiermacher. It refers to the process of circular understanding whereby we compare parts to what we already understand of the whole and vice versa. Schleiermacher usually used the term in speaking of individual texts as wholes. He assumed the Romantic notion of Friedrich von Schlegel and S. T. Coleridge that literary works worthy of the name possessed an "organic unity" as any living fauna and flora. The careful interpreter determines the precise role that every part or organ of a narrative contributes to its overall effect or life. A character like Jesus acting dramatically as he does in the Emmaus episode provides a special emphasis to themes underlying the entire work of art. To appreciate Luke's artistic intent requires reading every episode in light of the entire work of art. This is what we do when we compare the narrator's teaching strategy in one episode to the main character's in another. But even Schleiermacher envisioned applying the method more widely. A reader could read an individual work of art as part of a family of works, or canon, the sum of which provided a certain context for understanding what a particular writer was up to. This broader hermeneutical circle revived much of the patristic practice of allegorical readings, but now with an increased sensitivity to the particularities of each writer's contribution to a larger body of thought. There was, according to Schleiermacher's way of thinking, no room for the belief that the holy spirit inspired individual authors unconsciously to contribute their individual parts to the whole. He insisted that even if the holy spirit used writers as pens, it still could not have forced them to write what they were not conscious of writing (p. 7). This statement completes his whole understanding of this theory. A reader assumes that writers are conscious of what they are doing when they subordinate their episodes to the overall meaning of the work. A reader also assumes that writers consciously contribute their individual works to a canon of works—if indeed one is able to read that work canonically—as part of a larger whole.

Of course, this theory of interpretation is also circular. One assumes what a writer intended in order to prove that the writer intended it; a hypothesis becomes the evidence with which one begins. In the present case, we reason that Luke understood gnosticism, and our proof is that we find certain unique parables or episodes in his gospel similar to stories or episodes we find in the gnostic gospels. (We also assume that these fourth-century gospels reflect the written or unwritten gnostic teaching of the first century.) But in order to claim that the similarities between these narratives are more than coincidental, we need to assume that Luke knew what he was doing when he shaped his episode in a certain way. He deliberately and provocatively wrote his episode to contrast with the way a gnostic teacher or writer would handle a similar episode. This assumption turns out to be identical with what we want to prove. Therefore this kind of interpretation is always going to be more like elaborating a hunch than proving a point. It is going to be a useful exercise when, and only when, there is virtually no external and corroborating evidence to be had. At worst, it is a holding action; at best it freshens an appreciation of a familiar text by emphasizing what is unique about its various parts. In this case, what is unique appears when one understands the way different writers handled the same sort of episode. A comparison of this kind provides a generic rather than a historical analysis. That is to say, we compare different texts that we decide belong to the same genre, regardless of the time they were written.

This kind of analysis, with its attendant assumptions, directs the discussion in this chapter of Luke's handling of the themes of magic and timelessness in the Succession and Emmaus episodes, and in other features unique to his narrative. It does not matter whether Luke had actually read gnostic texts, although we can suspect he did. Instead, we consider what evidence there is that he was aware of their teaching and was confident of his abilities to appropriate them to his own orthodox purposes. He did so with great sympathy. He was drawn to preserve the best of the religious ideas many early Christian authorities viewed only with suspicion.

Broad Distinctions

To guide their comparisons, scholars such as Malcolm Peel now distinguish "gnosis," "gnosticism," "pre-gnosticism," and "proto-gnosticism." In Peel's terms, gnosis is knowledge of the divine mysteries reserved for the elite; gnosticism refers specifically to that unique form of religion developed in certain second-century sects that was first identified and combated by heresiologists of that century; pre-gnosticism is the particular set of theological ideas that emerge from Mesopotamian, Egyptian, Iranian, Jewish, and Christian spheres of influence, and that are found in their uniquely gnostic combination only in the developed second-century systems; proto-gnostic describes fully developed gnostic systems that emerged prior to the second century (pp. 142–43). Anyone wishing to compare gnostic and orthodox Christian scriptures would share the supposition that Peel identifies as the "proto-gnostic" assumption. One assumes that "proto-gnostic ideas and conceptions were utilized by certain New Testament writers, with such ideas occasionally exerting considerable theological influence" (p. 145).

Much of the work that has been done in this vein has stressed the large differences between gnostic and orthodox writing. Scholars often assume, as Jonas and Bultmann have, that there is an "essential gnosticism" that one can abstract from all of the gnostic writings. With their assumption, one explains each individual expression as another way of expressing certain abstract ideas common to many gnostic thinkers. In this way, it is easy to draw broad general distinctions between Jewish, gnostic, and Christian modes of thought.

It has been widely assumed, for example, that although they were written in an intellectual milieu aware of the Hebrew or Septuagint scriptures, gnostic writings encouraged abandoning close readings of them or *any* scripture. The gnostics wanted to free themselves for a new religious experience. Harold Bloom calls gnostic writing "strong because it is supermimetic, because it confronts and seeks to overthrow the very strongest of all texts, the Jewish Bible" (p. 72). In a term Bloom has made famous in other contexts, gnosticism is "misprision." By misprision he means that a writer is treating his literary forebears harshly. The writer deliberately and perversely misreads the older texts. The "purpose is to clear away the precursor so as to open a space for oneself" (p. 67). In Bloom's view, this purpose is not really directed against prior literature as such. It is directed against *anything* prior. The quintessential gnostic narrative reconstructs the "first chance" or the *now* pre-existing at any time or in any place.

Several other scholars make the same point with different emphases. Mircea Eliade distinguishes between the gnostic and the orthodox sense of time in general terms. In his view, the gnostic scriptures are generally indifferent to particular times and places. Even the identity of the individuals changes in the scene with the major voice. Their role is reduced to simple stimulus. They ask the questions that allow the major voice in the scene to reveal certain mysteries. This voice also takes on different forms or disguises. There is nothing specific in gnostic narratives whatsoever. The gnostic mind is archaic because it has no sense of history.

Eliade's main thesis is that Judeo-Christian religion is the first to distance itself from the tendency of the archaic mind to deny the significance of history. The process begins with the Hebrew prophets, who placed a value on historical events because they found them to manifest God's particular intervention in Hebrew history: "Thus, for the first time, the prophets placed a value on history, succeeded in transcending the traditional vision of the cycle (the conception that ensures all things will be repeated forever), and discovered one way time" (p. 104). Christianity amplifies this concept with its belief that the savior appeared at a historical time, to actual people, performed certain deeds, died on a certain day, and rose on another. Yet the older idea that real time was *in illo tempore* (literally "in that time" or in the mythic eternity before real time began counting) never completely disappeared. The Christian gospels speak of a time to come when time will be annihilated; and this was very early theologized into the doctrines of the second coming: "When the Messiah comes, the world will be saved once and for all and history will cease to exist" (p. 107).

Thus the gospels could be said to reckon a mixed economy of time. Actual events, particular characters, and distinct personalities have value to the extent that they belong to Jesus' specific history; but they do so precisely because they are part of a historical sequence of events leading to the eventual abolishment of time. The gnostic scripture reckons the same mixed economy differently. Its savior will make reference to the events of historical life. But usually he will insist that the value of such events is only what they manifest about the invisible, timeless cosmos. The appearances of this savior do occur to actual disciples, often with the same names as the disciples in the canonical gospels. But rarely do the minor characters display any distinctive personalities. They could be *any* devout listener; indeed, this seems to be the point of their virtual anonymity. The occasion for the meeting is usually a vision or a dream—circumstances in which humans stand outside of a particular time and place in literal ecstasy.

This is the basic insight of George Aichele, who describes the fundamental difference between Christian scripture and gnostic writing in terms of the difference between a timely, trenchant story and a timeless, spaceless myth: "Theologians of the Judeo-Christian tradition have stressed the importance to both religions of history—i.e., of linear temporality. Temporality is seen as fundamental to both the content of that tradition—the world created by God and moving inexorably under God's 'authorship' towards its end—and to its context—the believer (as individual and as community) in relation to God. . . . Thus 'story' is almost inevitably discussed as 'history' (linear time)" (p. 27). When we extend these ideas to our comparison, we find that Luke's Emmaus episode and others like it are more linear than most of those in the gnostics because the sequence in which things happen is crucial to the story. Also, the main character himself values history because it enables him to see between past stories and the present one he finds himself in, while past and present interpret each other. This is close to Joseph Frank's concept of spatial vs. linear form, which Aichele cites. In modern literature, Frank wrote, the spatial expands at the expense of the linear: "Just as the dimension of depth has vanished from the sphere of visual creation, so the dimension of historical depth has vanished from the content of major works of modern literature. Past and present are apprehended spatially, locked in a timeless unity that, while it may accentuate surface differences, eliminates any feeling of sequence by the very act of juxtaposition." "Paul Tillich has argued along very similar lines," Aichele adds, "relating spatially-oriented religions to tragedy, idolatry, polytheism, and nationalism, and relating temporally-oriented religions (the Judeo-Christian tradition) to human triumph over tragedy and unjustice, to the prophetic tradition, and to monotheism." In Tillich's words, "human existence under the predominance of space is tragic. Greek tragedy and philosophy knew about this. They knew that the Olympic gods were gods of space, one beside the other, one struggling with the other. Even Zeus was only the first of many equals, and hence subject, together with man and the other gods, to the tragic law of genesis and decay" (p. 33).

The Ancient Arguments against Gnosticism

As we now see, such comparisons and complaints are of long standing. Bloom cites Jonas citing Irenaeus complaining about the gnostics of his day: "Every day every one of them invents something new, and none of them is considered perfect unless he is productive in this way" (p. 70). The gnostic, Irenaeus goes on, never learns anything, "because learning is a process *in time*" (p. 72).

Elaine H. Pagels finds she can best compare gnostic narratives celebrating the mystery and spiritualness of the risen Christ only to the Emmaus episode in Luke and to the episodes in Acts and the Epistles featuring Paul and an otherworldly Jesus. To take one example she cites, the *Book of Thomas the Contender* features a dialogue between the resurrected Jesus and his brother Judas Thomas, allegedly recorded by Mathaias. The savior naturally assumes, as the disguised Jesus does in Luke, the role of a teacher passing on superior knowledge to an auditor who is walking with him: "So while you accompany me, although you are uncomprehending, you have (in fact) already come to know, and you will be called 'the one who knows himself' . . ." (p. 189). These episodes resemble the Emmaus episode and the depictions of the epiphanies of Paul in marked contrast to most of the post resurrection stories in the canonical gospels. Typically, the orthodox stories, including Luke's Succession scene and the other postresurrection stories it anticipates, stress Jesus' ordinary physical reappearance. Even after death, he appears as a man who could cook and eat fish and offer his wounds to be touched. These stories deliberately downplay any mystical and magical effects of Jesus' uncanny return from the dead.

Pagels wonders why the few scenes in the orthodox gospels such as the Emmaus episode and the epiphanies of Paul, which have much in common with directly mystical gnostic views, were not featured more in determining the content of orthodox Christianity. She answers her own question with her argument that orthodox doctrine in early Christianity carefully chose to avoid commenting on even its own texts when they contained elements that could suggest unorthodox readings. In the early years of Christianity, she says, unorthodox readings were most often gnostic readings or gnostic versions of traditional Christian stories. To counter their influence, the orthodox position stressed the ordinariness of the resurrected Jesus, his actual physical appearance in the flesh, blood, and form of his originally mortal self, and his appearances in this form to a few select disciples who held no doubts that they were actually seeing Jesus. According to Pagels, these emphases had political motives; belief in the bodily resurrection of Jesus legitimized "the authority of certain men who claim to exercise exclusive leadership over the churches as successors of the apostle Peter" (p. 6). Only a small number of people were privileged to see Jesus in the flesh, and if authority is vested only in them and their picked successors, then the lines of command will be short and tight. On the other hand, if the experience of a physically dead but spiritually living Jesus can be personal and spontaneous, the lines of command would all but disappear. The orthodox reading of the resurrection favored institutional organization, not as in the Emmaus episode a magical and personal experience; and therefore it was convenient for early orthodox Christianity to overlook the canonical texts (or features of them) that did not fit its agenda.

The general nature of this intellectual conflict has long been known. The dean of gnostic scholars, Hans Jonas, did most of his work before the Nag

Hammadi library was available, reconstructing gnostic texts from patristic citations. He points out that the gnostics returned the disfavor in which they were held when they could. The most orthodox of the gnostics, Marcion, included only an expurgated Luke (but containing the Emmaus scene) and selected letters of Paul within his personal canon of acceptable Christian works. According to Jonas's analysis, Marcion's tiny canon contained the only texts in which he could find the central theme of gnosticism: the alienation of human beings from both nature and God. In this scheme, human beings spend their whole lives as prisoners of their own consciousness. On their own, they can make no real, satisfying contact with anything else on earth or with any divine beings beyond the earth. They never make contact with nature because nature cannot respond to human needs. The only reconciliation with extrahuman life possible is between human beings and God, and this comes only at God's instigation. God reveals himself through direct knowledge—gnosis. This consists of a one-way infusion to which the passive human being renders him or herself open (much as the Emmaus disciples inadvertently did).

These ideas are conveyed more often by images than by abstract or philosophical language. The individual is pictured as alone in the world, frequently depicted as a stranger on a road, wandering with no clear sense of direction. An encounter with a voice or with a disguised figure whose identity often changes frequently begins the individual's enlightenment. The apparent beauty or order of nature is seen to be illusory, save for its appearance of vastness or magnitude, through contemplation of which an individual might come to recognize his or her helplessness. Jonas links these themes to the alienation experienced by many of the citizens in the Roman Empire, whose native cultures had been denuded of their identity and roots and even language. It is this condition that the gnostic savior addresses. The savior breaks into this closed system from without, and through the power of a special knowledge he defeats the fated powers that loom over the individual. The individual who responds openly has the chance of becoming authentic.

Pagels, Jonas, and other scholars can now better deconstruct the Fathers' polemics against these views precisely because the discovery at Nag Hammadi puts into their hands the same texts the Fathers read, the lot of which, it is supposed, fourth-century Christian authorities almost successfully burned. In Henry Chadwick's terms: ". . . the Church felt gnosis to be a *Doppelgänger,* a rival with the additional danger of teaching that orthodox faith and practice was a perfectly acceptable inferior level of spiritual aspiration, certainly not false, but a lower grade beyond which one might seek to rise with gnostic help" (p. 14).

Similarly we can now better deconstruct the primary narratives themselves, determining what compares and does not compare in episodes in the orthodox and gnostic scriptures. We can compare them because they both develop out of the same religious milieu, while heading off in very different directions, as many scholars have already noted. But I think the best way to make these comparisons is to heed the call of Malcolm Peel for closer, more nuanced readings. He says that when scholars read the Nag Hammadi literature closely, there turns out to be more individuality of expression in these texts than often immediately strikes the eye (p. 165).

Peel shows, for example, that the gnostics stressed the idea that gnosis and salvation occurred simultaneously in a kind of mystical, timeless "now." Yet there is often, in certain texts, a complimentary idea that a series of "nows" could be contained in a timely progression toward some future culmination. There is, in other words, an identifiable eschatology in gnostic thinking—an " 'already/not yet' tension" (p. 163). This makes it possible to compare their various views of history with some subtlety. To be sure, the orthodox stress the importance of historical process more than the gnostics do, but the differences are in degree, not kind. Likewise, the gnostics stress the importance of the spirit over the body and have much to say about the survival of the " 'pneuma-self' at death" (p. 163). Yet there are images of a rather substantial " 'resurrection body' of some type" in much gnostic writing (p. 163). Our comparisons of the genuine differences between orthodox and gnostic perspectives simply have to be more nuanced than the early polemicists and later idealists realized.

Closer Distinctions

Since the discovery of gnostic texts at Nag Hammadi, we can now make comparisons between narratives as narratives. Initially the comparisons were made only between similar phrases in both orthodox and gnostic writings taken out of context. In the introduction to his commentary, Fitzmyer lists Lucan passages derived from Mark, from "Q," and from "L" which have parallels in the Gospel of Thomas discovered at Nag Hammadi. This gospel is more a collection of sayings than a connected story (pp. 85–87). Fitzmyer shows in his commentary that most of these phrases originate with the synoptic tradition. This is consistent with the theory that most of the written gnostic works *we now possess* were influenced by the orthodox scriptures, not the other way around.

I propose to follow Pagels's lead in comparing the ways in which gnostic and orthodox scriptural narratives are composed. At this level, it is less easy to date the sequence of influence. That is because the gnostic way of thinking is very closely related to a style of telling stories in which characters are carefully prepared to experience an overwhelming event—both for their benefit and the benefit of the readers looking on (or if the stories were originally oral, for the benefit of the listeners listening in). This way of telling stories could very well have antedated any of the written documents we now possess, whether gnostic or orthodox. Let us say that Luke had heard, or even read, no longer existing stories told the gnostic way. They might have influenced his way of recomposing many of the written materials he had about the life of Jesus. They might have inspired his original compositions, such as the episode at Emmaus or the parables of the Forgiving Father and the Good Samaritan. Then, his particular imaginative reformulations might have inspired later, more resolutely gnostic thinkers and writers to write narratives with significantly different emphases.

But I think I can see that the distinctions between orthodox and gnostic ideas are finer in narrative form than in any other. Luke and the gnostic writers are equally concerned with the growth and change of human thought, with the magical moment when one way of thinking yields place to another. Furthermore, we find that when Luke examines this theme in the Succession scene, the Emmaus scene, and others, he uses narrative techniques for which we can find contemporary counterparts only in the gnostic scriptures. We also find that his narrative control defies precise comparison even with theirs. The difference points up the creative way Luke found to be orthodox.

To make this kind of comparison, we need to compare like to like. This is not often easy to do. Early orthodox rhetoric consists of several fairly distinct literary genres: the gospel narrative, the epistle, the commentary, the apology, and the polemic. The gnostic writings in the Nag Hammadi codices tend to combine elements of all these in single texts that continually shift modes, like a musical piece changing keys. Therefore I want to focus first on aspects of both literary traditions more fundamental than rhetoric, genre, or style. These are the mythic aspects emerging in certain common themes.

In addition to the large effects, Pagel compares a number of subordinate themes common to the gnostic narratives about a risen savior and Luke's narrative in the Emmaus episode. For example, as we have already seen in *Eugnostos the Blessed,* an anonymous first-person narrator announces in the first few lines that "the Savior appeared not in his first form, but in the invisible spirit. And his form was like a great angel of light. And his likeness I must not describe." We called this a "blind description." Another common narrative technique becomes apparent when the savior identifies the source of his teaching or wisdom. It comes from someplace above and beyond him. In this example, he states: "I came from the Boundless One so that I might tell you all things . . ." (p. 211); in Luke's Succession scene, neither the narrator nor Jesus says anything about the place he has come from. Instead, the appearance of the venerable characters Moses and Elijah only implies that the already-written scriptures provide the prerequisite premonitions for understanding his exodus or his point of departure. Apparently only after the resurrection, on the road to Emmaus, does Jesus himself come to command the specifics. Therefore, the narrator more pointedly withholds pertinent information in the later scene. We could call this technique a "deaf description." We are told about what we are not able (or allowed) to hear.

We can take another example from a gnostic text that Pagels mentions. In the *Sophia of Jesus,* the savior concludes his long address by saying that he has come to remove blindness from his followers by "telling" them the truth. He uses a standard synaesthetic metaphor for verbal revelation: it opens one's inner eyes. We have already considered two versions of this in Luke. In the Succession scene, a disembodied voice from above tells Peter and the other disciples enigmatically what the vision means. Then the voice becomes silent and the venerable characters complete their gradual disappearance, leaving Jesus "alone." The episode on the road to Emmaus, of course, concludes with Jesus' disappearance, leaving only ordinary disciples alone. Thus the second scene appears to complete the action of the first, and Luke's implied author incorporates both into one elaboration of a fundamental gnostic idea. In the *Sophia,* this is rendered: "These are the things [the] blessed Savior [said, and he disappeared] from them" (p. 228; bracketed words are editorial restorations). The implication in all three scenes is that now both the ordinary characters in the scene and the readers without must ponder for themselves the meaning of the transient visions they have seen. The savior will *not* remain.

We find comparable effects when we look beyond the specific texts that Pagels mentions to others in the Nag Hammadi library. The *Acts of Peter and the Twelve Apostles* (VI, 1) consists of a narrative about Christ in the guise of a pearl merchant named Lithargoel. He appears to Peter and other disciples as they take a journey after the crucifixion on a ship to the city of Habitation. Peter converses directly with the pearl merchant, who invites him to come to his city to find a pearl. Peter and the disciples agree to come and have a difficult journey, but because they renounce riches, they come through unharmed. When they arrive, Lithargoel disguises himself as a physician then reveals himself as Jesus Christ and commissions the disciples to minister to the sick and poor.

If we gather these common themes together, we can begin to talk about a myth of the Magical Risen Savior that each of these narratives casts in a particular form. An analysis of this myth provides a convenient way to talk about what the gnostic narratives and Luke's narrative have in common at their core. For the moment, we look beyond their different styles and literary contexts.

We could call the common narrative elements "mythemes," a term Claude Lévi-Strauss applies to the discrete distinguishable parts of the story available for unique narrative manipulation. Lévi-Strauss says these are elements of the story that sentences can describe; they have subjects, objects, along with modifiers, and express a coherent action. For examples, we could say that one of the mythemes of this myth is: "a religious figure with special powers appears to ordinary human beings." Other mythemes are: "these disciples are on a journey"; "the religious figure adopts a disguise"; "the disciples respond strongly to what the religious figure says, even without knowing who the figure is"; "the religious figure abandons his disciples to their own devices"; etc. These mythemes are organized into what Lévi-Strauss calls "bundles" with each telling or recording of the myth. This term reflects the concept that bundles of mythemes can be different and yet still recognizable as variants of the same "story" if the constituent mythemes are similar to each other. Lévi-Strauss does not talk of the genre of myth as much as a family of variants that make up a recognizable story from version to version.

In his view, mythemes are organized in two dimensions at once, just as language is divided by Saussure. There is a diachronic dimension, corresponding to the *parole,* or actual spoken form of any language. This is the plot, or the sequential order in which the story is told. There is a synchronic dimension, corresponding to the *langue,* or all the grammatical possibilities for speech in any natural language. This is the theme, created by the gathering of similar mythemes in the story, regardless of the order in which they occur. The diachronic "tells" the story and therefore is its narrative; the synchronic "gives meaning to" the story and therefore provides its heart. Lévi-Strauss believes that these two dimensions combine in each telling of a myth in such a way as to make possible the working out of a certain kind of logic. He calls it "mythical thought." It "always progresses from the awareness of oppositions toward their resolution" (p. 221). In other words, telling a myth is a process of working out contradictions by trying to discover a mediating position between them. The fundamental contradiction is always going to be between time and timelessness, the specific actions of the plot and their perennial meaning.

These terms and concepts allow us to identify certain elements in the Magical Risen Savior Myth that both Luke and the gnostic writers use in common. They come bundled differently in each version, but they are similar enough to be classified as belonging to the same family of myth. There is the same logic underlying all the versions of the myth. Consider, for example, the mythemes: "the appearance of the teacher is altered"; and "the nature of seeing and hearing are shown to be interchangeable." Luke's Gospel and several gnostic narratives bundle them together so that one happens as the other happens. As a result, human characters in the scene are taught by a teacher whom they do not recognize. The essential lesson they learn is that, although they "hear" what the teacher says, they do not at first "see" what he says. Only at the end of the story do they see who the teacher is at the same time that they "see" what he was telling them. This sort of gnostic learning appears to emphasize the importance of the oral nature of the teacher's teaching. You had to be there to hear it. Thus there is something concrete about the teaching. It was given at a specific moment to a specific group.

But according to the general accounts of gnostic thinking that we find in Hans Jonas and others, this notion would create a problem for a gnostic thinker. It runs contrary to the conviction that the moment of gnosis occurs with no regard for time or place. The logic of mythical thought recognizes that there is a contradiction here. Other mythemes now come into play to reinforce the spontaneous nature of the teaching. We could express one mytheme with the sentence: "There is no prior agenda to the teaching." For example, the continual questions the listeners ask the teacher give the teacher leads about what to say next. The questions provoke an unpremeditated teaching that meanders until reaching the ultimate revelation. We could express this essential mytheme with the sentence: "The actual words of the teacher are not as important as the culminating experience of understanding that the disciples have." This experience is the goal of the dialogue. It is more important than the specific words the teacher uses to prepare for the revelation. It is more interior and intimate and personal.

According to Lévi-Strauss, after mythic logic distinguishes contradictory ideas, the telling of the myth reconciles the contradictions. In the Myth of the Risen Savior, the contradiction is between the specifics of a certain time and place in which the scene is set and the universality of the transcendent teaching delivered there. For this contradiction to be resolved, it is crucial that the risen savior has a magical disguise in every version of the myth. He hides his physical presence so that the words may ring true by themselves. The person the disciples see is really there, and only apparently there. What the disciples think is real is only an illusion. In this way, the disguise mediates the contradiction between spontaneity and manipulation. What the disciples initially think is spontaneous is actually manipulated all along. They experience what they think is real only as a piece of theater. They can forgive being duped because of the pleasure of the discovery. They learn at the end that the disguise was for their own good all along. The savior cannot remain.

The Narrative of the Magical Risen Savior

We are now in a position to understand the different ways in which gnostic and orthodox writers could use this common myth. I begin by featuring the most elaborate narrative of the myth in the Nag Hammadi library: the *Acts of Peter and the Twelve Disciples*. The narrative begins with a first-person-plural narrator describing how "we" went down to the sea "at an opportune moment, which came to us from the Lord." Thus the narration is simultaneously first person and immediate, yet objective and omniscent. The narrator knows that "the Lord" is orchestrating the theater of the event. It is as if the narrator, in speaking in the plural form for a group, both experiences the action and understands it simultaneously.

But one paragraph later this narrator becomes singular. A character takes over the story, announcing that "I, Peter, was among those making the journey, and that I had a private conversation with the pearl merchant named Lithargoel. He invited my friends and me to come with him to a city to seek out a special pearl." When this Peter agrees to come, he gives no indication that he knows the identity of the merchant. The "we" who knows that the Lord instigates this encounter switches to the "I" who falls under the spell of the Lord in disguise. In the switch, the narrator loses omniscience and becomes bound by the limited perspective of all true characters. A reader might think it was Peter who was speaking at first as well, using the plural pronoun to emphasize his sense of belonging to a community. As he warms to the story, his report becomes more personal and immediate, in tune with the usual practice of gnostic narrators. But it is more than a change of pronouns; it is a change of perspectives. There are more surprises.

When Peter tells his friends what the pearl merchant said to him personally, they are overjoyed. They make their way to the city to which the merchant has invited them. They rest in front of the city gate. As they do, the narration becomes first person plural again, as if, when Peter rejoins the group, his story becomes theirs to tell. As before, the plural narrator becomes omniscient, reporting that when the merchant Lithargoel met *us* at the gate, "he had changed." "He had the appearance of a physician, since an unguent box was under his arm, and a young disciple was following him, carrying a pouch full of medicine. We did not recognize him" (p. 268). Now the narrator resembles Luke's narrator in part. The plural voice tells the readers that the merchant is disguised as a physician, even while it still withholds the information about who is behind the merchant's disguise.

At the moment of recognition, the narrator's identity changes again three times. First the narrator becomes an objective, third-person voice, very much like Luke's narrator. This narrator reports that Peter asks the new stranger to take them to the merchant Lithargoel. The stranger says that he will, but expresses amazement that the disciples know the name of the merchant, and then dramatically calls Peter by his proper name. Peter is shocked and responds, the objective, impersonal narrator tells us, "to the Savior." With this word the narrator, like Luke's narrator, tells the readers more than the characters know. The physician is the disguised merchant Lithargoel, and the disguised Lithargoel is the Risen Savior.

In this narrative, however, the revelation to the readers comes only a few sentences before the revelation to the inner characters. " 'How do you know me,' asks Peter, 'for you called my name?' " (p. 269). At this point, the narration becomes descriptive. The figure in the disguise of the physician loosens his clothes and reveals himself to the disciples as Jesus Christ. He does not disappear at this moment, as he does in the Luke Emmaus scene. Rather, it is the objective anonymous narrator who disappears. The narrator becomes the plural "we" again. "We prostrated ourselves on the ground and worshipped him" (p. 269). The third change occurs when Jesus takes over the narration directly to bring it to a conclusion. In direct discourse Jesus admonishes the disciples to take his teaching into the world.

Genuine gnostic narratives such as the preceding one are essentially unstable. Perhaps this is because spontaneous gnosis is at cross-purposes with a written text; pure, unmediated experience can only take place once, without anyone being able to recreate the moment authentically for anyone else. Pheme Perkins has recently written that the majority of the dialogues in the Nag Hammadi library "still operate within the conventions of a world or oral tradition" (p. 32), and at this time and place, the oral tradition made for rather informal and loosely organized recitations. Following Walter Ong, he says that literacy, with all its stabilizing constraints, had not yet begun to exert an influence from within: ". . . the tight linear organization of argument or of modern narrative plot is out of the question" (p. 32). From this perspective, what Luke might have done is simply to cast quasi-oral written narratives into more consciously written narrative forms.

But this is still not to say that Luke necessarily improved upon the narrative style he absorbed. We recall the rudiments of Plato's idea of artistic imitation as an expanding telescope, pulling away from the object under view. In this case, the experience is the prime moment, the dialogue that made it possible is secondary, and the text that passes on the dialogue is tertiary. Each representation further dims the original. Therefore there is something aesthetically appropriate in the failure of most gnostic narrators to stay in one place or hold a single identity. The blurred or protean narrator escapes from the confines of specificity.

The effect can be both artistic and profound. Remarkably for either an orthodox or a gnostic text, Jesus' teaching in the *Acts* includes doing practical and spiritual work together. He tells the disciples to give material things to the poor as well as teach them, and cure the physical ailments of the sick as well as rectify error: "Heal the bodies first, therefore, so that through the real powers of healing for their bodies, without medicine of the world, they may believe in you, that you have power to heal the illnesses of the heart also" (p. 270). His complex teaching matches the complexity of the narrative. The extraordinary resources of the protean narrator combine gnostic and orthodox perspectives simultaneously. In fact, in this rendition of the Magical Risen Savior myth, the teachings of the narrator and the main character are even more synchronized than they are in Luke.

The complexity is artful. We do not have to agree with an analysis offered by the translators in the *Facsimile Edition* of the *Acts*. They explain the shifts in narrators as evidence of clumsy editing. They speculate that the material revealing the physician as "the Savior," marked by the shift to an objective, impartial narrator, might be secondary: "It compromises the identification of Lithargoel with Jesus, which is most important for the narrative. The physician is the intermediate figure between the two" (p. 52). In other words, in their opinion, the narrator suddenly and inappropriately informs the readers that there are two disguises in effect here, and that Peter had responded "to the Savior" when he thought he was only speaking to the physician. The aside appears to be inconsistent, because until this point both the readers and the characters do not know that the person behind the two disguises is the savior. The editors seem to have two questions here. First of all, why tell the readers that Jesus adopted two disguises when the characters never know? And secondly, why tell the readers who the physician is just before the characters in the scene make their discovery? The answer could be that the shift in narrators and the accompanying creation of two levels of perception (one for the characters in the scene and one for the implied readers) is but another instance of the different levels of perception beloved by gnostic narrative writers. We can just as easily speculate that the apparently premature narrative revelation to the implied readers is deliberate. They get to anticipate and thus to feel more intensely the revelation enjoyed by the minor characters in the scene.

Professors Murdock and MacRae also take a dark view of narrative inconsistency in the preface to their translation of the gnostic tractate *The Apocalypse of Paul* (in *The Nag Hammadi Library in English*). They attribute it to bad writing: "The inconsistency may perhaps be attributed to literary carelessness rather than to multiple sources, for at these points in the narrative no clear 'seams' can be detected on other grounds" (p. 48). In both cases it is somewhat dismaying to find the spirit of Dibelius (discussed in the introduction) rising among the scholars of these fresh new texts. Already they are warning us not to take the texts seriously as literature. Instead, to the extent that we can find a consistency between the shifting narrative perspectives and the gnostic notion of shifting levels of perception, we can discover a significant reiteration, if not an intention. This is what Luke discovered from his acquaintance with his gnostic narrative colleagues.

Luke's Magical Risen Savior

We can take these mythemes that we have been discussing to constitute important elements in the common myth of the Magical Risen Savior. If we find these mythemes in a number of gnostic texts but only in Luke among the orthodox writers, then there is common ground between them, and the more mythemes they share, the more they appear alike. The translators of the *Acts of Peter* make more or less the same point when they comment: "The emphasis upon apostolic poverty and the polemic against the rich are even rooted in the New Testament. Though the tractate does not seem to proclaim distinctively gnostic ideas, it is clear that gnostic interpreters would have no trouble relating to such themes as the stranger, the journey, the hidden pearl, and the expensive garment of the world" (p. 265). Thus, in their view this is neither a canonical text nor a strictly heretical text from the orthodox perspective, and it thus comes perhaps the closest to mapping out the common ground between the two traditions.

But neither they nor Pagels suggest that sharing mythemes means sharing ideas, no more than Fitzmyer suggests that Luke thinks like the Septuagint translators just becauses he borrows their Greek vocabulary, idioms, and even thought patterns in places. We all recognize in one way or another that an author's narrative style shapes mythemes like a potter shapes the common clay into uncommon patterns. Recall again Luke's arrangement of the Succession scene. The narrator addresses the implied reader, while one character, the disembodied voice, instructs the disciples, and the implied author instructs the interpreter by suggesting how the more or less mute tableau in which Jesus, Moses, and Elijah appear reiterates what is said in the scene. In the related Emmaus episode, the arrangements are slightly different, but the effect is very much the same. Now the main character instructs the disciples, the narrator the implied reader, and the implied author the interpreter. In each scene, each pedagogy is separate and consistent, yet each appears the cognate of the other two. The resulting narrative is much more stable than anything we find in the Nag Hammadi library.

Thus we can say that one significant difference between gnostic and orthodox Christian narratives of the Magical Risen Savior is the difference between their narrative styles. Myth is an amalgamation of story elements whose relationships have not been set. Jesus or a messenger from God can appear again and again in gnostic gospels in many different forms. His mythical identity can take many forms and return from any place, including the usually terminal place of the grave. He can say anything to anyone, although in a gnostic mythic version he will tend to say things within the realm of gnostic images and thinking. Because the identity of Jesus and the kinds of things he can say and the sorts of characters he can say them to are not set, there are myriad possibilities for retelling the myth. Every time the myth is told, of course, it is narrated, and it becomes fixed in a narrative.

Usually, in gnostic narratives, the narrator speaks in the first person—either the person to whom a revelation is given, or Jesus, or some disembodied voice from another realm. The first-person narrative is the most immediate narrative in the literal sense of the term. It appears to be the least mediated and the least distanced. In this context, the idea behind this narrative technique appears to be that anyone who has had a revelation desires to share the narrative with anyone who will hear of it.

Gnostic gospels are mythlike in that they invite or tend toward further reformings and shapings. The only way to stop them from being told, as the orthodox seemed to intuit, is to supress the publication of the tellings, burn the codices, and disperse the readers, as the orthodox did. The third-person narratives of the orthodox gospels, on the other hand, tend to police themselves. There are far fewer possibilities for retelling once this kind of narrative restricts the field of what it will report. The major restriction is imposed by its realism; the events described must satisfy certain elemental rules of plausibility. These rules do not exclude the miraculous, if the miraculous can be made to fit an otherwise plausible social situation. An orthodox Christian narrative such as Luke's stresses the continuities between the Jesus before and after his death and resurrection in the resurrection narrative, and the consistency of what he says in short realistic narratives and the long set speech at the heart of each gospel. This Jesus appears only to people who knew him before. He appears in places that are familiar to both him and his followers. He says things that extend his earlier teaching. He has a plausible human memory, and the enlightenment he passes on builds on earlier insights and teachings. In fact, in Luke, the resurrected Jesus on the road to Emmaus takes pains to tie the events of his own life into the stories and implications of the already written scripture. In the same way, Luke's narrator ties the events of the Succession scene to those of the Emmaus scene so that the second extends the first.

In other words, Luke stresses plot over theme in an attempt to end the proliferation of the myth. He gives the myth a final form that bears no more retellings. Narrative restrains myth's natural errancy. Every detail of this process we can enumerate describes another resource that literary technique has to tie meanings down—to make them orthodox.

Gnostic Teaching versus Fiction

Another way to describe Luke's debt to gnosticism is to say that he learned how to write fiction from his meditation on gnostic teaching now represented in the Risen Savior Myth. He learned how to resolve the contradiction between realism and calculated effect in telling that or any story. It is no aesthetic crime to beguile one's readers if one's purpose is benign. His preface self-consciously admits to Theophilus that the following narrative will not be true-to-life. It will provide a "connected narrative" that will get at the truth of things not apparent in the unadorned reports of the eyewitness. He thereby appropriates for himself the license to shape the details of the Transfiguration scene he takes from Mark into a Succession scene that anticipates many of the essential features of his gnostically inspired Emmaus scene.

He learned from the teaching conveyed by the myth that the actual form of a story is insignificant. Form or fiction pales before the experience of understanding what the underlying meaning is. While they are reading, the readers of a narrative are like the disciples fooled by a disguise. Only when they grasp the meaning of the words do they understand what the disciples saw when the disguise dropped away. What I describe here is what Hans Jonas calls the gnostic moment of knowledge. In the gnostic system, it is the only form of knowledge worth having. This is what Luke understood.

Luke simply took his license in fiction a step further than the gnostic writers did. Even if the actual form of a story can be shaped according to a writer's perspective, it still can be shaped very carefully. In the two scenes featured here, voices emanate from some one place privy to the scene. The narrator speaks, God speaks, even the implied author speaks through a deliberate choice of words. Each voice provides a perspective. But the stable narrator's voice is authoritative. It provides the limiting perspective on what can be seen or heard—what is revealed and withheld. Third-party objectivity joins the scene. The events are looked at, reported on. The narrative does not simply flow or exude as in mythlike narratives.

Luke's is a realistic narrative in Hans Frei's sense of the term, where the narrator's point of view remains fixed and coherent, and therefore conveys the impression that the narrative is comprehensible. Realistic narrative of this kind lends itself to minds that take up a stance. It is the expression of a coherent community—its *kerygma,* or "teaching." C. H. Dodd comments that the unique literary qualities of the Emmaus episode make it the most polished of all the "Appearance episodes or pericopes" to be found in either the orthodox or gnostic scriptures (p. 43).

Reconciliation: The Gnostic Spirit

It is not surprising that, with these fundamentally different ways of looking at the world and religion at the time when the gnostic texts were buried, gnostic and orthodox believers seemed little inclined to think about what they shared in common. They were not interested in the reconciliation of disparate views but in the consolidation of what each thought was right thinking. To do so today could be an exercise in wistful thinking about what might have been if each group had been more open to defining the Christian experience. There are traces of this in Pagels's book when she points out the reappearance of gnostic ideas in Lutheranism, Quakerism, modern charismatic religions, and in the thinking of Christian mystics, medieval and modern. She finds attractive the emphasis on the value of femininity for the religious experience in some gnostic texts.

But Pagels is fundamentally a realist. The major point in her book is that orthodox thinking had an instinct for the sorts of dogmas that would create a church that would hold together in its early years and, as it turned out, become increasingly powerful once it was recognized as the state religion of the Roman Empire. The orthodox had an instinct for the concrete, the direct, and the simple. They believed that Jesus really rose from the dead. He appeared to Peter and other disciples in the flesh. Those who believed in the reality of the resurrection and the authority of its early witnesses could rally a community around a few essential common points. Their belief in the realness of the passion of Jesus prepared them to accept as authentic the suffering of the early Christian martyrs—and this further served to draw the community together and to spread its influence through its exemplary steadfastness.

To this point, most of the scholarly work that has compared gnostic and orthodox texts favors the approach Pagels, Jonas, and Aichele use, emphasizing the theological differences between the two traditions. This is, after all, what the gnostics and the Fathers themselves were doing, and it is only with the rediscovery of texts on the losing side of the controversy that we can today appreciate the depth and the nuance of their differences. I, too, have been following this line of thought by emphasizing some critical differences in literary style between the two. But all of us can do so in the spirit of one of the most startling of the gnostic scriptures. The *Gospel of Mary* seems to be aware of the difference between gnostic and orthodox religious beliefs. Yet its narrator holds out hope for tolerance and perhaps for even more—for an ongoing parataxis of comparison between the two perspectives.

The Gospel of Mary appears at the end of the recent edition of the Nag Hammadi library collection of gnostic texts, as if it were its proper coda. Scholars estimate that it is a fifth-century work. It has two parts. In the first part, the resurrected Christ is engaged in dialogue with his disciples, who raise questions for him to answer; in the second part, Peter asks Mary to tell the disciples of a vision she has received. Some of them react to her description with hostility, until Levi reminds them that the savior loved Mary more than he loved any of them. They adjourn and go out to preach.

There is very little narrative material here at all. Most of it is in dialogue form, with the savior, Peter, the disciples, and then Mary speaking in the first person. The most remarkable scene occurs when Mary recalls a vision that she had of the savior. Although four pages are missing, what remains appears to be typical gnostic teaching, very vague and cosmic and mystic. The savior returns to the familiar theme of not being recognized by those who could not understand his true, extrahuman nature: "I was not recognized. But I have recognized that the All is being dissolved, both the earthly (things) and the heavenly" (p. 473). What is remarkable is not the gnostic teaching. It is that the disciples in the scene do not appear to be gnostic disciples at all. They are orthodox. One of them called Andrew reacts with anger and disbelief at Mary's "strange ideas." His dismay represents, perhaps, the dismay of the orthodox followers of the original apostles, who by this time were actively prosecuting gnostic teachers as heretics.

If Mary represents gnostic thinking and Andrew orthodox thinking, then the narrative at hand is neither gnostic nor orthodox in spirit. For neither character is allowed to have the last word. Instead, another called Levi speaks up. He admonishes both Peter and Andrew for their hostile reaction to Mary, someone Jesus loved after all, he reminds them. He says, "Rather let us be ashamed and put on the perfect man, and separate as he commanded us and preach the gospel, not laying down any other rule or other law beyond what the Savior said." With these words he breathes forth a spirit of tolerance. It would allow each teacher to go his or her separate way, according to his or her individual light. After Levi's speech, an impersonal narrator concludes the narrative with the words "and they began to go forth and proclaim and to preach." Each is to begin his or her own personal exodus. Here is a narrator as close to the perspective of Levi as Luke's narrator is to Jesus. Both narrators are open to a plurality of interpretations. It is sad that the voice of this narrator remained buried so long with all the other more resolutely gnostic narratives.

Levi stands for an evenhanded awareness of why the mythemes of the Magical Risen Savior occur more frequently in gnostic writings than they do in the orthodox writings—Luke's Emmaus episode excepted. These mythemes lend themselves very well to gnostic scripture writing because Jesus is somewhat disembodied in each. In the resurrection scenes, he has a body that no other human being could claim to have had. However real, it had experienced the termination and then the return of its life forces. It was a body transformed, even if only to return to possessing the form of the very real, fleshly body that it had had before. This was more or less the orthodox position. Any attempt to try to imagine what this body looked like or felt like would lead to fantasy because neither writer nor reader would have had any previous real experiences of such a thing. A story about such a body would lend itself less well to orthodox writing for the same reasons. Such a story requires a considerable amount of rhetorical control in order to contain precisely the free-ranging associations that the gnostics want to cultivate. Here the effort must be to embody Jesus, to fix him in a place, and to make both that place and his own presence palpable and consequential. But Levi, aware of the differences, does not force a choice between them. He says that one should let each person with each point of view get on with the ordinary business of the day. That business creates the cantonnage we all wrap around the precious religious insights we nurture in our hearts.

Something of Levi's tolerant spirit breathes in both Luke's Succession and Emmaus episodes. In the first, Moses and Elijah fade away gradually after sharing a common glory with Jesus and establishing their common interests with him in the never-ending exodus of the spiritual life. In the second, Jesus himself disappears after establishing an infectious enthusiasm in two of his disciples, who are now left to interpret the scripture on their own. They need not rely overly much on the authority of any teacher, magical or otherwise. If we find both scenes refreshingly liberal, it hardly matters who inspired whom, whether Luke learned from gnostic teachers, or gnostic writers learned from him. Gnosis, or insightful knowledge, now means attending to several different kinds of teaching happening simultaneously. The reader finds that they are each related and distinct. The precise relationship between them cannot be defined. Gnostic breezes blow through the lattices of narrative.

Narrative Gnosticism

Having made our comparisons, we can now add another definition to Peel's gnostic lexicon cited at the beginning of this chapter. This is "literary" or "narrative gnosticism." Harkening back to the notion of Stanislaw Eile, we can say that narrative gnosticism conveys the special aspect of the gnostic worldview which was amenable to narrative storytelling. To the extent that it was amenable, the traditional gnostic cosmic sense of time had to be subordinated to the ordinary narrative demands for distinct point of view, place, and an ordered sequence of events. Narrative gnosticism, in other words, could not hold itself aloof from the demands of realistic representation as a more abstract philosophical or theological gnosticism could. Images that might elsewhere be amorphous became bound to the exigencies of literary form. Even if the narrator's point of view could shift in a narrative like the *Acts of Peter,* each time it does shift, the story has to be told from a distinct point of view. It was the narrative form of gnosticism that inspired Luke's orthodox revisions.

Granted, we have seen there is no evidence that *written* gnostic narratives came to the hands of any of the orthodox evangelists, even if there is a broad consensus that gnostic ideas were in the air when they wrote. It is thus impossible to say for sure, as perhaps some scholars would like to, whether Luke would best be called a proto- rather than a post-gnostic Christian. Such a definition would presuppose that gnosticism is doctrinaire, and that Luke could be rated as either an early pioneer or a later polisher of definitive, gnostic doctrines. Rather, gnosticism refers to a way of thinking, available to be discovered by many religious thinkers who might not have ever had any contact with the literary and philosophical forms that gnosticism filled in the first four centuries of the Christian era.

Yet, the evidence displayed here suggests that Luke did more than discover certain gnostic ideas inadvertently. He did less than adopt the gnostic ideas of his own time in their entirety. Rather, he found certain gnostic notions of learning fascinating and important, and he played with them extensively in his own imaginative re-formation of Mark's Gospel. One way we measure his success as a writer is that his gospel appealed to such very different readers as Marcion and Tertullian, each of whom was convinced that he could interpret Luke's gnosticism correctly.

Perhaps Luke had at least heard gnostic storytellers or preachers who used the universal techniques of suspense, plot, characterization, and point of view in airing their gnostic views. These literary devices would even affect the content of gnostic thought to the extent that they featured realistic characters like Peter and Mary in realistic circumstances experiencing the shattering moment of gnostic insight.

Perhaps Luke even had gnostic narratives like the *Acts of Peter* before him as he began composing his ordered account. They might comprise a part of his unique "L" source. This source might have contained not only stories or sayings about Jesus. It might have contained gnostic narratives of the Risen Savior that demonstrated new techniques for rendering new kinds of storied events. Or Luke might himself have been one of the first writers to render oral narrative gnosticism into a more definitive form. He himself might have inspired the *Acts* writer. Because it is not possible, or even necessary, to determine how much he adapted the form, we need not observe the well-established distinctions between oral and written narratives.

Whatever the case, Luke was first and foremost a writer of narratives. He could therefore have been as acute as any dedicated writer in appreciating how he could adapt new literary devices for his own special narrative vision.

Treating Luke's Gospel as a slyly imitative, even impertinent text is something very different from what Charles H. Talbert does when he declares his "moral certainty" that Luke-Acts was written to serve as a defense against gnosticism (p. 111). In my view, when we compare Luke's Gospel to gnostic narratives, Luke's borrowings appear affectionate and more subtle than critical. In the next chapter, we consider why strong efforts have been made to assure that his borrowings would not become widely known.

Chapter Three
Critical Responses to Luke's Narrative Gnosticism

Jesus said, "Be what you like but remember that after me it's the straight
action and no more dressing up."

Russell Hoban, Pilgermann

Once out of nature I shall never take
My bodily form from any natural
    thing.

W. B. Yeats, "Sailing to Byzantium"

The Enduring Polemic Against Gnosticism

Let us call Luke's narrative gnosticism a silent arrangement of
scenes intended to provoke the reader into personal insights. The reader
first responds to the arrangements expecting that there is some discrete
purpose behind what the implied author arranges and what the narrator
reveals and holds back. There is a sense that there is a disguised purpose in
the narrative. It takes an educated imagination to catch its implication.
Now let us ask the question, Has any orthodox biblical interpreter read in
such a way as to respond directly to the narrative arrangement or narrative
coyness? If there is something intrinsically gnostic about Luke's narrative,
surely it could not have been missed during almost eighteen hundred years
of interpretation, even by readers not inclined to want to find it there. I ask
this question of the tradition in order to seek some assurance that what
seems to me apparent about Luke is not simply my projection onto the
narrative arrangements of a purpose that is only my own. Have others read
this way?

The short answer is yes, they have, but only rarely and fitfully.
The basic reason they cannot sustain any interest in the narrative arrangements is that there is, among orthodox biblical scholars, an enduring po-

lemic against anything gnostic in the Christian scripture. It stems from the first debate about how Luke's Gospel should be read. As it turns out, Luke's Gospel was the first work of Christian scripture to be the object of discussion on how Christian scripture should be read. This debate pitted two highly opinionated readers against each other. One was the gnostically inclined Marcion, the other the orthodox apologist Tertullian. Their debate began the tradition of one of the major branches of orthodox Christian interpretation that continues even today.

A related question is, Can this tradition return to its roots for a new orientation? Could the triumphant orthodox readers now safely engage the narrative gnosticism of Luke's Gospel, or any other gospel? If so, we can capitalize on the new appreciation for narrative gnosticism that the Nag Hammadi library kindles in many scholars.

Before proceeding I wish to offer several acknowledgments. Any criticism of the orthodox tradition found here is offered in the same spirit with which many of its members criticize each other. If something has been overlooked, let us look at it. Admittedly, there are good reasons why narrative gnosticism in the New Testament has been overlooked. We have already considered the political reasons that Elaine H. Pagels describes. Other reasons stem from various legitimate interests that traditional biblical interpreters have in looking at what they consider to be sacred texts in their own highly sophisticated ways. The most specific reason, however, is that appreciating Luke's narrative gnosticism is tantamount to appreciating his gospel as literature. Many traditional biblical scholars have recently made it emphatically clear that they are not interested in reading the Bible as literature. Those of us who pursue a literary reading of the Bible are like children returning home to the farm from school with some new ideas of how to plow the north forty. It is incumbent that we explain ourselves.

The tactic here is to focus exclusively on the tradition of reading the Emmaus episode in Luke's Gospel. Pagels points out that this is the most gnostic of episodes in the orthodox gospels. It provides a special test case for determining how the biblical interpretive tradition handled narrative gnosticism. What we learn from the handling of this scene could be extended to the handling of many other scenes in Luke. If narrative gnosticism remains more or less invisible where it is most obvious, it is not likely to be seen where it is less so. We thereby limit the scope of the inquiry to something that could fit into a reasonably sized book. It is also with length in mind that we pass over vast amounts of provocative Lukan scholarship, much of it sensitive to literary nuance. What we are after here is one small, persistent oversight that has significant consequences for the current discussions about what it means to treat the gospels as artistic literature.

The goal of this criticism is positive suggestion. Even orthodox interpretation could appreciate a heretofore mostly obscured aspect of Luke's narrative artistry. The narrative gnosticism of the Emmaus scene has already been shown to illuminate other episodes that bear its traces throughout the narrative. They include the parables of the Good Samaritan and the Forgiving Father, the comic scene with Zacchaeus, the tragic scene with Peter, and the Succession scene with Moses and Elijah, Peter, James, and John. This chapter features their diffusion throughout the structure of the narrative.

Early Arguments among the Fathers of the Church

By several accounts, Luke's first appreciative critic was Marcion of Sinope in Pontus. Marcion was, in the eyes of the orthodox, a notorious gnostic writer of the late second and early third centuries, although more recent scholars have disputed whether he was a Christian or a gnostic. In a well-known early-twentieth-century monograph, Adolph von Harnack claimed Marcion was not a gnostic at all because for one thing, as we shall see, he derived his scriptural canon exclusively from Christian writings. Rather, he was a Christian who entertained certain gnostic notions, such as the need to reject the Jewish scriptures, the humanity of Jesus, and belief in the bodily resurrection. More recently R. M. Grant refined Harnack's view by saying that it is more accurate to view Marcion as a Christian with a presumption that Christianity was more authentic when stripped of any Jewish roots. E. C. Blackman sees him as characterized less by sectarian affinities and more by his "pedestrian mind" and his unwillingness to engage in any of the free-ranging allegorical comparisons between Jewish and Christian scriptures favored by the Christian authorities (p. 82).

The ambiguity of modern opinion about Marcion's religious affiliation is interesting for several reasons. For one, it reiterates a certain ambiguity in the early Latin Father Tertullian, perhaps Marcion's harshest critic. He treats Marcion's ideas seriously as if they erred from correct opinion in emphasis and detail, rather than by a complete misapprehension. This suggests that, to the extent that Marcion can be considered an errant Christian in his thinking as Harnack more or less does, the debate that his interpretation stirs among early, more resolutely orthodox Christian thinkers clearly establishes the first guidelines of orthodox biblical interpretation *from within the tradition*. The guidelines stem from the efforts that various early Christian thinkers make to avoid the extreme theories of interpretation of people who thought somewhat like themselves. For another reason, as the recent discovery of the Nag Hammadi library shows, every so-called gnostic pronouncement raises more questions than it answers about just what gnosticism is, Marcion's included. When we read Luke, or Marcion on Luke, or Tertullian on Marcion, we are engaging in explorations of many elusive and provocative affinities between different kinds of religious ideas. All three writers strive to discriminate where gnostic and orthodox thinking coincide and where they diverge.

Whatever Marcion's precise religious affiliation, it is well established that he fashions the first recorded response to the Emmaus episode that survives. He does so, it turns out, in a distinctively gnostic manner. It is ironically appropriate for anyone such as Marcion with the typical gnostic suspicion of written documents to have his views recorded only in the documents of others. The originals of his tracts have been lost—probably deliberately destroyed by those who disagreed with their opinions. We only know of his reading through the words of the early orthodox critics Epiphanius, Tertullian, and Origen. They cite him to condemn him. Nevertheless, some gist of his thought survives because his critics appear to take care to get right what they condemn.

According to Epiphanius, Marcion indicates the importance of the Emmaus episode to his reading by an act of selective omission. In one place Marcion says that the authentic canon of Christian scripture should contain only the charismatic material from the Epistles of Paul and a severely expurgated version of Luke's Gospel. Marcion cuts from Luke chapters one and two, the episode of the Temptation in the Desert, the parables of the Forgiving Father and the Good Samaritan, and several references to the writings of the ancient Hebrew prophets, as well as to Moses, Joshua, David, and other venerable heroes. In short, he deletes any inkling in the text that there are any scriptural or religious traditions relevant to Jesus' story. This includes the reference to Jesus interpreting for his disciples "all the Scriptures" in the Emmaus episode. But Marcion does include the episode aside from this cut, and thus has its magical teaching loom larger in its diminished context (XLII,xi,4–7).

His cuts show that even a gnostic theologian could be insensitive to traces of narrative gnostic ideas, such as those contained in the parables of the Good Samaritan and the Forgiving Father if they were tainted by association with other more orthodox ideas about the close connection between two religious literary traditions. The debate we are talking about is not, properly speaking, a literary critical discussion at all. It is theological and has to do with the broader question of the importance to Christianity of its Jewish heritage. According to the Dutch scholar P. G. Verweijs, Marcion simply cannot abide the Old Testament portrayal of "a jealous and stupid God" (eifersüchtiger und ein unwissender Gott). He is a typical gnostic in that he is more hostile to Jewish scripture and less to Jewish culture and its people than many early Christians were (p. 335).

According to Tertullian, who relies on Epiphanius, Marcion cuts the gospel down to the size of his theological belief that there is a fundamental antithesis between the Gods of each testament: "so that his Christ may be separate from the Creator, or belonging to a rival God, and as alien from the law and the prophets" (p. 189). The God of the older tradition still promises an earthly Messiah to come. The God of the newer tradition brings a spiritual salvation available to anyone, now, whatever his or her religious or historical circumstances.

From these accounts, it appears that Marcion does more than give Luke a strong reading. Through his cutting, he wants to establish the standard text that a community would read, and thus to have his expurgated Luke become one of the few orthodox texts in a very small scriptural canon. As it turns out, the tradition we now call orthodox biblical interpretation won out against his desire to set a standard canon. This tradition successfully restored to the Christian canon the unexpurgated Luke, the other gospels, and the bulk of the venerable scriptures. But along with its liberality, as we shall see, came severe restrictions on how that ample canon should be read—restrictions that keep alive a prejudice against strong, personally opinionated readings of the sacred texts, especially those that would explicitly deny a clear connection between the venerable scriptures of the Jews and the newly emerging Christian scriptures.

Thus, even if Marcion cannot be properly called a literary critic of the Bible, his theological views on the inappropriateness of reading Jewish and Christian scriptures together *implies* a way of reading. His implication will be rejected and replaced with an explicit model of reading. This explicit model will determine the subsequent nature of biblical interpretation even until our own day.

Tertullian versus Marcion

Tertullian, a contemporary of Marcion, devotes the fourth book of his *Adversus Marcionem* to a line-by-line restoration of Marcion's expurgated Luke. He plays especially close attention to Marcion's cutting in the Emmaus episode. Not surprisingly, we learn that Marcion omits that part of the conference between Jesus and the two disciples which relates to the prophetic predictions of his suffering (verses 26–27). He replaces the words *hoi prophaetai* (the prophets) with *humin* (to you). Jesus' admonition to the disciples now reads simply: "how slow you are to believe what was said *to you.*" In the next verse, it is described how they draw close to the village. Thus, in Marcion's version, the episode at Emmaus more emphatically features a magically disguised teacher who refers only to his own past teachings while engaging the disciples in new ideas. This Jesus becomes spiritualized to the extent that he appears less connected to and concerned with any other stories or teachings of the past. In the new episode, he grants awareness of himself gratuitously at the moment of insight when he appears and disappears from mortal men. Verweijs makes the interesting observation that Marcion makes Jesus appear less kindly. He no longer has any concern for any religious ancestors, and he appears more forbidding to his own disciples, in keeping with the gnostic notion of the alienation from human beings of God or his messengers (p. 336).

Presumably Marcion also omits the reference to the scriptures that one of the disciples makes at line 32 in the orthodox version, when he exclaims how excited they were when Jesus was explaining the scriptures to them. Neither Epiphanius nor Tertullian says anything about this cut, however. Tertullian remarks in the fourth book several times that Marcion will often leave things in which one would think he would cut out "either to prove that he had not cut anything at all, or else that he was fully justified in what he did cut" (p. 430). At any rate, Tertullian shows that he is wise to both Marcion's theory and his method. As we see, he respects the subtleties of what he considers to be Marcion's perversities.

Tertullian begins engaging Marcion by citing his overt justification for making the cuts. Marcion insisted that the true gospel needed to be purged of all the extrapolations added by those he called "Christian Judaizers." They were trying to advance a claim that the two traditions were related. Tertullian admits that he appreciates the germ of insight here. In an argument often still advanced today, especially by Jewish scholars, he insists on the radical difference between the two testaments: "I do not deny that there is a difference in the language of their documents, in their precepts of virtue, and in their teachings of the law." Tertullian probes the intellectual structure behind this truism: "For as there is nothing, after it has undergone a change which does not become different, so there is nothing different which is not contrary to its former self" (p. 176). To put a finer point on it, Tertullian says: "Diversity is a . . . *condition* of innovation" (p. 178). He points out that God even made the world to manifest this truth. Bright dawn follows the dark night; gentle spring comes hard upon harsh winter. The critical difference is that for Marcion, Tertullian says, every new instance stands alone. That which is new is of a different order altogether from its source. He cannot see any connection between the story of Jesus and the venerable tradition of older stories. In his system, every story is distinct unto itself in the same way that every moment in time begins a new era. Every human decision bears the imprint of a unique, divine intention. Tertullian, on the other hand, insists that something new can resemble its source. Their kinship allows the possibility of unity not only between the different testaments, but between the different books in the Christian scriptures. "Never mind if there does occur some variation in the order of their narratives . . . there is agreement in the essential matters of the faith" (p. 180). In other words, and figuratively speaking, the butterfly is the worm transformed; or to put it in Tertullian's phrase, Jesus' story *sententias re-*

formaverit "reformed the determinations" of God. Thus Tertullian insists on the appropriateness of verses 26 and 28 to Luke's text. In his Luke, Jesus is described as reminding the disciples of all that was said of him "in all the Scriptures."

Thus far Tertullian's critique of Marcion's reading calls it to task for its unwillingness to read the text as it was written. As such, it rings true. But as we might expect, as a man with strong ideas himself, Tertullian does more than restore the integrity of the text. He proceeds to fill in its silences with his own dogmatic findings. He says, "It was well that the unbelief of the disciples was so persistent, in order that to the end we might consistently maintain that Jesus revealed himself to the disciples as none other than the Christ of the prophets" (p. 190). Nowhere is there any language in Luke's Gospel to the effect that Jesus was the "Christ of the prophets" or, indeed, that Jesus was the Christ at all. The narrative says only that there were passages in Moses and the Prophets which referred to Jesus. But Tertullian is confident that he is dealing with matters of fact here, even when the text does not literally support his reading. He presumes the text has a meaning as clear to him as Jesus' appearance was to the disciples on the road. Furthermore, he says, this appearance itself was of a real man, the same man who had lived before his death: "At no time even after his resurrection did he reveal himself to them as any other than what he appeared to be before their eyes—just as they had always thought him to be" (p. 192). This is a very strong reading of the indefinite phrase "their eyes were held, and they did not recognize him."

In all fairness, Tertullian is, properly speaking, no more a literary critic than Marcion is. According to Gérard Vallée, the theological disputes between the so-called gnostics and the early Christians Tertullian, Irenaeus, Hippolytus, and Epiphanius were really always about organization and authority, whatever their ostensible topic (p. 92). They addressed the question of whether direct, personal experience could determine religious truth (as the gnostics more or less believed) or whether designated authorities had to verify explicitly the meaning of every religious truth (as the orthodox more or less believed). Pheme Perkins claims that even the Nag Hammadi narratives "seek to appropriate the authoritative tradition of Christianity by placing one or more of the disciples in the role of a legitimately commissioned Gnostic teacher" (p. 58). Orthodox narratives, in contrast, such as Luke's Succession and Emmaus scenes, feature Jesus as the only verifiable teacher. Tertullian here is not so much misreading Luke as articulating certain already-established, orthodox dogmas on the occasion of refuting a reading of Luke.

We can say, however, whatever their ultimate purposes, both Marcion and Tertullian read Luke correctly. They recognize Luke's narrative insight that the story of Jesus breaks new ground. But as readers of the narrative (at least), they err in different directions. On the one hand, Marcion overlooks the narrative's paratactic suggestion that Jesus' story relates to those in the venerable scriptures. He insists that the new ground is an island. On the other hand, Tertullian overlooks the narrative's paratactic reticence about precisely what that relation is. He insists that Jesus' story is the highland toward which all the previous stories have inclined. The debate they began between their equally inappropriate certainties still holds sway today.

Hans Jonas, the eminent modern student of gnosticism, notes that when Marcion defined his canon, he was the first person to perform any "text-critical work" on a large body of literature pretending to be Christian scripture. However, "he sides with the Jewish exegesis, against his Christian contemporaries, in insisting on the literal meaning and rejecting the allegorical method, which the Church applied to the Old Testament for the purpose of establishing its concordance with the New" (pp. 139–40). Marcion agreed with the Jews that their messiah was yet to come. In his view, Jesus was an altogether different being whose coming changes not the world but the spiritual condition of humankind. In other words, Marcion included the Emmaus episode in his expurgated scripture because it contained images of an otherworldly, spiritual being. This was Marcion's concept of a properly gnostic Risen Savior. Interestingly, even at this late date, Jonas feels strongly enough about what Marcion did almost 1,800 years ago to accuse him of being "high-handed" (p. 145), while offering no corresponding criticism of orthodox interpretive excess. The tradition to which Jonas feels he belongs has a long memory for outrage.

Similarly, Tertullian's polemical response is the first body of work to crystalize the growing dogmatic insistence in Christian orthodox circles that the story of Jesus used the older scriptures as a preamble. Elaine Pagels believes that early Christian apologists had a vested interest in establishing the belief that Jesus actually rose from the dead and appeared to a few select disciples. This would restrict the first authentic experience of the risen Jesus to a small number of men who could then be claimed as the precursors of another small number of men. This group in turn insisted on its privilege to pronounce on matters of faith. The church hierarchy needed a narrow point of historical reference to justify its concentration of power. Pagels cites Tertullian as an early defender of both the doctrine of the bodily resurrection and the authority to declare heretical anyone who dissented from that view. He states emphatically that it is heretical to dissent from the literal interpretation of Jesus' bodily resurection (*De Resurrectione Carnis,* p. 2). He argues against Marcion that in the unreported discourse in the Emmaus episode Jesus upbraids his disciples precisely for their inability to believe in his bodily resurrection (p. 194). In *De Praescriptione Haereticorum,* he argues that Jesus adequately instructed his disciples on this occasion and on others before and after his resurrection, so that there now can be no mistake about what orthodox belief should be. The scriptures have been "explored," as Jesus did on the way to Emmaus. The reports on right thinking are in.

To hold this belief, Pagels writes, required a mind that could be satisfied with paradox. By its nature the doctrine would not withstand skeptical or rational thinking. There could be no tolerance for any sort of personal insight about what the narrative said on the basis of a reference to the text's narrative implications. Thus there is a connection between this dogmatic insistence about the resurrection and about the inclusion of the venerable and Christian scriptures in the scriptural canon. Both dogmas were different manifestations of the notion of "reformation," as Tertullian put it. The new scripture reformed the old, just as the resurrected Jesus reformed his dead body into a newly living man. This would explain why many orthodox interpretations, taking their lead from this early debate, are compelled, as we shall now see, to stress the reality of Jesus' presence and the continuity between the older scriptures and the new. At the same time, it explains why the interpretations often show signs of unease. The magic and enigmatic silences in the narrative resist definitive readings. When the strain shows, the effects can be very interesting.

Origen versus Marcion

Origen (185–254), another of Marcion's contemporary critics, also presses the orthodox point of view that the new canon must include the old. He cites, among others, Luke's Emmaus episode as a proof text for his doctrine. In his great work of doctrine and theory "On Principles," he compares both scriptures to adjacent and contiguous fields: "cultivated with plants of every kind, and out of sight, buried beneath it, are hidden treasures of 'wisdom and knowledge' *sophias kai gnoseos*" (p. 340). One gets at this gnosis by having free range to cross the scriptures at will and wherever one finds promising ground. He also uses the metaphor of a cooking pot into which the interpreter pours many ingredients from many different texts and stirs them together into nourishing spiritual fare ("Commentary on John," p. 196). His gnosis is different than Marcion's intuitive conviction. It is bookish and aggregative. The interpreter eventually digs out or spoons out of every narrative a "type" (*typous*) of something "spiritual" (*pneumaticon*). It is only after this research is firmly in hand that one then "transgresses" or leaves behind the literal meaning to seek out a higher, spiritual meaning. Until this point of affirmation, interpretation is as deliberate as reading a map or following a recipe ("On Principles,"pp. 137–40).

Other evidence of his instinct for the concrete is that Origen likes to base every transgression on solid facts. For example, he is the first writer in the orthodox tradition to single out the Emmaus scene for a specific reading in one of his homilies on Luke. As he does so, he states his orthodox opposition to anyone who believes that the disciples only imagined Jesus to have been talking with them. He was really there. But Origen shares with Marcion some affinities for idealist abstraction. His concept of what was real was wide enough to include the ineffable, as we see when he singles out for comment the special magic in the scene. He explains that Jesus possesses "a body intermediate . . . between the grossness of that which he had before his sufferings, and the appearance of a soul uncovered by such a body ("Homilies," p. 1900). He goes on to say that Jesus could shift back and forth between his two bodies at will and bedazzle the two disciples. In this way, Jesus reinforced dramatically a specific point about the unity of scripture. The two scriptures were separate bodies of language, but the meanings of each could transform into those of the other.

This is not quite what Tertullian had in mind. Instead of arguing for an underlying historical continuity between the two bodies of Jesus and the two bodies of literature, Origen refers to a realm of reality transcendent over anything physical. There all things become one. This is not far from Marcion's way of reading the world. Indeed, according to one modern commentator, Jean Daniélou, who tends to equate Platonic with gnostic dualism, the neoplatonic Origen had a fatal weakness especially for the gnostic notion that "temporal events are an image of what takes place in the world of pure spirits." This notion was "different from both the rabbis' and from Philo's, and not connected with the exegesis given by the Catholic writers. . . . We can only call it gnostic" (p. 194). If we follow Père Daniélou, Origen, it seems, could incorporate gnostic ideas into his own way of thinking even in the process of refuting them. The magic trick in the Emmaus scene drew him in.

Alas, it is just this sort of imaginative play that gets Origen in trouble with more literal-minded authorities. Epiphanius sets what he considers Origen's gnostic interpretation of the Emmaus scene alongside of Marcion's mutilation and condemns them both (p. 201). Jerome thought highly enough of Origen's homilies on Luke to translate them into Latin. But he warned against being beguiled by Origen's interpretation of the Emmaus episode (*Contra Joannem Hierosolymitanum*, p. 401). According to Daniélou, Theopolis warned other interpreters of his errors officially in the year 400 at the Council of Alexandria. The Ecumenical Council of Constantinople condemned his notion of Jesus' resurrected body in his reading of the Emmaus episode in the year 543. Discretion (and silence) concerning the theologically trickier elements of a narrative passage was the better part of interpretive valor.

Early Patristic Refinements

To avoid a similar fate, other orthodox interpreters aware of these early debates hew close to Tertullian's line. They stress the undeniably realistic elements in the episode. One strategy was to look past the magic in the scene, where one could become tangled in dangerous explanations, and instead focus on the reactions of the disciples. Their reaction was "realistic" even if the things that occasion it belong beyond the pale. The patriarch of Alexandria, Athanasius (293–373), praises in a sermon the "fire" of the two disciples' zealous belief, comparing it to the fiery inspiration laying hold of Jeremiah and the blinding transports of Paul (p. 1981). Another related strategy was to stress the ordinary physical presence that Jesus took on while walking, talking, and eating with them. Jerome (320–420), a contemporary of Augustine's, writing to Pammachius about Jesus' appearance in the episode, dwells almost hypnotically on the word "real." He "really" (*vere*) walked with Cleopas; conversed with men with a "real" (*vere*) tongue; "really" (*vero*) reclined at supper; with "real hands" (*veris manibus*) took bread, blessed it and broke it, and was offering it to them (p. 387). When there was a rare discussion of the disappearing act, or how it was that Jesus was able to disguise himself during the greater part of the encounter, the interpretations become vague, usually saying something about Jesus' divine nature or making an abstract point about faithfulness. We sense caution in the twenty-third Sermon of Gregory the Great, delivered in 588 two hundred years after Jerome, whom he cites, wrote to Pammachius. His original reading includes his speculation that the whole scene has two meanings: what really happened as the scene reports—and what the disciples thought about what happened. In a nice twist, he says that the "eyes of their body" could not see as clearly as the "eyes of their heart" (p. 1182). Their faith in what Jesus was saying, in other words, was stronger than their senses could confirm. Gregory shifts the emphasis away from the magic in the scene to the reactions of the disciples to what Jesus says. His maneuver proved compelling. The Venerable Bede repeats Gregory's interpretation word for word one hundred years later (p. 111). Smaragdi Abbatis cites both Gregory and Bede two hundred years later still and quotes them word for word.

But if these Fathers were careful, others could find some intellectual adventure in reading the episode. One relatively safe approach was to imitate what seemed to be Jesus' way of reading. One searched "in all the Scriptures" for other stories and metaphors to illuminate a reading of Jesus' story. Ambrose (340–397), the bishop of Milan, an open admirer of Origen's interpretive style and another of Luke's earliest interpreters, refers to the Emmaus episode in one of his better-known sermons. He develops the idea that the biblical character Isaac provides a good model for the Christian soul.

He compares the Emmaus episode to several others in the Hebrew and Christian scriptures picturing characters with souls on fire. They include the episode at Pentecost, the vision of the last days, Jeremiah feeling a "fire in his bones," and Moses confronting God in a burning bush. Ambrose moves so fluidly between testaments that he can say without pausing to explain himself that it was "Christ, loving Moses" who appeared to him in the burning bush (pp. 515–19). One hundred years later, St. Caesarius of Arles is just as fluid in making a similar pastiche of many different biblical passages. He uses passages from both testaments, including the episode in John's Gospel of Jesus transforming jugs of water into wine. He uses them to elaborate upon Jesus' lesson in scripture reading to his disciples, which he says "turns the water of the Hebrew scriptures into the wine of his fulfillment" (p. 655). We could say that this allegorical reading catches something of Luke's narrative implication with its metaphor. The fermentation of wine from grapes is something like the transformation of venerable stories into new plots.

This familiar practice later became known generally as "allegorical" reading, whereby one passage was always calling to mind another. It was assumed that at some level of abstraction, all the texts of scripture meant the same thing. They all encourage charity, Augustine claimed in a letter to Jerome (p. 431). His most extensive reading of the episode occurs in sermon 232 of his Easter Sunday Sermons. He weaves bits and pieces of all four gospels' resurrection scenes together. He draws attention to this episode as one of several incidents where disciples were not able to believe their eyes or reports they have heard of Jesus' return from the dead. Augustine chides them for their lack of instantaneous faith. In a parenthetical aside, he expresses amazement that one of the disciples characterizes Jesus as a mighty prophet: (Is He that, O disciples? Was Christ, the Lord of Prophets, only a prophet?)" (pp. 1115–25). Augustine goes on to cite other gospel passages where other disciples acknowledge Jesus more fulsomely as "son of David," "son of God," or "the Christ." It is as if he chides the Emmaus disciples for failing to understand the other Christian scriptures sufficiently.

This is undoubtedly an unfair if only rhetorical flourish. The disciples could not have read scriptures that had not been written yet. Indeed, the scriptures derived in part from the oral testimony they themselves might have given. But Augustine, who has read widely in other passages, is able to make an acute observation at this point in his sermon that is very close to a description of a narrative strategy directed toward anyone, like him, who can read the written texts. He begins with a hortative: "Let us now attend to what we hear when the Gospel was read today . . . so that we may appreciate how great a favor was bestowed upon us by His kindness in that we believe what we have not seen" (p. 1115). The phrase "that we believe what we have not seen" echoes the statement Jesus makes to the doubting Thomas in one of John's postresurrection scenes. By calling this episode to mind in a discussion of Emmaus, Augustine implies that Jesus is using a similar strategy in both scenes. Jesus is a master psychologist and teacher. He knows how to draw his disciples out of their disbelief. But at the same time, Augustine explicitly applies this strategy to people like his listeners who themselves have not seen Jesus—beyond reading about him in texts such as these. As Jesus' teaching was to his disciples, so the scripture is to us. Both are humane strategies taken to overcome our natural inclination not to believe what we have not seen.

Another great interpreter will be even more explicit. St. John of Damascus is considered to be the last of the Greek Fathers and brings to a culmination most of their wisdom in his seventh-century compendium *The Font of Knowledge*. In the process of making an extensive comment on the Emmaus passage, he extends Augustine's hint that Jesus could be purposefully dramatic. Remarkably, he says that one of Jesus' human traits was that he could "pretend" (literally, "act according to a pretense" *ta de kata prospoiaesin*) as he does when "he made as if he would go further" in this episode. John explains: "he was merely assuming a human way of acting as required by the advantage and profit to be gained thereby" (p. 525). In developing this idea, St. John distinguishes three ways of describing Jesus after the resurrection that assure us, each in its own way, that he really did what the gospels say he did. One he calls "actual." Jesus is said to have the same wounds before and after his resurrection, as well as the need to eat. The second he calls "according to nature." He means that Jesus was able to perform miracles before and after his resurrection. Finally he uses the phrase again "in pretense." Here he means that Jesus is just as capable after he rose of making convenient fictions (making as if he would go on) as he was when he wept before the tomb of Lazarus whom he knew ahead of time he would raise from the dead. He also points out that it was part of Jesus' teaching style to ask rhetorical questions.

I submit that this notion is remarkably close to a modern interpreter's insight that Jesus is made out to be a character in the gospel narratives who can assume a role to make a point. It is not far from the related notion that an author might contrive to arrange a narrative episode in the same way. What is different, of course, and this is by no means a trivial difference, is that St. John, like Augustine, easily assumes that Jesus actually acted theatrically and pedagogically, whereas a modern critic might only be commenting on how the narrative made Jesus appear to act.

But two late Latin Fathers close the difference further with even subtler readings of narrative strategies at work in the Emmaus episode. Abbas Wernerus cites Augustine in a homily in the year 956 and develops his idea that the episode represents the reality surrounding every individual Christian. Christ is present to us, as he was to the disciples on the road to Emmaus, but not visibly. We must learn, as they did, to harken to his teaching even when we are unaware that he is teaching. This silent instruction is most likely to occur while we are reading scripture (p. 675). Wernerus does not speculate at all on the mechanism of the silent teaching. He says nothing about the provocative arrangements of the scene. But he does trust that the reader is taken in hand by some force or another. The learning the reader gains goes beyond anything that can be accounted for in the literal words of the text.

A century later the Venerable Godefried cites Wernerus and takes his idea a step further. He says that this episode signifies the limits of all written discourse. "We are not able to interpret the meaning of what the evangelist writes by means of singular words. Rather, like the disciples in the scene, we experience the fear that comes from sensing with the eyes of our heart that there is more going on in reality than we are able to account for with our ordinary senses" (p. 807). Remarkably, Godefried intuits the deliberate reticence in the episode. He has the sense that both disciples and readers are expected to *experience* their lack of understanding as part of a deliberate strategy on the part of Jesus and the writer. Thus, he extends what happens to the disciples in the scene to what happens to any faithful reader of the scene. As he does, he sees, as St. John of Damascus did, but even more explicitly, the similarity between Jesus' pretense with the disciples and the writer's strategy with the readers. Both "victims" experience a premonition of a meaning that is beyond the literal sense as a "fear" of the ineffable. This fear is part of our puzzling response to the written scene. At the same time, it describes our sense of the unaccountable wonder of God. Thus, although Godefried interprets Luke with the language of the orthodox tradition, he draws from the episode concepts that would have been well understood by the gnostic thinkers whom the orthodox authorities had long since silenced. This indicates that the unexpurgated text that Tertullian restored was itself able to preserve the essence of unacceptable ideas until such time as an interpreter was able to see them. Then, like a magician, the narrator of Luke's episode suddenly makes materialize what was only apparently invisible.

Thus, to admit with Pagels that the political necessities of the first Christian millenium guide the orthodox reader's eye to see certain things, and not other things, in a scriptural episode such as this one, it is not to dismiss what the orthodox interpreters have to say. Rather, once we understand them, their reconceptions create the opportunity for our appreciating their unexpected insights. The modern critic Paul de Man talks about the prejudicial blindness of critics as the course of their greatest insights. It provides the barrier that can suddenly fall. When we allow for the restraints under which these interpreters worked, we take advantage of the particular acuities of insight they discovered.

We find the same pattern of blindness and insight as we read on in the tradition. Each instance is another affirmative answer to the first question raised at the beginning of this chapter. There are intimations of Luke's gnostic reticence in the orthodox tradition of interpretation. As we continue our survey, therefore, we can begin to focus on the second question raised at the beginning of this chapter: Would it not be legitimate to sharpen the orthodox insight that there are interesting teaching strategies at work in the creation of the gospel narrative? Are they not worthy of being attended to in detail?

Scholastics and Reformers at Emmaus

There is a change in mood, if not basic method, in reading this episode when, approximately in the eleventh century, the so-called "scholastic" period begins and the patristic period ends. A certain desperate intensity disappears. There had always been the fine pressure of decision and dogma behind every scriptural interpretation of the Fathers. They must get things right, they feel, or heathenism of one sort or another will break through the gates. The great medieval scholastic theologian Thomas Aquinas (d. 1274) is calmer and more reflective when he seeks out the opinion of these venerable authorities. By his time, he can be confident that much is known about scripture; many disagreements have been resolved and many doctrines rest secured in language as ornate and buttressed as a Gothic cathedral.

He titles his review of the patristic interpretations of the four gospels a "Chain of Gold" (*Catera Aurea*), indicating that he considers their interpretations linked together into a single revelation about the salvation of the world. Each link in a chain is shaped, self-contained, and solid in itself. As he takes up each gospel text and each episode within each text, he does not so much read what they say as read how they have been read for a millenium. He cites one authority after another, as if their harmonizing voices bespoke a single conviction. In Aquinas's hands, interpretation is as deliberate as taking books down from a shelf.

But Thomas does not cite everything that has been said; even the writer of the massive *Summa* has a sense that books can only contain so much before losing their shape and sense. When he takes up the Emmaus episode in his *Chain,* he selects from the tradition the ideas that strike him, probably because they are ideas that already preoccupy him. As he does, he reveals as much about his own mind as he does about the tradition and the original scriptural text that inspire its response.

Thomas is especially drawn to the Emmaus episode for its descriptions of Jesus as a magically gifted teacher. He not only teaches about faith, he does so with powers beyond the power of reason to describe. Throughout his writings, Thomas is preoccupied with questions of faith and faithfulness. His was the age, after all, when the rediscovery of Aristotle's elaborate descriptions of rationality had intensified a dissatisfaction with reason as a device for achieving ultimate assurance. To be sure, Aquinas is not the first to notice that these are themes touched upon in the Emmaus episode.

He cites Gregory, who says that Jesus refrains from manifesting himself outwardly to anyone who doubts him inwardly, and he cites Theophylos's bold speculation that Jesus turned a certain uncontrollable otherworldliness to his pedagogical advantage: "at this time he had not such a body that he was able to abide longer with them; and he used it that he might increase their affection for him. He was invisible so that their doubts might be made manifested and thus cured" (p. 341). Aquinas combines these ideas into one complex and satisfying idea. Faith penetrates appearances to see what is really there.

As he continues his literature review, Thomas gives less space and emphasis to those who have searched "in all the Scriptures" for passages Jesus might have been relating to the two disciples. This is not so pressing an issue for Thomas, perhaps because the canon has been so long established. In his commentary he briefly cites Chrysostom's discussion of the sacrifice of Isaac as an indication of to what great lengths a Christian's faith in God sometimes must extend. He recalls Venerable Bede's echoing Jesus' admonition to his disciples by saying that all Christians should seek out Old Testament antecedents frequently (p. 342). He is satisfied that any reference Jesus would have made here would have only reinforced the fundamental idea that faith is the paramount Christian virtue. Altogether Thomas's handling of the Emmaus episode indicates that, for him at least, the ground of dogmatic discovery has shifted from reading the scriptures to playing in the speculative mind. That play focuses particularly on the knotty question of the relationship of real evidence and evidence that must be taken on faith. In the *Summa,* he cites patristic commentaries which use the Emmaus episode as evidence that Jesus had the ability to eat real food after his resurrection. This, in turn, was evidence that he had a real body after his resurrection—a doctrine of faith for which there was, therefore, concrete evidence (III, p. 432).

This intellectual play would characterize the readings of other interpreters after Thomas who chose to feature other moments in the episode. They would also pick and choose among those authorities who had written from the same perspective. Orthodox interpretation by this time has full coffers, and one can draw from them at will the coin that would make the necessary purchase. For the sake of brevity, we need only concern ourselves with significant reiterations or elaborations to prove the point that the tradition does not change in essential assumptions, even as its "techniques" become variously more rational, historical, linguistic, or psychological.

The next interpreter after Aquinas with anything substantial to say about the Emmaus episode is the Renaissance humanist and churchman Desiderius Erasmus (1469–1534). He devotes more words and textual space (twenty columns) to the Emmaus episode than any other commentator in the history of its interpretation—almost a third of his entire paraphrase of Luke's Gospel (pp. 469–84, especially p. 473). The commentary occurs in a large work he titles a "Harmony" of the New Testament. In contrast to Aquinas, he returns to the patristic view of the passage. He lays emphasis squarely on the survey "in all the Scriptures." He speculates that Jesus must have cited texts from Isaiah, Jeremiah, Daniel, Hosea, Zachariah, Habbakuk, Lamentations, Psalms, Laws, Deuteronomy, and Genesis, which he himself cites with relish and at great length, using for his authority the speculations of sundry Fathers. But he has no intention of simply reviving patristic allegory for its own sake or using it to serve dogma as the Fathers did. The theme of Erasmus's commentary is brotherhood at a time when various Christian thinkers, his correspondent Martin Luther among them, were discovering harsh things to say about each other's beliefs. He hopes this episode will harmonize rancor.

He introduces his speculative survey with favorable words for the affection of the two disciples, obviously long-time friends, and the kindness with which Jesus encounters them and instructs them. His survey is done with the idea of showing the analogous genial compatibility between the older and newer scriptures. Several times he expresses his hope, and what he believes is Jesus' hope, that the Jews will join the Christian family in believing that Jesus' story belongs to their common salvation history. In other words, Erasmus imagines Luke's Jesus in this episode desiring to break down the distinctions between Jews and Christians, at a time in ecclesiastical history when, to his dismay, various Christian factions were making dogmatic distinctions fatal to their venerable communal belief.

Erasmus can do this and come to different conclusions than earlier, patristic commentators did about what Jesus might have said precisely because he can take advantage of the gospel's textual parataxis. Luke is silent on what the implied author, narrator, or character would say on the matter of the relationship between the older scripture and the new story. And of course, none of these textual authorities expresses anything definite about the relationship between the traditional church and the new spirit of reformation in the air. In Erasmus's new reading, the venerable gospel could be found to recommend maintaining continuity with the past. By focusing on the question of the Jews, he is both cryptic and coy. Certainly if Jews could join with Catholics, Catholics could remain in contact with Protestants. Perhaps they could not agree on a common belief. But they could engage in an endless but fraternal discussion of what belief could be.

The mood of Christian interpretation changes again as the reformation continues apace. It becomes more rancorous despite even the best efforts to enlarge the understanding of what was orthodox thinking. Martin Luther featured the Emmaus episode in a sermon for Easter Monday in the year 1511. He has something of Erasmus's spirit when he stresses the friendliness of Jesus toward the two disciples: "See with what care Christ gave himself to these two weak believers, how he did everything to help their weakness and strengthen their faith, because he saw and knew why they were so troubled and why they had withdrawn from the other apostles not knowing what to think or hope. . . . But because these two were in such great danger of unbelief, he suddenly joined them, as if after his resurrection he had nothing else whatever to do" (p. 226). But Luther also has some very strong ideas about the difference between weakness and stupidity. He sees in the two disciples representatives of "ignorant and inexperienced people like our great popish jerks (*unsere groben Kloess, die Papsts*) who do not understand the rudiments of right beliefs (p. 224). We hope he did not have the gentle Erasmus in mind.

Yet despite his own weakness for polemics, Luther shows himself sufficiently in command of his wits to be the first commentator I have found to notice that Luke withholds from the reader information the reader would dearly love to have: "Now it is true," he goes on to say, "that we would all dearly love to know just what passages the Lord quoted concerning himself. . . . Since Moses [the Pentateuch] contains little or nothing of a plain statement of that of which Christ here speaks" (p. 230.) Luther does not, however, take this to imply that such plain statements would be impossible to supply. Rather, he believes that the reader must do the necessary work with the holy spirit providing guidance. Thus he takes Luke's reticence as a strategy. Luke holds back so that God can reveal the truth directly to the properly "pious and simple minded" (*frome einfeltige*) (p. 231). This is a remarkable statement in the history of the interpretation of this passage. It revives Marcion's sense of the special freedom from definition the written scripture had; it revives the narrative gnostic notion (at least) that insights occur spontaneously at the gratuitous behest of God. The slogan associated with Luther, *sola scriptura* ("only scripture"), was not inconsistent with the narrative gnostic notion that truth came in the form of individual insights.

But if there was the breath of a gnostic spirit in Luther, it was firmly circumscribed by a reverence for the tradition to which he firmly believed he belonged. He concludes the sermon with the standard patristic observation that the passages to which Jesus must refer are doubtless the same ones we find that the apostles quote in their sermons in the Acts of the Apostles and in the Epistles. Like the Fathers, Luther glosses this text with other scriptural texts as if they all had a common source of truth.

Reformation polemics had considerably soured the atmosphere in which scripture was interpreted by John Calvin's time (1509–1564). His tone is very different in his "Harmony" of the four evangelists published some fifty years after Erasmus published his. We cannot take his attitude toward the papists as possibly jocular, as we can Luther's. And when he handles the question of Jesus' perspective on the older scriptures in the Emmaus episode, he is harsh where Erasmus would be amiable. He employs the rhetoric of pronouncement and condemnation for his interpretation: "In order that Christ may be made known to us through the Gospel, it is therefore necessary that Moses and the Prophets should go before as guides, to show the way. It is necessary to remind readers of this, that they may not lend an ear to fanatics, who, by suppressing the *Law and the Prophets,* wickedly mutilate the Gospel; as if God intended that any testimony which he had ever given respecting his Son should become useless" (p. 360). Under Calvin's withering gaze, "readers" can become venial, lazy students, quick to forget essential facts. If some of them can have wicked intentions as they read this episode, then prior intention is of paramount importance when reading any scriptural text. In Calvin's view, intention had better be aligned with rightful thinking.

For Calvin, rightful thinking is above all empirical. He will not argue for a miracle when a practical explanation is possible. Jesus vanished from the disciples' eyes "not because his body was itself invisible, but because God, by withdrawing their vigor, blunted their acuteness" (p. 360). He goes on to say that these disciples were like myopic readers who cannot see what is plain before their eyes. "Their eyes were held" at the beginning of the episode, he says, to bring home to them and to us the readers "how great is the weakness of all our senses" (p. 355). In each instance, Calvin implies that we see what we are predisposed to see, and that attending to our predispositions is the first step in the process of careful, rightful thinking. The next step is to abandon those predispositions. The reader needs to see precisely what the text says and does not say. To some extent, Calvin practices what he preaches. He follows Luther in noting that Luke's Emmaus episode does not spell out the scriptural passages that Jesus shares with his disciples. He does not so much say that the text is silent. He says simply that *he* must be silent. He retires from considering just what the connection is between the two scriptural traditions with an evasive statement that such a question "passes beyond the measure of my present labors" (p. 360).

That is a remarkable statement. Calvin manages to suggest that the narrative of Luke is literally silent about an important matter in Jesus' teaching. At the same time, strictly speaking, he leaves open the possibility that another interpreter, taking other measurements, might be able to supply the missing links. For all of his perception and modesty, Calvin, like Luther, maintains the fundamental orthodox assumption. Correct readings reveal correct meanings. The correspondence will be exact whenever it comes. Thus for Calvin and others, there is something eschatological about biblical interpretation. The hope persists that what cannot be known now will someday be revealed. The measure will be found.

It would be interesting to speculate, therefore, what Calvin might have thought about Cornelius à Lapide's (1567–1637) freewheeling interpretation of the Emmaus scene some fifty years later. In view of the history we are reviewing here, it appears as an unabashed regression to the earliest methods of Christian interpretation. Lapide, a counterreformationist and pietist, revives Origen's notion that Jesus possessed a magical body after his resurrection. Its very magical powers were the first "argument" Jesus used in proving and confirming his resurrection. Lapide concludes that Jesus is similarly present but invisible in the eucharist (p. 977).

It is doubtful whether Calvin would have approved even the Protestant John Albert Bengel's (1687–1752) careful, scholarly interpretation of the episode some one hundred years later. Bengel admits more overtly than Calvin that the Greek phrase in the episode *ta peri eauton* "the things concerning himself" is indefinite. The things in the older scripture are left unspecified in the gospel. But Bengel has no trouble asserting as the Fathers did before him: "There is no doubt that the passages alluded to were the same as those which the apostles subsequently were wont especially to quote" (p. 221). He evokes the tradition to fill the silence of the text. Lapide's and Bengel's arguments both imply that what is invisible is more important than the plain sense. In retrospect, Calvin's awareness of the limited "measures" of his labors is far more prescient.

Unfortunately it has not become traditional. After Bengel there is evidence that the interpretation of the Emmaus scene regresses even further from his clear-eyed, literal reading. At least it does at the hands of Hugo Grötius (1583–1645). Grötius is the great late Christian humanist. His commentary on the New Testament features the Emmaus scene almost as prominently as Erasmus's does. But now he adds to Erasmus's long survey of the biblical prophets Jesus might have had in mind several secular prophets and philosophers as well. He quotes Pisander, Democritus, Sophocles, Cicero, and Plato at length. These writers appeal to him because each has something sensible to add to the definition of what it means to be a fully human Christian (p. 494). Furthermore, Grötius, like Lapide and Bengel, is attracted to the invisible elements in the scene. He follows Origen on the idea that Jesus could do with his body what he wished after his resurrection (p. 506). But he reminds us of what the Church Father Basil said about the mysterious nature of Jesus' presence in the episode: "We should not enquire too closely how it was done." This could mean that one should be satisfied with the meaning of the mysterious disguise rather than its mechanics. But as Grötius seems to mean it, the mystery simply stands beyond the reach of any human understanding. In other words, rather than note the deliberate, or at least the literal obscurity of Luke's text, he looks beyond the literal, literary narrative. He decides that the meaning of the passage resides in the meaning of the event it depicts. And *that* is beyond the ability of even the disciples on the scene to understand. Grötius concludes with an assertion of the limits of human understanding to know. This is another version of the eschatological hope in orthodox interpretation. The truth is out there someplace. In due time it should be revealed.

The Devout Moderns

As far as I can find, Luther's and Calvin's close, literal, and brief acuity has no counterpart in the history of the interpretation of the Emmaus episode until the work of the great German theologian and scholar Friedrich Schleiermacher at the end of the eighteenth century. The spirit of empirical interpretation that breathed in the early years of the Reformation breathes again. Once again someone pays attention to the importance of what the scriptural text *withholds*.

In his commentary on Luke's Gospel, Schleiermacher reads the Emmaus scene as central to the literary strategy underlying the three resurrection scenes in Luke. He notes that the previous scene with the women at the tomb breaks off without development because "Luke was in such haste to come to the history of the two disciples of Emmaus that he neglected to bring the former narrative to a conclusion" (pp. 296–97). With this remark he clearly attends to what we have been calling the implied author's arrangement of scenes. In Schleiermacher's view, the author is more concerned with the dramatic development of his own narrative sequence than with relating certain perhaps true but irrelevant facts. Schleiermacher reiterates his point about artistic motivation in these scenes several ways. He writes: "the preceding incidents are only related so far as they had to provide the disciples of Emmaus with certain expectations. . . . Is it possible to resist the impression that the first account originated only by way of reference to the second narrative? The latter is evidently the nucleus of the whole" (p. 297).

This is exciting. From this perspective, Schleiermacher could have continued to make observations about the narrative syntax or the dramatic arrangement of scenes, as I do in the first and following chapters. Indeed, his method directly inspires my own. But like Luther and Calvin, he does not sustain the rigor of this close, literal reading of the implied author's arrangements for long. He drops his speculation about the aesthetics of the narrative arrangement. He proceeds to sift the scene for clues about the actual historical circumstances it represents. He examines the "minuteness of the details" in the scene, such as the naming of one of the disciples, and the *verbatim* record of the private conversation the two of them have as they wend their way. They indicate to him that the source of this unique episode could only have been "from the original oral narration of one of the two, and therefore most probably of Cleopas who is therein named." On the basis of other scholarly theories about the composition of Luke's Gospel Schleiermacher has been discussing, he argues further that Cleopas was probably the first person to have committed the oral report to writing. Later Luke drew on his source.

Thus we see that Schleiermacher is finally interested in the strategy of the narrative arrangement only insofar as it provides evidence for authorial intention or editorial history. He has no real interest in the aesthetic strategy as such. He looks beyond the implied author in the scene to the once-living writer who wrote the text. As it turns out, he is not very impressed with what he finds.

He concludes his commentary on the entire gospel with the statement that Luke was not "an independent writer" (*unabhängiger Schriftsteller*). He was "only a collector and compiler (*nur Sammler und Ordner*) (p. 301). His implication is that any truly admirable writer would only write logically. Any apparent surface illogic or alogic that he finds in the Emmaus scene must be evidence of heavy-handed tampering with the record. With such hermeneutical predilections, one perforce could not notice any parataxis. Inferential gaps in the narrative would simply appear as unfocused writing.

As we have seen, Schleiermacher's flickering interest in narrative strategies as vehicles of intention is not unprecedented. A thousand years before he wrote, Origen and John of Damascus were aware of authorial "fictions" and character "pretense" in scripture. The reformists Luther and Calvin remarked on the provocative authorial silence of the text. But unfortunately, for all of Schleiermacher's new and vigorous interest in authorial intention in interpreting the scripture, he could not sustain his interest in narrative strategies significantly longer than his forebears.

I think Schleiermacher's lack of attention to the narrative qualities of the scripture is not unprecedented. Furthermore, his theory and method in particular probably indicate an inherent limitation in the tradition of biblical interpretation. Those in the tradition always remain true to the assumption that scripture contains "deep" meanings. These deep meanings can range from the inherent *gnoseos* Origen wanted to dig out of the broad ground of the united scripture to the actual authorial intention Schleiermacher can almost see playing beyond the shadows of the literary language and to the "overall complex pattern" of meaning Sternberg is certain can be found. Deep meanings always consist of some extratextual reality thought to be superior to anything mere words can say. Consequently, those in the tradition can *never* see that scripture is artistic. I mean something more than scripture's possessing literary ornaments which those in the tradition do frequently note and appreciate. Recall John of Damascus's appreciation of Jesus' dramatic skill and Luther's appreciation of the narrator's reticence. Rather, I mean the artistry of narrative suggestion and implication that deliberately refrains from stating a definitive meaning. There are only other things to be imagined about what it implies.

Indeed, even in Schleiermacher's hermeneutics we can still find the spirit (if not the overt method) of allegory at work. In this commentary, it appears in the form of a tendency to let information about matters that happened outside the text itself speak to that text as one of its explanations. Now, instead of privileging the older scriptures as a ground for understanding the new, one privileges the history of its composition. The same principles operate today in what is called redaction criticism, or the study of the history of the composition of the text. They operate in *Sitz im Leben* criticism, or the study of the historical circumstances surrounding the composition of a text. They operate in kerygmatic interpretation, which puts every scriptural text into the hypothetical context of the development of church teaching. In this case, Schleiermacher does a little of what will become all three types of modern biblical interpretation. The narrative syntax does not appear as interesting to the commentator as the underlying or prior history to which the surface meaning appears to aspire to reveal.

According to Hans Frei in his illuminating recent study *The Eclipse of Biblical Narrative,* Schleiermacher's hand lies upon every subsequent biblical commentary that ignores its narrative connectiveness or syntax to talk about apparently deeper and more important meanings. Frei points out that Schleiermacher's reform of Christian interpretation was salutary in many respects. It curbed the worst excesses of interpretive license practiced since the days of Origen. No longer could interpreters make claims for a deeply underlying spiritual meaning based on the flimsy evidence that a text in Genesis, for example, might use the same word or image as a text in Revelation. But this good came at a price. A sense of narrative was lost, whereby one narrative might appear akin to another, or one passage in a narrative appear as preamble or postscript to another. In its stead enter the methods of biblical dissection—form criticism, kerygmatic criticism, redaction criticism, the search for sources, the highly refined philological studies comparing discrete text to discrete text—all with an eye to discovering an intention or a meaning or a reality behind individual passages. Silence any talk of narrative magic; ban any notice of parataxis. One can only notice the gaps between elements in a narrative if one is inclined to read a narrative as a narrative—that is, a continuous series of juxtapositions, many of which are left (provocatively) unconjoined.

Several times Frei states that this state of affairs still reigns (pp. 12, 16, 324). In the shadow of this eclipse, the narratives of the Bible come to seem "aggregative rather than organic, their sequence disconnected and merely ranged together, one incident or group of sayings to the next" (pp. 310–11). Today, form critics continue to see the text as a collection of pericopes and their groupings as the prevailing literary writings, while redaction critics look beyond the groupings to the religious ideas the final editor must have had in mind in arranging them this way.

I basically accept Frei's metaphor of an eclipse of awareness about the narrative in modern biblical scholarship. This is the very light that my study hopes to encourage to brighten again. But I also think my review to this point indicates that the light of this awareness in this tradition has always been rather dim. Past scholars felt free to link very different narratives with their allegorical readings but offered only rare observations about how individual authors put together particular narrative strategies.

We find instances of Schleiermacher's influence that Frei describes throughout the nineteenth century. G. L. Hahn, a scientific German commentator, repeats Schleiermacher's observation that the exactness of language in the episode is a clue to its original source in an eyewitness account. But rather than comment on the way Luke might have exploited his raw materials, Hahn continues by taking issue with other German commentators who have naturalistic explanations for why the disciples could not see Jesus. It was, in his opinion, the result of a divine miracle (*göttische Einwirkung*) because the passive verb in the phrase "their eyes were held" implies that an outside force did the holding (p. 34). Hahn does have interesting things to say about the purpose of the miracle. It was to draw attention to Jesus' teaching in a special way. It tried to get the disciples to listen to a rather prosaic account of how they should instruct themselves. They need not be bedazzled by the spectacle of a man coming back from the dead. But Hahn does not develop the idea that the scene contains various teaching strategies working in conjunction with each other. Instead he follows tradition in speculating about what Jesus must have done as he interpreted the scriptures. He decides that Jesus must have compared specific texts in the Pentateuch with others in the Prophets, much as Christian exegesis has done ever since.

Less scientific commentators would concentrate more exclusively on the dogmatic conclusions that could be drawn from the scene. Like Hahn, John J. Owen, a nineteenth-century English commentator, rejects the various naturalistic explanations for why the disciples could not see Jesus, such as their being blinded by excessive grief. But he argues for a miracle on psychological rather than linguistic grounds. There had to have been a powerful force holding their eyes if they were not to have become suspicious that it was Jesus talking to them while their "hearts were burning" as they listened (p. 64). Like Hahn and Owen, Henry Burton, another contemporary English commentator, notes the exactness of the language in the episode. He sees it as evidence that Luke must have been the second and modestly unnamed disciple. But when he gets to the miracle, he lets out the stops: "And thus, opening their Scriptures, putting in the crimson lens of the blood, as well as the chromatic lens of the Messianic glory, the disciples find the cross all transfigured, inwoven in God's eternal purpose of redemption; while the sufferings of Christ, at which they had stumbled before, they now see were part of the eternal plan of mercy, a Divine 'ought' of great necessity" (p. 411).

In our own century, the same orthodox critical assumption still reigns. This is the assumption that the scripture is not really narrative in the sense of being individual texts with discrete arrangements of meaning. Augustine is quick to leap from one text to another without regard for the integrity of an individual text or subtlety of meaning. Schleiermacher doubts Luke could control the many sources of his material. "Without a doubt these are unliterary writings," the twentieth-century biblical scholar Dibelius writes of the gospels. "They should not and could not be compared with 'literary works'. . . . They are collections of material. The composers are only to the smallest extent authors. They are principally collectors of tradition, editors. Before all else their labour consists in handing down, grouping, and working over the material which has come to them" (cited by Kee, p. 5).

An example of modern redaction criticism applied to the Emmaus episode is H. D. Betz's essay arguing that the Emmaus episode was not originally a part of Luke's Gospel. Instead, it was edited into the gospel after the church had decided that the Lord's Supper was to be her primary religious ritual. Therefore the scripture had to be made to appear to anticipate its importance. An example of kerygmatic interpretation is Eric Franklin's book arguing that the Emmaus episode reflects the teaching of early church members that bread was to be taken as "a sign of fellowship with the risen, exalted Lord . . . empowering them with the life of the kingdom and with the promise of the fullness of the future" (p. 149). An example of intentional criticism is provided by John Drury's discussion of the Emmaus scene in his recent and influential commentary. He features not what Jesus might have said when interpreting "all the Scriptures" but what Luke was doing using phrases from Deuteronomy when he writes this scene. He claims that Luke used Deuteronomy because he believed his history writing to continue what the Deuteronomists had done. Like his Jesus, Luke began by examining scripture and then transformed its stories into a midrash, or a retelling. The new version featured Jesus as the new hero doing the same sorts of things the old-time heroes did, but now in a new way. In Drury's view, Luke believed that there was nothing in any scripture text that resisted its creative revision. In effect, Luke believed he was rewriting the already written scripture rather than writing a new scripture. This assumption allows Drury in his turn to compare texts written in very different times and languages as if one was the literary cognate of the other. Consequently he can restore to modern exegesis much of the interpretive range of the old allegory. He is a traditional partisan in a new way. He assumes Luke is right in doing it because these old stories could stand the correction that would finally make them clearer about their underlying Providence. In our terms, there is a syntaxis between Old Testament and New.

In general, interpreters like Drury still downplay the magic in any narrative text considered to be sacred in order to emphasize its "normativeness," as Krister Stendahl puts it, by which he means the aspects of a story that exemplify how to act or think or believe religiously. Another good example is I. Howard Marshall's recent learned commentary on Luke's Gospel. His remarks on "The Walk to Emmaus" describe the appearance of Jesus as having nothing to do with magic. It has only to do with the psychology of the disciples. "The truth, previously hidden from their eyes, dawns, and they realise it is Jesus." To explain further, he uses theological terms: "The most puzzling feature is perhaps the initial blindness of the disciples, but this is more theological than legendary in character. . . . The lack of recognition is more due to a spiritual blindness by the disciples than to something unusual about the appearance of Jesus . . ." (pp. 891, 893).

The more sectarian the interpreter, the more affirmations of faith predominate. Burton Scott Easton: "Underlying the story two distinct motives appear; Christ was manifested to certain disciples at a eucharist; and Christ originated the Old Testament apologetic of the Church" (p. 362); Frederick W. Danker: Luke . . . emphasizes that suffering is the prerequisite for glory" (p. 111); C. B. Caird: "Humanly speaking, [the disciples] failed to recognize Jesus because, like many a modern sceptic, they were convinced that miracles of that sort could not happen" (p. 258); "We look in vain for Old Testament predictions that the Messiah must reach his appointed glory through suffering. . . . What Luke is here claiming is that, underlying all the Old Testament writings, Jesus detected a common pattern of God's dealing with his people, which was meant to foreshadow his own ministry" (p. 258). Caird thinks this would include Daniel 7, Hosea 5–6, and Isaiah 6–9 and 40–55. Eduard Schweizer: "The turning point does not come through a miracle but through Scripture. In table fellowship Jesus gives them the reality of his presence; his word takes the form of a visible gift"

(p. 373). The disappearance is explained as "an extreme way of saying that when God enters into human life and is recognized as God, the divine is never in a position to be apprehended" (p. 373).

The best example of a commentary with more discrimination and less affirmation is Joseph Fitzmyer's definitive two-volume *Anchor Bible Commentary* on Luke's Gospel. Fitzmyer devotes eighteen pages to the Emmaus episode (almost as much as Erasmus) as he carefully sifts through the language of the text and the many scholarly opinions that have been ventured as to its meaning. He is continuously judicious. He says, accurately, in the spirit of Luther and Calvin, that "the modern reader will look in vain for the passages in the OT to which the Lucan Christ refers . . . ." (p. 1558). There is perhaps the implication here that modern readers no longer have the freedom the readers of the past had relished. Later he says in his line notes: "It is not surprising that the 'Servant' of Isaiah 52–53 was eventually identified with a messiah in the Jewish tradition; but it still remains to be shown that this identification existed in pre-Christian Judaism or in Judaism contemporary with the NT" (p. 1566). He adds that although it might be "tolerable" to cite here passages Luke mentions elsewhere in the narrative, Luke himself "supplies no specific references" (p. 1567). Furthermore, it "is far from certain" that Luke based his account on Mark 16:12–13 or any other source used by any other evangelist; it is more likely derived from a source unique to Luke and therefore one that needs to be read in Luke's own context, rather than comparatively with another gospel (pp. 1554–55). Fitzmyer analyzes the peculiarly Lucan use of virtually every word and syntactical and stylistic patterns in the passage to reinforce his point. Then, after considering other scholarly opinions about other kinds of postresurrection appearance stories, he concludes again that "the appearance-stories cannot be harmonized; being too different from one another in character and detail" (p. 1557). It is an episode that belongs exclusively to Luke. When Fitzmyer considers the parallels another scholar has found between this episode and the one with the Ethiopian eunuch in Acts, he states: "One cannot deny the similarity of structure in the stories, but there is also enough dissimilarity to caution one from overinterpreting the former" (p. 1560). He reads closely indeed.

But when Fitzmyer takes up what he calls the "eucharistic" motif in the episode as Jesus breaks bread with the disciples, his restraint yields to a personal and dogmatic pronouncement close to the concerns of his Catholic beliefs: "The lesson in the story is that henceforth the risen Christ will be present to his assembled disciples, not visibly (after the ascension), but in the breaking of the bread. So they will know him and recognize him, because *so* he will be truly present among them" (p. 1559). He is still careful: "We know very little about liturgical celebrations in the first century" (p. 1560). But at the end of his line notes, Fitzmyer's last words on the episode reiterate what appears to him to be the most important motif in the scene: "What is above all important is that the disciples report that they knew him 'in the breaking of the bread' (v. 35) and not by seeing him" (p. 1569).

The Limits of Commentary

The reason why even a most discriminating biblical scholar such as Fitzmyer will also affirm faith is, of course, because he has faith. The reason why he will use the form of modern learned commentary in making his biblical interpretation is because its structure implicitly encourages a faithful affirmation. The minute discriminations of language lead logically to a "general understanding." And this general understanding is usually taken to be the underlying, or hidden message of faith: a deep meaning. To put it another way, on the one hand, the scholar sifts through the scriptural text one chapter or one unit at a time, with a critical survey of other opinions appended to the translation and discussion of each discrete fragment. Every article about a particular passage or every book about a particular theme thereby appears to be gist for an eventual commentary's mill: its raw material as it were. On the other hand, the commentary either begins or ends by summarizing the overall sense of the passage, and in the case of learned commentaries, the overall critical consensus about it. The summary gathers everything that has been done to date together, and this permits the commentator to abstract the meaning of the text. This abstraction, in turn, inclines toward the affirmation of the true or underlying meaning of the passage. The commentary gives the impression of scholarly and spiritual exhaustiveness. What more could be said?

I have two answers to that question. The first is that one could talk about the narrative arrangement that the commentary format eclipses. These are its patterns of paratactic juxtapositions *between* the discrete parts that the implied author leaves for the reader to ponder. They are like synapses at the endings of nerves. They are not connectives; they are the implied space through which connections need to be made. The aesthetic or artistic aspect of a narrative is the pattern of implications its gaps imply. To notice them, one has to notice the conflicts in a scene or a whole work—the connections that are not explicitly made. The only way to notice them is to consider all the conflicts that are left unresolved. They cannot be noticed if one chooses only the details in a scene that seem consistent with one another or consistent with some overall theme the author seems to be building. They might be; the harmonies and the themes might be there, and it is good to attend to them, especially when we have the sense, as we might with the evangelists, that they are celebrating harmonies and wonderful themes. But to write a narrative is to create netted patterns of silence like those between the words in a spoken discourse or the words in the lyric of a song or the notes in a work of instrumental music. These silences say nothing literally, but they invite the recording mind to draw inferences and so enter into the creation of the particular work of art. They are there in the gospel narrative like they are there in every narrative; and they are worth attending to.

The second answer is that one could pay attention to the narrator. The narrator is not God, an apostle, a prophet, or even a contemporary of the events the narrative describes. The narrator is an artifice, no "natural thing," a gold-enamelled bird, as Yeats put it, singing "of what is past, or passing, or to come." Again it is in his words in the poem "Sailing to Byzantium," "the artifice of eternity." The spell it casts is the closest we can come to this realm in this life.

A few modern biblical scholars have made passing but acute observations about these two intrinsic narrative authorities. Hans Dieter Betz comments on the Emmaus episode: "We as the readers of course, know better. We know that the real situation is reversed: Cleopas and his friend, in the last analysis, do not know what had happened, although they were eyewitnesses of the so-called *bruta facta*" (p. 43). Jean Starobinski notes the same strategy in Mark, whose narrator, he says, arranges the point of view in such a way that the reader "sees" more than the characters within the scene whom Jesus decries as "blind." Thus "the text is structured in such a way that the reader (or hearer) is made a disciple of Christ *ipso facto*, by the interposed narrative" (p. 335). Other readers could make these kinds of observations more extensively.

To read the biblical narrative as an implied author's arrangements and as a narrator speaking, we need to extend our scholarly detachment even further than Fitzmyer allows himself to do. As we see, when he reads certain passages such as the one about "all the Scriptures," he is able to maintain great respect for the limits of what the words say. He definitely forbids the now apparently idle speculations that have excited Christian interpretation on this scene for almost two millenia. Luke's Jesus does not clearly define the relationship of his story to the venerable scriptures that preceded it. On this point, his view is compatible with that of a contemporary Protestant scholar of the New Testament, Brevard S. Childs. He comments on Luke's use of the Old Testament: "Above all, Luke does not attempt to Christianize the Old Testament, but to let it speak in its own voice of the coming salvation. This characterization is not to deny that Luke's own perspective and the Hellenistic environment provided a filter through which the Jewish Scriptures were read. After all it was the Septuagint which he consistently used. Nevertheless, the major point to be made is that Luke's explicit intention was to relate the story of Jesus to the story of Israel" (p. 115). Samuel Sandmel, a contemporary Jewish scholar, agrees in these terms: "Luke wishes to avoid the charge that Christianity was new or marginal; he insists that it is central and truly ancient. Though he does not go so far as some of the later Church Fathers, who made veritable Christians out of the Biblical forebears, Luke points the way to the next step" (p. 98).

To take "the next step" in discriminating among the different narrative strategies in Luke's narrative in the next chapter, I eschew the commentary structure. Only in this way can we consider how Luke's implied author employed narrative parataxis throughout his gospel. Only in this way can we hear the narrator speak. In the epilogue, I reflect on and define the method being used. What follows is a reading of Luke's Gospel in light of the Emmaus episode that I hope belongs with, and extends, all the readings that have already been made of it in the last eighteen hundred years.

Chapter Four

On the Road to Emmaus

Felix, qui potuit rerum cognoscere
causas/
What a pleasure to discover the
underlying causes.

Virgil, Georgics *II*

Joseph Fitzmyer is right to feature the theme "on the road" in Luke's Gospel. Like Abraham, Joseph, Moses, and Ruth before him, Jesus wanders for a good part of his story, not toward the promised land as they did, but rather from place to place within Israel, now divided into several petty fiefdoms under overweening foreign domination. As he wanders, his words and adventures allude over and over again to the older promises and stories, tracing out a new way to understand them as no longer time-bound, place-bound, or even book-bound: "It is written . . . but I say to you . . ."

Luke's narrator traces Jesus' wanderings with more display of purpose than any legitimate character, even Jesus, can ever have. A character has to appear uncertain about where his or her story is going in order to remain true. A character is made interesting by the quality of the inquiry after the meaning of a life. But a narrator knows where the story is going from the first words of the narrative the reader reads. Luke's entire narrative of Jesus' wandering builds toward the climax of the episode on the road to Emmaus, where two disciples have something like a gnostic experience, as we have seen. But now that we proceed toward that narrative climax from the beginning of the gospel, we can appreciate how the narrator prepares for Jesus' gnostic experience as well. He finally learns who he is. He finally learns how properly to teach the others.

There is an obvious point of difference between the gnostic experiences depicted in the narratives of the Nag Hammadi library and in Luke's narrative. The so-called gnostic gospels are always fragmentary as narratives even when they appear to be more or less complete as texts.

They feature a singular, overwhelming moment of insight. There are many such moments in Luke. We have considered some of them in parables of the Good Samaritan and the Forgiving Father and in Peter's tragic recognition of his own ignorance and weakness in the courtyard. But they are linked together to illustrate the progressive education of the main character. The moments of insight he has, or arranges for others, are preambles for insights yet to come. When the gospel concludes with its series of enigmatic scenes, the Emmaus scene paramount among them, the disciples within the scenes and the readers without are left to their own well-exercised devices: "how our heart was burning."

Luke's fascination with the necessary progression of insights explains why he is the only evangelist to present not only the birth, as Matthew also does, but also the early years of Jesus, beginning before he could speak. Only Luke features Jesus as an insensitive, precocious child whose decision to remain behind in Jerusalem dismays his parents. Only Luke features Jesus as a callow youth whose inept first effort at preaching almost gets him killed. When his Jesus takes command of his circumstances in following scenes, it is clear that he has learned something about himself. For Luke, something like gnosis is the prerequisite for Jesus' becoming a teacher.

No one can make a claim that Luke's narrative hews to any modern standard for a *Bildungsroman*. He inherits and includes a considerable amount of traditional material about Jesus in the form of the individual pericopes which usually show Jesus dominating the circumstances in which he finds himself. These resolutely self-centered discourses resist plotting. Like the other synoptic evangelists, Luke clusters many scenes by verbal or thematic association, for example, presenting food and healing scenes together. There are many instances of paratactic silence that only suggest how Jesus might have learned to think and to teach more effectively. But nonetheless there is a sufficiently obvious narrative arrangement of unique material. Luke was able to diffuse his theme of progressive gnosis throughout the narrative. He brings it especially to bear on the provocative and ultimately unanswerable question that intrigued Jesus, his disciples at Emmaus, and Luke's earliest readers: What is the relation of Jesus' story to the venerable scriptures? They do not appear to anticipate his peculiar story line and especially its astonishing denouement.

To appreciate Luke's progressive narrative approach toward the question (if not the answer), we need something like Marcion's affinity for gnosis; Origen's fascination for intertestamental relations; and Alter's, Sternberg's, and Kugel's sensitivity to parallelism. We also need an appreciation for narrative parataxis, and occasionally the modern biblical exegetes' analytical acuity. We need above all a willingness to consider the narrative as a narrative—a forest with a certain dimension and shape—not just a plantation of countless branchy trees. To borrow a metaphor, we need the perspective of a swinger of birches.

Providential Arrangement versus Realistic Detail

Even before Jesus is old enough to speak, Luke's implied author arranges the narrative to suggest the subtle departures his conventional story will take. In the first scene, an angel comes to Zechariah, a pious old man praying in the temple. He has left Elizabeth, his pious, barren wife at home. The angel promises Zechariah that his wife will bear him a son. The reader who knows the venerable scriptures recognizes another Abraham before him. Like Abraham, Zechariah does not believe what he hears. His wife is to be another Sarah. Their plight also recalls that of Isaac and Rebecca, Jacob and Rachel, Elkanah and Hannah. All were childless until late in life when they became the parents of a child who became an important character in the next generation of God's people. The reader well read "in all the Scripture" has an idea of what to expect.

But even before the angel speaks, the narrative drops several paratactic hints that their story is not to be only or merely typical. Both Zechariah and Elizabeth are called "blameless," and not a word is said about their discontent, even though they are childless. Yet when the angel appears before Zechariah, he says, "Zechariah, your prayer has been heard: your wife Elizabeth will bear you a son." Due to a paratactic reticence, the reader cannot be sure whether Zechariah just made this prayer, selfishly thinking of his own predicament during the august moment of his ritual presence in the inner sanctum, or whether the prayer has been long-standing. Later, when Elizabeth does become pregnant, we hear her bid farewell to the hateful humiliation of childlessness she has borne all along.

Clearly these symbolic characters have feelings and frailties. Gabriel's command that John be raised as Nazirite—"He shall never touch wine or strong drink"—recalls the hallowed figures of Samson and Samuel, men whom angels enlisted at the same age for lives of heroic abnegation. It is not an altogether consoling recollection for a parent to have before a son is born. Samuel died disillusioned in the midst of a civil war, Samson eyeless in Gaza. The grim hint in the angel's otherwise happy allusion turns out to be prophetic. We learn in chapter nine that an anxious and befuddled Herod has John beheaded in prison.

These details give God's grand abstract plan, unrolling since the time of Abraham, strands of realistic narrative texture. We are reading two kinds of stories at once. One is an epic story of God's unfolding grand plan. The other is a realistic story of how the plan affects the lives of the ordinary characters it conscripts. When Luke takes these kinds of narrative pains to be sympathetic to the old style of scriptural story, he is not doing so because he wishes to dismiss that style altogether. He refines it in order to use it, honoring it even while he is setting the style up to be replaced by another. Even the different styles are evoked by parataxis. We are aware of the old while perceiving the new and wondering about their relation to each other.

Luke's inventiveness with the older forms is bolder in the following scene. The reader has already been led to expect the birth of an extraordinary child as a firstborn son. If the story follows true to form, that son will be the elder brother of a second son who, like Isaac or Jacob, will become a much more important character than the elder Ishmael or Esau. The reader anticipates that John will have such a brother. True to one's expectation, Gabriel next appears to a younger woman, Mary, and makes the same promise. Strictly speaking, it is not unprecedented for the "brothers" in a typical biblical story to have different mothers, as Isaac and Ishmael did— Sarah and Hagar respectively. There is another precedent in the two mothers, Leah and Rebeccah, for the twelve sons of Jacob. But other details are without precedent. Gabriel comes this time to the future mother, not the father, as in all previous stories. He finds her at home, not in a particularly sacred place. Most significantly, rather than being barren as all the previous married women had been, she is unmarried and virginal, empty in the way an apple basket is before picking day. This child is to have no certain father. Compared to Zechariah, she simply wonders how the angel's promise can come about, whereas Zechariah was incredulous about a much more probable pregnancy. The reader has a sense that the rules governing biblical narrative conventions are being changed here.

In addition, Luke's new narrator has a sensitivity to narrative variation that exceeds that of angels. Gabriel, for all his perspicacity, cannot read precisely the variations in the parallels that he is in the process of setting up. When he sees that his greeting "troubles" Mary, he takes it to mean that she is as frightened as Zechariah was when he saw him in the temple. He tells her "not to fear" (*nae phobou*), while the narrator says only that "she is troubled" (*dietapachthusae*) over what his greeting might mean. Her response is private and personal. It is as if she has the foreboding that whenever a divine being takes notice of you at all, life is about to become very unsettling.

Her silence lies at the center of the scene. Even the narrator appears unaware of Mary's thoughts as Gabriel relates the extraordinary promise: "You shall conceive and bear a son, and you shall give him the name Jesus. He will be great; he will bear the title Son of the Most High; the Lord God will give him the throne of his ancestor David, and he will be king over Israel for ever; his reign shall never end" (1:31–33). It is remarkable that she only questions the biology of the prediction, not its religious or histori-cal dimension: "How can this be? . . . I am still a virgin." When the angel tells Mary "how this is to be," that the holy spirit will "overshadow" her, the implied reader cannot comprehend what the literal statement means. Such an explanation for a conception is completely unprecedented. No story in the venerable scriptures ever suggested that even an improbable birth required more than an especially favored sexual union.

The reader does not even hear whether she is to conceive while a virgin or yield her virginity at the angel's command. Yet Mary within the scene either understands what Gabriel says or is willing to abide in trusting igno-rance. "Here I am," she says. This is her moment of inspired gnosis. But even the angel who inspired it does not appear to understand completely what she thinks. Her motives are less predictable than Zechariah's. She is thus less reducible to the stuff of caricature or type. She keeps her own counsel, into which even the omniscient narrator does not pry.

As the third scene continues to make parallels between these two stories, we begin to see how much narrative parataxis can imply once certain patterns have been established. In the first two scenes, an angel comes down into the story with prophecies for two characters within it. One character, Mary, moves unbidden across the narrative landscape to visit another, Elizabeth. As she does, she joins their two stories together of her own free will. She occasions another allusion to the venerable scriptures. When she greets Elizabeth, Elizabeth tells her "my baby leapt in my womb." This recalls two stories in Genesis. One recounts the struggles of the twins Perez and Zerah while still in the womb of Tamar, the other, those of Jacob and Esau while still in the womb of Rebeccah. These chil-dren had been wrestling for access to the birth canal and the primacy of the firstborn. In this new story, the two brothers are in adjacent wombs. The one biologically destined to be born first magically dances a jig of joy that his younger brother even exists. Such is the silent implication in the scene. What is overt is its realistic and palpable manifestation. With Mary's greet-ing of Elizabeth, both women share an unambiguous joy they create for each other. Elizabeth's particularly anticipates the gnosis of the younger son in the parable of the Forgiving Father. She appears overjoyed the moment she discovers the importance of even a secondary role.

In these and similar ways, the implied author's sensitive, realistic detail-ing brings the grand abstract plan down to earth. What remains obscure in the story is part of the message: the workings of God in this story startle and disorient characters hitherto preoccupied with very different, usually mundane concerns. What remains obscure to them, even while they try to cooperate, preserves their integrity as characters who have to view things differently than narrators or even angels. It makes them heroes who do more than they understand.

In this regard, the second part of Mary's scene with Elizabeth is all the more startling. At this point early in his narrative, the implied author employs a narrative technique so fresh and unexpected that it seems as miraculous a discovery as the angel's message was to Mary. He has her break out of the narrative altogether to sing a song directly to the reader. With her *Magnificat* she looks back on previous stories about deposed monarchs and exalted common people, about the promises made to Abraham and to Israel. She looks forward to the generations who "will count me blessed." For the length of her song, she has a prophet's range of vision and a psalmist's sense of rhythm, both surprising in a young woman who had stammered in the presence of an angel three months earlier. Her newfound voice is as surprising as the pregnancy the angel predicted. As Mary sings, she resigns her role as symbolic counterpart to Elizabeth as well as her role as a realistically flabbergasted young woman. She becomes, for a moment, the story's narrator, able to comment on the significance of her own role in the story of which she is a part. Her song is similar to those that Brecht's characters sing when they step out of character and comment on their stories in order to keep the audience alert to its underlying logic of ideas. The comparison is not anachronistic; Brecht claimed the technique was natural in didactic literature. Nor is the comparison exact. Mary does more than comment on her story. She demonstrates the authority that characters have over either the grand design or the realistic rendering of the story they are in. There is more to her than either can recount.

The only counterpart to this moment in the narrative occurs when her son Jesus, at the end of the story on the road to Emmaus, will be able to command a comparable understanding of his place in the grand design of things. He, of course, will whisper rather than sing. She has no counterpart in any of the orthodox gospels. We have to look beyond them to that different Mary in the *Acts of Peter and the Apostles* who was also favored with a special vision. From this comparison we can see that Luke shares some gnostic writers' high regards for the intelligence of women. Here is another episode that Pagels could have added to her short list of gnostic-like New Testament episodes.

Varieties of Narrative Parataxis

When Mary's song ends, the implied author's grand design appears to regain control of its parallel structuring. In the next chapters, he continues to compare John's early life with Jesus'. Two lines recount John's birth, while it takes twenty to recount Jesus'. John is born at home, with friends and neighbors nearby; Jesus is born "on the road," in a strange town, in a stable, with strangers nearby. John's family's friends and neighbors hear through word of mouth about his birth; shepherds hear from angels that a messiah has been born, a baby now lying in a manger. John's birth delights the friends and neighbors; the angels' appearance first terrifies the shepherds. The angels tell them, as Gabriel told Zechariah and Mary, not to be afraid; heavenly hosts fill the skies with the praise of God. The shepherds converse, go to Bethlehem, see the child, describe what they have seen, and astonish their audience. Mary ponders what is happening. The shepherds return to their fields glorifying and praising God.

These broad parallels are another form of narrative parataxis. The juxtaposed scenes *imply* questions about what is similar and what is different in each story. The reader could say that in contrast to John's, Jesus' home is anywhere. His family includes the lowest social classes and the highest heavenly beings. Whereas John is domestic, Jesus is cosmic. In the following scenes paralleling the early adventures of the newly born brothers John and Jesus, the implied author varies this form of parataxis in wonderful ways.

Initially it appears that the tables turn and John becomes the featured brother. This time twenty-one lines recount John's circumcision (1:59–79), with only one for Jesus (2:21). John's story is more detailed and emotionally absorbing than Jesus' will be. This time John's neighbors are astonished and even frightened by what they see and hear. They expect the child to be called Zechariah for reasons the narrative does not disclose. Elizabeth knows the child is to be named John, again without our knowing why. Perhaps other scenes occurred out of sight in which Zechariah wrote out for her all that he had seen and heard. In any case, when Zechariah writes "John" and simultaneously regains his speech, the friends and neighbors, not knowing what to make of all this, are "afraid" (*epi pantas phobos tous perioikountas autous,* 1:65). Here, as in the Emmaus scene, the readers and characters know different aspects of everything that happens, making reality strange all around.

Characters and narrator together amplify the narrative richness. Zechariah writes the word "John" where he could have indicated with a far less elaborate (and less telling) gesture approbation of what Elizabeth has said. Perhaps he has a sense of theater; perhaps too he has a sense of narrative, a sense of where, in fact, he as a character exists. His subsequent song, like Mary's *Magnificat,* reveals his sense of being a part of an extended story moving out of the past, beyond him and his son, into the future. It is his gnosis, and it is one he has come to with some apparent intellectual effort. He was not able to understand what the angel said to him in the temple with the same apparent ease with which Mary came to her understanding at her house. Now Zechariah can see enough to sing:

> Blessed be the Lord, the God of Israel, because he has
> visited and wrought redemption for his people,
> And has raised up a horn of salvation for us, in the house
> of David his servant,
> As he promised through the mouth of his holy ones, the
> prophets from of old . . . (1:68–70)

The implied author allows Zechariah to celebrate his Jewish sense of sacred history at the beginning of this new episode. Jesus' teaching on the road to Emmaus appears only to render his poetry into prose.

As a character, of course, Zechariah has no idea what is coming in the narrative rendition of his story and in his song that will change its significance for the reader. But the narrator does. The voice drops a stitch in the reporting of the scene of John's circumcision to report the subsequent effect of the rumors and hearsay about these as yet untold events: "All the neighbors were struck with awe (fear), and everywhere in the uplands of Judaea the whole story became common talk. All who heard it were deeply impressed and said, 'What will this child become?' For indeed the hand of the Lord was upon him" (1:65–66). There is teasing ambiguity in the lines. In the line "all who heard it," "all" could refer to all the neighbors present in the scene, and "it" to Zechariah's new-found speech; or "all" could refer to all the people in the uplands of Judaea and "it" to the whole story about John being narrated here. Either the intimate group or the larger group could wonder "what will this child become?" Therefore either group would represent the proper attitude implied readers should have for the story they are reading. Knowing its precedents merely compounds the difficulty of understanding the new narrative's use of them.

Whatever the ambiguities in the John scenes, we imagine that if we could get the narrator off to the side and ask the right questions, we could straighten things out in our own minds. Not so with the Jesus scenes. Even if we broke through the veil, jumped the fence, and got into a corner of the story as a bystander, we would still stand amazed as its minor characters do. For example, according to Luke's great modern commentator, Joseph Fitzmyer, no precedent has been found for the ritual of "their purification" that follows Jesus' circumcision. This is a ritual the ancient texts prescribe only for the recent mother (p. 341). The narrative describes at 2:22–38 a third and more elaborate ritual of the "presentation." Once again strangers rather than friends praise and wonder over the child. Once again what makes the scene uncanny is that everyone in the scene seems to know exactly what they are doing, while neither the reader nor the scholar can be sure. (See Fitzmyer, p. 344).

At the beginning of the first scene with Simeon, the narrator tells the implied readers some details about the presentation of firstborn males in the temple and the terms of the offering. We have a brief sketch of Simeon and his dreams. We hear that the holy spirit has already alerted him and now guides him into the temple and up to the child Jesus. The spirit is the facilitator of his gnosis. The central moment consists of Simeon speaking in verse and in general terms about the "deliverance," "light," and "glory" which the child he holds will bring to Israel. He speaks in the same vein to Mary. "This child is destined to be a sign which men reject; and you too shall be pierced to the heart. Many in Israel will stand or fall because of him, and thus the secret thought of many will be laid bare." The secret of his thoughts will not be laid bare until later in the story. What he says, the center of the episode, the whole story has to explain.

We get even less relevant information from Anna in the second scene. To a hypothetical bystander, her words would follow upon Simeon's remarks to Mary. But in the narrative economy of the implied author, it is a separate episode prefaced with background that seems to be a weird rehash of themes already moving in the book, but to no apparent purpose. We hear who her father is, her age, how long she was married—information much more specific than we seem to need. And then we hear hardly anything about what she has to say at this moment, only the general statement that "she talked about the child to all who were looking for the liberation of Jerusalem." The narrative suggests that we are to read her as a symbolic barren woman with no possible hope of children who looks for a son for the whole people rather than just for herself. This time the narrative is much more obscure than in the scene with Simeon. No other place in the gospel will make it clear why we have to be told her exact age and the name of her father. It is typical of this gospel that there are realms of understanding beyond the text that the text does not disclose.

The final scene in the group confuses two of its major characters. The background informs us that Jesus' parents were ignorant of Jesus' whereabouts after a festival and had many questions when they find him discoursing with teachers in the temple back in Jerusalem. We are left to wonder what Mary "treasures" in her heart from the experience and whether she herself understands what Jesus means by calling the temple "my Father's house." All three episodes come down to showing that Jesus is not an ordinary son. There is something alien, literally unfamiliar about a child about whom strangers and parents are compelled to wonder and speak abstractly. John's early days, extraordinary as they are, are ordinary in comparison. A different, fuller story about him could probably tell all in a way we could understand, whereas more such details about Jesus would push us further into the dark. There is an aura of the gnostics' alien God about him.

Enlarging the Providential Narrative

Luke's fourth set of parallels embraces almost the rest of the narrative. John's public life is recounted in several scenes of his preaching (Luke 3:1–20) and in two short scenes later that treat his imprisonment (7:18–30) and execution (9:9). Jesus' public life, including his imprisonment and execution, is recounted in all of the scenes that follow those of John preaching. In this way, the grand abstract plan of the implied author extends over the remainder of the gospel. John is like the heroes and prophets "from of old," in Zechariah's words. Jesus is like John.

But there is one exception. There is no antecedent in the John story whatsoever for Jesus' resurrection. Thus at that point in which it occurs in the narrative, in Luke's ultimate chapters, the narrative breaks free of the supporting canon of stories that John's story represents. Luke's ultimate chapters mark the point where his narrative comes fully into its own. And as it does, magically, the previously clear connection between the earlier stories and the most recent one becomes ultimately obscured. Not even Jesus clears it up, because the character Jesus, like the narrator, can no longer be certain what the connection is. Comparison no longer computes; parallel lines become tangent. The second story can no longer be thought to cancel the previous story out. They become independent precisely because that is the only way they could continue to constitute a provocative parataxis with each other.

My point now is that Jesus' obscurity on this point represents the height of his mind. He has learned how *not* to be certain about a critically important literary and religious issue. Only a rare mind can rest at ease before that which will not allow itself to be reduced to an idea or a dogma. Now we trace the continuing education of Jesus as depicted in the narrative. This education is punctuated with moments of gnostic insight. They create the intelligence he displays in the episode on the road to Emmaus. It is this intelligence that the implied author and narrator reflect in the narrative's final assessment of the relationship of his story to the venerable scriptures which preceded it.

The Early Education of a Teacher

It is the standard premise behind many biblical interpretations, especially older ones, that what appears unusual in one text can eventually be explained by comparing it with another text and isolating the essential variables. The Emmaus episode appears to be what we could call "an episode of disbelief." Similar episodes include the postresurrection scenes which Augustine first brought together for comment. In them, certain disciples, such as Thomas, hear about Jesus' appearance, or in the case of Mary, actually hear a resurrected Jesus speaking, without believing what they have heard until seeing Jesus before them. One motive behind presenting such scenes is to have the reader identify with the initial doubt of the character in order that the reader might share his or her eventual affirmation of belief. "My Lord and my God," declares Thomas. "Rabboni" (Master), cries Mary.

What is unique about the Emmaus episode in comparison to these is that Luke is the only gospel writer to feature a magic trick in describing how minor characters change their minds about Jesus. When a change of mind like this occurs in other scenes in other postresurrection accounts, a natural explanation is implied or can be derived as to why the minor characters could not at first recognize Jesus. Matthew reports that when Jesus appeared to his eleven disciples on a mountain in Galilee, they worshipped him "but some doubted." Presumably they were unable to believe what they were seeing, and presumably Jesus addresses this doubt when subsequently "he drew near and spoke to them . . ." (Matthew 28:18). John has two scenes of delayed recognition. In the first, Mary is at the open tomb and, upon hearing two angels asking her why she is weeping, "turned around and saw Jesus standing there, and she did not know it was Jesus . . ." (John 20:14). In the second, the disciples are fishing as Jesus stands on the beach, "although the disciples did not know it was Jesus . . ." (John 20:5). In each instance, Jesus appears where he is not expected and so is not likely to be recognized until, as in each instance, he acts characteristically and steps through the veil. He addresses Mary with an intimate phrase and the disciples with advice. Here the cause of the failure to recognize the unexpected could lie plausibly in the natural psychology of the other characters. Nothing is done deliberately to keep them from seeing what is there.

Some witnesses of Mark come closest to matching Luke's narrative with a cryptic "he was manifest in another form to two [disciples] as they were walking on their way into the country" (Mark 16:12). But this passage is part of a section (Mark 16:9–20) that does not seem to have been a part of the original manuscript. It is often not read as part of Mark's Gospel at all. In any case, the phrase leaves out so much that it is difficult to determine what the probable implications could be. "Another form" could be anything from a different facial expression and demeanor from the one he had used previously with Mary Magdalene (Mark 16:9) to an appearance as an angel or a phantom. Perhaps it was purely a mental phenomenon. Significantly, nothing is said about the reaction of the two disciples in Mark. The narrative of the suspect passage is so unspecific that is within the realm of its legitimate implications that the disciples could have recognized Jesus instantly despite, or even because of, his "other form." Only Luke brooks no naturalist explanation. His Emmaus episode nurses its magic.

And he compounds the effect. There is a second magic trick at the end of the episode (or maybe the climax of the setup) when, after Jesus maintains his disguise while he walks with the disciples and then stops for a meal with them, he is recognized for who he is an instant before he disappears altogether. His *tour de force* is equally unprecedented among the other gospel texts usually noted for their sympathetic borrowings from one another. Strictly speaking, it is magical, not miraculous, because in the gospel context, miracles always involve the transformation of one substantial thing into another: a few fish and bread become many, water becomes wine, ordinary garments become dazzling, an unwell person becomes well, the dead return to life, etc. Nowhere else does something or someone simply dematerialize. The only other scene that can possibly be compared with this magical disappearance also occurs in Luke's Gospel. Jesus' first preaching in his home synagogue outrages his townspeople and a crowd drives him from the town and makes as if to push him off the edge of the hill on which the town is built. "But he passed through their midst and left" (4:30).

Thus we do well to begin looking for precedents for Jesus' magical teaching of the Emmaus scene in the precincts of Luke's own narrative that describe Jesus teaching. It is a likely place to begin if we are to make good on our claim that his narrative bears reading as a coherent work of narrative art. As we do, we discover that the gospel narrative changes. In the first four chapters we have already considered, the implied author arranges the scenes, the narrator comments, and minor characters respond to their circumstances. The later episodes feature the major character, Jesus, speaking. The narrator supplies helpful editorial asides to make the teaching clear. The implied author arranges scenes to suggest there is growth in the thinking of the major character, especially on the issue of his place in the pantheon of heroes who preceded him.

In addition, we find in the first scene of Jesus as a teacher, climaxing, as the Emmaus scene does, with a startling disappearance, that the implied author is already focusing the narrative on the theme of changing minds. This early episode also includes a description of Jesus' teaching about himself while making reference to scripture, even citing chapter and verse. It occurs right after Jesus has gone off to the desert "full of the Holy Spirit" and has returned "armed with the power of the Spirit." The narrator adds that "reports about him spread . . . and all men sang his praises" (4:15). The word for reports (*pheme*) could mean either fame or notoriety; it means both, as we soon see. Jesus begins his first public lesson by reading a text of Isaiah:

> The spirit of the Lord is upon me because he has anointed me;
> he has sent me to announce good news to the poor,
> to proclaim release for prisoners and recovery of sight for
> the blind;
> to let the broken victims go free,
> to proclaim the year of the Lord's favor. (4:18–19)

This time the reader gets to hear Jesus' specific text and can thus detect the boldness of his application. Jesus changes the words by replacing the phrase in Isaiah 61:1–2, "to bind up the broken hearted," with the phrase "to let the broken victims go free," taken from Isaiah 58:6. He makes the text sound more militant, in keeping with his iconoclastic mood. He indirectly justifies his liberty when he then makes a bold claim that his is the face behind the *persona* of the servant whom Isaiah has speaking here: "Today in your very hearing this text has come true." If he really were the servant, of course, he would be expected to know what he was talking about. A fascinating play of innuendo and nuance follows. At first the crowd does not seem to pay Jesus' incredible assertion any attention. They murmur admiringly at his "gracious words," appearing to take pleasure in his surprising elocution ("Is not this Joseph's son?") rather than in what he says. It is the ultimate small-town put-down to refuse to see anything about a person except that he or she is the grown-up child the town has always known so well.

Jesus drops any further attempts to make or elaborate his claim but rather gives his next words a sarcastic twist. He insinuates rather crudely that his audience is merely small-town provincial when he says, "No doubt you will quote the proverb to me: 'Physician, heal yourself' and say, 'We have heard all your doings in Capernaum; do the same in your own country.' " This is curious because the text has not yet recorded any trip to Capernaum, and we imagine that the proverb literally warns against hypocrisy, not spite. There is clearly some resentment under the surface here such as one often encounters in a provincial place. Jesus opens up a wound, anyway, when he drops all talk of the claim and dwells on his reception. "No prophet is recognized in his own country," he says, a phrase that he illustrates with stories from the careers of Elijah and Elisha, out of which he obviously intends, and his audience perceives him, to be making savage innuendos.

In one story, Elijah goes to a foreign town after leaving home, disgusted with the corruption he has found there (1 Kings 17). In the second story, Jesus' implication is less obvious. In this one, a young Israelite girl slave tells Naaman, the foreign warrior who captured her, to go to Israel to seek a cure for his leprosy. He does so, and the king there is distressed with the request because he fears retribution if the cure fails. Elisha offers to cure him but does not display any social graces when Naaman comes to call. Elisha stays in his house and sends out word that Naaman is to cure himself in the Jordan by following out a repetitious and silly ceremony. Or so it seems to Naaman, who starts to leave in disgust, complaining that he was expecting a highly dramatic cure effected in a spectacular way by the prophet himself. A servant manages to talk Naaman into trying the cure anyway; he does and it works. He returns to press payment on Elisha, who refuses it. One of Elisha's servants runs after Naaman and extorts a payment for himself. When Elisha hears about it, he lets the servant keep the money, but curses him with leprosy (2 Kings 5). Jesus' point seems to be that he, like Elisha, is a genuine article, and disappointing only to people too bound up in their prejudices to be able to take advantage of the wisdom he has to offer. Whatever his point, his purpose is to insult his audience, and he is an enormous success. His audience knows their literature well and takes words of *this* kind at least very seriously. They try to tear him to pieces.

In direct contrast to his deportment with the disciples on the road to Emmaus, Jesus' early tactics with his own countrymen are not calculated to win him disciples. Granted, he knows his message about himself is bound to be controversial. That does not excuse or explain deliberate provocation, however hurt the young preacher might have been. The purpose of the narrative arrangement of this scene, putting it first among several other scenes in which Jesus meets opposition, is not so much to criticize Jesus as to show that he quickly grows up. He is never again so callow. The narrator matches Jesus' early boldness with bold suggestion that at the very beginning Jesus had much to learn about public appearances and how to go about changing minds.

The narrative parataxis implies that Jesus has learned something by the time he reaches Capernaum in the next scene. Now the crowds marvel at his "authority," which suggests that he has integrated his demeanor and his message. Now it is a demon who cries out against him, a more appropriate foe, and Jesus' words still the violence instead of instigating it. The crowd marvels at the performative power his words have: "He gives order to the unclean spirits with authority and power, and out they go" (4:36). Luke uses the same word "rebuke" (*epetimese*) to describe the style of words Jesus uses to exorcise this demon and the demons he meets a little later on crying out that he is the son of God (4:40–41), as well as to cure the fever afflicting Simon's mother-in-law. It suggests that Jesus makes a literally devastating insult and conjures up the image of a warrior making good on the ceremonial insults exchanged with some chaotic force before joining battle. The word *epetimese* also nicely suggests how much more effectively Jesus has learned to use his words than he had at the beginning. When we compare Jesus' deportment in these episodes to his deportment in the episode of Emmaus, Luke makes us see the enormous, almost magical strides Jesus has taken in his maturity as a speaker and as a teacher. What he has learned is what *not* to say, how to teach by opening up what he is saying and doing to almost endless implications.

Jesus appears to have had something like a moment of gnosis in coming to this realization. Perhaps it came at the hands of his fellow townspeople as they were attempting to throw him off a cliff. Luke passes over his moment of insight. But because Luke is the only evangelist to show Jesus as a poor teacher, he is also the only one who manages to capture all of the traditional scenes of Jesus teaching as episodes for his theme of Jesus' growth. Jesus learns how to change people's minds by getting them to think in certain ways, rather than trying to replace one set of notions or scriptural readings with another. Jesus does this by illustrating a teaching with a vivid visual effect. He pairs words and pictures to suggest that the one interprets the other paratactically.

Jesus' Maturity as an Interpreter

Once he learns this basic technique, he then learns to use it in ever subtler ways. In the next event (5:1–11), Jesus takes control of circumstances rather than responding to them. He orders Simon to put down nets after he has finished preaching from his fishing boat. Simon's response hovers between a complaint, an expression of exasperation, and a self-conscious exclamation of his willingness: "Master, we were hard at work all night and caught nothing at all; but if you say so, I will let down the nets." When he does, the real weight of the symbolic catch is great enough to threaten to ruin both the symbol and the catch, as the boats trying to haul it in begin to sink. Simon's response hovers between wonder and fear: "Go, Lord, leave me, sinner that I am," an expression of a fear that being around a person with this much power to do good is going to be a dangerous thing. Mortals are more comfortable with less overwhelming pleasures and goods. In the next scene, Jesus is more subdued. He cures a man of leprosy, refashioning the words of the man's request into a simple imperative: "Indeed I will; be clean again" (5:13).

The following four events mark an increasing maturity in the way Jesus handles conflict. The resistance becomes more or less organized and official; Jesus cures and preaches in calculated defiance of what the authorities will think. Jesus' most wonderful moment begins when, as he is preaching, a paralytic floats down on a stretcher lowered by ropes from a hole in the roof (5:17–26). It is an opportunity on a silver platter. Jesus says, "Man, your sins are forgiven you" as much to bait the lawyers in his audience as to respond to the faith of the suppliants. He knows the lawyers will construe his remarks as blasphemous. When he senses their thoughts, he asks a tricky religious-legal question—is it easier to cure or forgive?—in order to box his opposition into an even tighter conundrum. Then he bursts it open. As a sign that the invisible thing is as easy for him to do as the visible, he cures the man with the same kinds of words he used to forgive him. The gesture is at once theatrical and performative, polemical and kind.

Jesus' utter control catches the opposition off guard and dazzles the crowd. He uses the same approach and tactics when he ostentatiously goes in to eat with a disreputable tax-gatherer (5:29–39), when he and his disciples pick corn on the Sabbath (6:1–5), and when he cures a man in the synagogue on the Sabbath (6:6–11). Each provocative act maneuvers those who complain into the position of petty hypocrites whose grasp of the letter of the law stifles generosity, spontaneity, and intelligent kindness. Jesus has traveled a good distance between the synagogue of his first sermon and this one. And we can measure that distance in two ways. For one thing, Jesus is more confident about how to teach; for another, he is less explicit in what he wants to teach. He himself is learning the art of pedagogical parataxis: to let one thing suggest another.

But however interesting our discoveries, we should take stock of what we are doing before continuing. When we compare what Jesus does in his hometown to what he does in Capernaum and beyond, we are using a kind of comparative reading of scenes we do not find in the Fathers, modern biblical interpreters, or in Jesus' method in his first preaching scene. Now we are comparing different episodes in order to derive underlying themes or causes. But we are going only as far afield as these adjacent episodes. We consider a paratactic gap as small as the space between paragraphs or pericopes (episodes). Frank Kermode refers to a similar arrangement of adjacent episodes when he finds in Mark's Gospel an aggregation of what he calls "incalations" (p. 51). These are stories intruding into other stories and appearing to comment on each other. He says that their net effect is an aura of secrecy. Each individual reading reveals a different pattern of implications when one episode intrudes upon the other.

The point I am working toward is that the early narrative scenes represent Jesus gathering his wits about him. With them Luke presents another variation of paratactic structure. His implied author connects one scene to another without any overtly discursive rhetoric suggesting a smooth continuity between them. We do not see a strictly progressive development in Jesus' thinking. We see him doing this, and then that, and then yet something else. But the implied author articulates the structure. He breaks the change in Jesus into three moments. First we see him being infused with high spirits. Then we see him trying out his new message and power with almost disastrous results. Then we see him gaining command of what he has to say as he moves among the ordinary people of the countryside. Furthermore, Luke's scenes have Jesus matching message and action. He hails and honors and heals the ordinary people he claims he has come to enfranchise, thereby showing that he learns from his own experiences who stands to lose and who to gain from what he promises. Perhaps by following the logic and progression of these connected scenes, we experience as directly as did Jesus the growth of his own thinking. Each separate scene contains simultaneously the separate insights of the writer, the main character Jesus, and the implied reader. Each scene points to the necessity of Jesus creating for himself a sense of purpose that does not need to be spelled out in great detail.

Venerable Precedents

Just as Jesus refines his teaching in the early scene, so Luke's narrator refines the possibilities of biblical narrative parataxis in this arrangement of early scenes. Where else could Luke have learned this narrative technique for depicting a changing mind than in the very venerable scriptures his Jesus is learning to interpret in new ways? We turn again to Robert Alter's reading of these venerable scriptures.

According to his analysis, they contain many important stories depicting a central character changing his or her mind to meet the challenges of the biblical God. It is critical that such central characters be more than automata or allegorical representations if they are to appeal to real readers as real models. They have to be lifelike and complex, and their personalities have to be capable of change if their stories are successfully to recommend the change of heart, *metanoia,* that their God continually demands. In this way, biblical narrative realism in the depiction of character serves the biblical moral imperative for balancing personal freedom and necessity of change.

Yet in comparison with modern narratives, biblical narratives appear to operate under a handicap. They shy away from depicting a character's thinking or motivation, almost as if narrative omniscience of the modern secular kind would constitute an invasion of the character's inner sanctum. It may well be that the gospel writers, like the writers of Hebrew biblical narratives, simply did not know how to speak about motivation in character or to represent progressive thinking, in much the same way that earlier visual artists did not know how to create the illusion of perspective in two-dimensional art. Be this as it may, as Alter shows in his reading of Abraham's preparations for the sacrifice of Isaac, what the writer would not or could not allow the narrator to do could still be part of the literary effect. The great silences of Abraham and his son in the scene suggest patently the depth of their bewilderment. Theirs is the dilemma of being caught up in the hands of an inscrutable God.

In this scene, and throughout the Hebrew Bible, inner thought and motivation are suggested paratactically. The reader is given one scene or series of episodes, and then another, and is left to imagine what must have occurred in the gaps between them to have made such change possible. We extrapolate Abraham's unspeakable reverence for God out of our being shown God telling him to kill his son, and then our being shown his setting about to do it. We see Jacob crudely beating his brother Esau out of his birthright and then later being cheated out of his heart's desire by Laban. Still later we see Jacob elaborately and cleverly cheating Laban out of much livestock, his daughters, and even his household goods, and greeting his elder brother on the way home with respect and deference. The seven years it takes Jacob to learn to be coy indicate how slowly he learns, but that in fact he can learn. It takes Joseph even longer. We see him first as a callow youth boasting of his self-aggrandizing dreams before his brooding, murderous brothers. Then we see him some twenty years later as a mature government official leading his brothers through an elaborate ritual of mutual atonement for all their failings to each other. We see Moses stammering before God, protesting his lack of skill in public speaking. Then we see him handling Pharaoh eloquently and later still persuading even God to change his determination to destroy his followers worshipping before the Golden Calf. In perhaps the Bible's most terrible scene, the narrative parataxis which indicates a change of mind is even more tightly drawn. David says nothing when one of his soldiers, Uriah, refuses to return home to sleep with his wife, Bathsheba. David had ordered him first home from battle and then to the bed of his wife in hopes of covering his own adultery with Bathsheba. She had become pregnant with David's child while her husband had been in the field. After David has heard Uriah's refusal, he abruptly orders Uriah back into battle. He sends along a secret note to his commander to see to it that Uriah is killed. In the terrible moment between giving the refused order and the accepted order, the reader can only imagine how swiftly David calculates the odds. It is perhaps better for all concerned that the narrator cannot describe the mechanics of his thinking.

In these narrative instances in the Hebrew Bible, the gaps left open between scenes or between movements within a scene represent a character's freedom to act in ways that neither God nor circumstances could determine. The freedom to decide what to do comes out of nowhere, much as creation did when God first summoned it into being. It could be said that at every moment when a biblical character decides what he or she will do, the world of biblical story is created anew out of the stuff of human imagination and will. As creators of their own destiny, all biblical characters bear the privilege Abraham was granted at the beginning of his story in Genesis 12:1–9. God speaks to Abraham much as he spoke to chaos at the beginning of time. A voice sounds from no place in particular with an order for change. But the scale this time is vastly smaller and more exquisite. Now one fleck of matter, one man, is ordered to leave one country and go to another. In all the world only two places are important: Abraham's origin and his destination. By moving between them, Abraham shows himself willing to get into the story God sketches out for him.

These two places represent a psychic space as well. A gap opens this time between God's command and creation's response. God speaks and Abraham listens and decides for himself to obey God. The spoken word does not instantly transport him into the desert as it transformed chaos into order. The response this time is not an echo but a compliance. The French critic of narrative Gérard Genette describes as "an anachrony" any textual reference to the past or the future in regard to the moment in the story when the narrative was interrupted to make room for the anachrony. This temporal distance he calls the anachrony's "reach": "Every anachrony constitutes, with respect to the narrative into which it is inserted—onto which it is grafted—a narrative that is temporally second, subordinate to the first in a sort of narrative syntax . . ." (p. 48). "Prolepsis" is the term Genette gives to an anachrony that anticipates later events in the narrative. Often in the bible narrative prolepsis gestures toward yet another gap. Just before recording God's second speech about the place to which he has gone ("I give this land to your descendents . . ."), the narrator tells us: "At the time the Canaanites lived in this land" (12:7). This parataxis indicates that God leaves something out in his words of command and promise. There is a narrative suspense about what is going to have to happen for Abraham to take up residence where the land is already inhabited. The story promises to become a history. Not only does Abraham have to respond to God's command to get into his story, he is going to have to go about fulfilling the promise with his own wits.

We find a similar resourcefulness in Luke. What Luke has learned is how to hint that Jesus' understanding of his place in the pantheon of heroes grew by progressive steps from an initial, startling insight at the brink of a cliff. His mind matured. Yet there was something magical about his growth of mind, as there always is when anyone learns anything. Narrative parataxis of this new kind is able to hint at this magic whereby ignorance becomes transformed into knowledge. Jesus, the mature teacher, would be able to represent this natural magic in the spectacular trick he plays on his disciples in the Emmaus scene. It represents in turn the culmination of Jesus' thinking on the relation between the two scriptures. We now turn to the next, and very intricate, arrangement of scenes the implied author provides to convey the next steps in the education of his major character.

The Sophisticated Gnosticism of Luke and Jesus

First of all, we consider the various ways in which Luke "timed" the narrative. This leads to an appreciation of the sophisticated timing of the episodes following the Sermon on the Mount, which culminate in the episode on the road to Emmaus. The timing closely relates to the course of Jesus' education.

We return to the gnostic effects on the composition of this gospel for insights about time. Origen came close to getting it right when he gave what was later condemned as a gnostic interpretation of the Emmaus scene. In Luke's Gospel, Origen said, Jesus moved in a timeless realm of story. He could recall the stories of the venerable scriptures to his disciples because these stories existed in the eternal "now" of their being read. They happen at the same time that the reader lives in. The reason why Jesus can imagine himself a fellow character with Elijah and Moses and appear comfortably with them in the Succession scene is that, in his mind, their stories can exist simultaneously in any lively imagination.

To put it simply, as Marcion and Origen did, there is something otherworldly or timeless about Jesus. There is something gnostic in his disposition. In Luke's Gospel, he is never completely at ease dealing with the real people of his times, even his closest followers, for all his immersion in the real time of the real world. He has his face set "on the time when he would be taken up into heaven" (9:51). This is conveyed in a number of ways, many of them dramatic. Jesus appears to be comfortable in dealing with the preternatural devils inhabiting the body of the wild man of the Gerasenes and less comfortable dealing with the people of his own town. What makes the scene uncanny is that Jesus and the devil or devils understand each other's every bizarre word and gesture. Their brief interaction implies an enormously complex culture someplace else in some other time, much as two foreigners talking spiritedly in their exotic language and gestures would to passersby who could not understand them. The demons greet Jesus by name. He handles them with easy words. The demons know pigs make a better abode than the abyss, even if they suspect that they will live there only for the brief, wild moments while the possessed pigs are rushing off the cliff, and Jesus sympathetically lets them go. There is a hint that Jesus shares with the demons a cosmopolitan, occult world. The many devils call themselves "Legion," a loan word from Latin designating a unit in the fiercely efficient Roman army—a fitting image of evil for a captive people. When Jesus vanquishes Legion, he raises a fist against the Roman empire for the first and only time. Yet he appears more intimate with the demons, even in the midst of violent argument, than with the inhabitants who kept the possessed man chained and who afterward ask Jesus to leave.

Their quotidian world is resolutely provincial, no matter who the stranger might be (8:26–39).

One narrative touch makes the reader experience a confusion of realms somewhat like that of the people of the countryside within the scene. It is not clear what is happening in the scene after the cure of the madman of the Gerasenes. The text reads, "so Jesus got into the boat and returned. The man from whom the devils had gone out begged leave to go with him; but Jesus sent him away. 'Go back home,' he said, 'and tell them everything that God has done for you' " (8:37–39). Does Jesus go away and come right back? Is the sentence about the man wanting to be with him supposed to be understood as a wish expressed before Jesus got into the boat, and that Jesus was returning to whence he had come, and not back to the land of the Gerasenes? We have seen Jesus sending people away before and urging them to be silent. Now, in this scene, there is a hint that he does not feel comfortable with an ordinary human being after his heady conversation with a creature from his own realm. Offhandedly, he associates himself with God again.

Similarly, Jesus speaks at ease with the miraculously appearing Moses and Elijah. He then rebukes Peter for his mundane desire to make a shrine out of the place where the miracle occurred. This otherworldliness is also conveyed in Jesus' parables of the Good Samaritan and the Forgiving Father, where it is the character whom the worldly-wise value least who emerges as hero, the bearer of the moral message. "How dull you are," he admonishes the disciples he meets on the road to Emmaus. They are not able to read the broad context of his story as it extends from the earliest written texts to the interpretations he now provides. They cannot read beyond the historical moment in which they are living.

Any discussion of gnostic timing also applies to parataxis. Now it appears as all the narrative devices that represent or allow access to a psychological state. Luke arranges the narrative to show that Jesus' mind is alien to, set apart from, the doings of the world. It is juxtaposed. He makes no clear and smooth connections between the way he thinks and the way things are. He moves in time and yet stands outside of time. The scenes and sayings that convey this separation throughout the narrative prepare the reader for the final scenes in which the risen Jesus appears in the world but not of it. These are the themes, as George Aichele suggests, that Luke or any orthodox gospel writer inherits from whatever acquaintance he has had with gnosticism. I believe that Luke's narrative response to the theme of time created new possibilities for both theology and literature. In my opinion, whatever is literary about Luke's theology is gnostic, and precisely that part of it escapes a definitive or temporal explanation.

Time in the Gospel of Luke

The events in the opening chapters of Luke's Gospel run on biological time: the months of pregnancy between conception and birth. By its measurements, the implied author appears to distance Jesus' story from a typical gnostic narrative of God or Jesus. Luke's Jesus belongs in history, in a real place. He is far from a disembodied being.

The first scene has Gabriel come to old Zechariah to announce the beginning of the pregnancy of his aging wife, Elizabeth. The second has Gabriel come to a young Mary to announce the beginning of hers. Mary visits Elizabeth in the third scene at the time of her quickening. The births of both children occasion the next cluster of scenes. Among them is a scene in which Jesus is described as twelve years old when he stays behind to talk to the elders after his parents have left Jerusalem to return to Nazareth. Presumably he is now mature enough to be allowed the independence his parents had accused him of abusing. Jesus is later described as being thirty years old the first time he is recognized in public at the baptism by John (3:23). Luke is the only gospel writer to express any interest in Jesus' age. His unique sense of biological timing implies the importance to him of Jesus' ordinary physical and mental development. His Jesus is first of all an ordinary man with the same origins and development as all of us. He teaches other ordinary people as a peer about the opportunities available to anyone who walks the everyday earth.

Luke even subordinates the ritual divisions of time to biological time. He has Zechariah chance to draw an opportunity to perform an important ritual in the temple's inner sanctum just at the moment when the angel appears to him. Luke thereby implies that "the lot" which chose him was either rigged on high or served as a convenient moment for God to make a critical intervention in a religious ritual to announce a birth. Luke's narrative of the early events in the lives of these two characters suggests that traditional ideas about holy times and places are becoming obsolete. His Gabriel chooses to meet the future mother of Jesus in her own home during an ordinary day. The parallels in what the angel says to Zechariah and to Mary suggest that the other details in each scene are also meant to be compared. A woman in her own home on any ordinary day can be as blessed and as gifted as a priest in the temple during an especially consecrated time.

Luke also subordinates secular historical time to the lifetimes of his characters. Luke links Jesus' birth and John's public life to contemporary historical events by listing the rulers in power when both events occurred (2:1–3, 3:1–3). But in the first case, the registration ordered by Caesar Augustus which brought Jesus' parents to Bethlehem serves only as the convenient occasion to have Jesus born in a place appropriate for a literary allusion. The angels who announce his birth to the shepherds tell them that a new messiah or Christos or "anointed one" has been born in the city of David. It was to David that Nathan the prophet predicted that a son was to be born into his family who would establish a new and lasting order of peace (2 Samuel 7). In the second case, the list of rulers in office when John is old enough to begin his ministry serves to introduce the name of Herod who will prove to be John's and Jesus' nemesis. His craven behavior in the arrest and execution of both will serve to complete the cycle of parallel actions in both their stories. His part in the execution of Jesus, furthermore, provides an occasion for the final chapter of Jesus' story, which recounts his rising from the dead. These scenes have proved so compelling to generations of readers that two thousand years later they continue to frustrate the strenuous efforts Herod made to suppress the reports that were going around about Jesus. It was like trying to stop a river with his hands. The list of rulers also frustrates the efforts of scholars who discover, as Fitzmyer and Brown report in their great commentaries on the opening scenes, that there was never a moment in actual history when the leaders Luke mentions ruled at the same time or at the time Luke said they did. For Luke, secular history is merely a loose collection of names and places to be embroidered as his story requires.

Luke inherits other ways of timing his narrative that also lend an aura of definitiveness to the story. All four gospel writers time the episodes recounting Jesus' arrest, trial, condemnation, and execution almost identically, in each case in a manner very different from the way they time the rest of their gospels. Here events are closely linked and causal—one scene and its events lead inexorably to another as Jesus is taken through a judicial process of foregone conclusions. This kind of timing implies that strict chronology is the method of telling time that authorities use. To fall into its patterns is to fall into the hands of those who set the public agenda.

By these strategies, the first his own, the second shared with the other gospel writers, Luke comes to grips with what could be called the inherent gnosticism of early Christian scriptural sources. Most of the episodes we find in Luke's Gospel or any of the other orthodox gospels are timeless or at least unspecific as to time. Many begin with an indefinite temporal phrase such as "once," "then," "when," "next," "afterwards," "one day," "on Sabbath," "later," "during this time," "while he was speaking," "there happened to be," etc. The episode so introduced usually features a dramatic event involving Jesus and minor characters. Typically the event quickly results in a moment of tension either from a conflict between Jesus and his detractors or from the surprising and often unsettling demands Jesus makes of his audience or they of him. Then something Jesus does or says releases the tension as if he were winding a watch to the point where the spring gives way. Episodic time could also be called charismatic time.

Its use implies that significant events are all unique and virtually have the same importance. They occur in a series of continuously present moments at the instant when desire and satisfaction are suddenly and gracefully brought together. Every gospel portrays the mature Jesus as the master of the charismatic moment.

There are prosaic explanations for this in source theory. Both the indefinite and the conditioned future phrases probably reflect the common sources that all four gospel writers shared. There might have been collections of undifferentiated vignettes about Jesus collected from the stories in circulation about the extraordinary things Jesus said and did. Various discrete episodes about Jesus' deeds or teachings circulated orally, or perhaps even in written form, before each gospel writer gave a particular narrative shape to the loose collection that came to hand. Each episode is a pericope, or a nugget of language whose form is older than the narratives we find them in. In this primitive form, pericopes were amenable to being used by gnostic narrative writers who almost always feature a character like Jesus at a charismatic moment, providing a disciple with an unexpected experience which changes his or her life.

Beginning with material like this could have been a curse or a challenge for an orthodox writer, of course. To a great degree, the charismatic episodes Luke and the others inherit defy patterning, as gnostic experience would. The episodes imply that revelation is local, unpredictable, and recurrent and thus would be more appropriate to an epigrammatic, aphoristic, or episodic scripture, such as a collection of Zen koans. They are not so well suited to a narrative scripture with its emphasis on the significance of plot or a sequence of connected events leading to a denouement, and all the other devices narratives use to convince readers that their stories represent reality.

Perhaps it was Mark who first discovered several principles of order that could be imposed on the pericopes that would preserve their integrity while harnessing their energy to singular themes more amenable to dogmatic synthesis. For one thing, Mark and other gospel writers like Luke who follow his example draw the episodes of Jesus' life into a rough plot that gives it some sense of direction. Thus they counter any impression of randomness the episodes might provide. In each gospel, at some point Jesus announces that from this point on he will be making his way toward Jerusalem in order to hasten the denouement of his story. The episodes that follow frequently condition their indefinite future with a reference to his goal such as "as he was making his way toward Jerusalem" (Luke 13:22). This rough plotting implies that if the bright moments in Jesus' life have any meaning beyond themselves, it comes from seeing them against the dark backdrop of the ending Jesus himself deliberately refuses to avoid.

There were other principles of order, as well. Each writer was free to arrange the sequence of these independent episodes consistently with a logic that might be made to appear. For example, there is a typical inner patterning that encircles events in the beginning of Jesus' public ministry in Luke's Gospel. Several scenes recount cures (4:16–5:26). Discussions of sin occur within them, suggesting illness as a metaphor for sinfulness. Scenes then follow in which sin is the major topic (5:29–6:5). Then there is a scene in which Pharisees construe the way Jesus cures to be a sin (6:6–11). Throughout these scenes, allusions recall older stories, either explicitly with references to Elijah, Elisha, and Naaman (4:25, 28), or implicitly in the cures Jesus effects in imitation of theirs. The sequencing is diffuse but significant, clustering together scenes under one rubric and connecting them with other clusters by associations. Smaller patterns are worked within the clusters; larger ones connect even widely separate clusters. The many references to Elijah, the man who ascended into heaven in an older narrative, indicate throughout that there is a precedent for Jesus' most extraordinary feat. This "ripple patterning," as it could be called, allows an almost infinite series of associations and implies that who Jesus is and what he teaches cannot be cast definitely in words.

This patterning reveals another facet of the genius of narrative parataxis. Each scene remains discrete, but comments on the scenes before and after it by an almost infinite series of juxtapositions of words, images, phrases, and concepts. Divining the possibilities is almost an endless process, and so in itself, the thematic patterning was not enough. The orthodox gospel writers needed to pour the shimmering stuff of the pericopes into their various molds of narrative. In this way, the spirit of gnostic individualism remained only in the differences among their various definitive narrations.

Thus everything Luke does to make his story coherent or realistic is done to convince all of his readers beginning with Theophilus that his ordered narrative presents a trustworthy guide to the understanding of a real Jesus. He uses the structure of biological time and the techniques of the *Bildungsroman* to suggest that Jesus developed his thinking over time. It is essential to his purposes that, as we have seen, Luke have Jesus fumbling with his first exposition in public. Luke needs to show Jesus gaining a considerable amount of practical experience before he could teach real people effectively, in order to make clear the fully human accomplishment of his sophisticated teaching on the road to Emmaus. Luke thereby dramatizes that Jesus has to condition his great inspirations with a common touch. He has to learn, as any realistic character does. And one of the things he learns to value is the ordinary people he has come to enlighten and who very quickly bring him down to earth. This is another implicit message of the episode of Emmaus. Ordinary people, one without a name the other with a name that has no currency wider than this scene, are the most appropriate audience for his message. They are most receptive to it when they believe themselves to be in more or less ordinary circumstances.

We are reminded of Luke's preface to Theophilus again. Just as it takes real people to shape Jesus' message, so it takes a "realistic" or "connected narrative" (*kathezaes graphai*) to make that message available to those who come along after the eyewitnesses with a need and a desire to see for themselves who this Jesus was. To put this in slightly different terms is to draw out another implication of Luke's narrative logic. Just as Luke's narrative represents the reality Jesus faced and which forced him to accommodate his teaching to his audience, so a realistic narrative of the sort Luke concocts now constitutes the only medium through which readers can now see Jesus. Jesus and the narrator then begin with the same kinds of problems. They need to make what they want to say seem realistic, lifelike, or down to earth.

Paratactic Theology

Having laid out the parameters of an implied author's handling of time, we can now appreciate how wonderfully it reflects the main character's sense of time in the later chapters of the narrative, from chapter 6 to the end. This sense of time is the main point Jesus conveys in his teaching. He is teaching about the relationship of his day to sacred history, as well as the relationship of any worldly time to eternity. As we look back and forth from the implied author to the character and from their sense of time to their teachings, once again we consider the genius of narrative parataxis. But now we are looking into the places in the narrative where the spaces are very small and cunningly related. Luke attunes, or better fine tunes, the realism of his narrative to make of it the correlative of the special earthbound but still ethereal nature of Jesus' teaching style. We discover that in the reciprocity a breath of gnostic otherworldliness returns. We find that Jesus' teaching style is never finally down to earth, for all its momentary appearances. Even while the disciples on the road to Emmaus think they are listening to an ordinary man, they are listening to a magician touched by heaven, whom the ordinary moment and place will not contain in the scene's final moment. To the extent that Luke's narrative features the Emmaus scene and diffuses the scene's spirit throughout the entire narrative, it cannot be realistic or down to earth either. Facts melt because they are corporeal. When imagination stirs in the reader, it is as if the spirit of gnosis breathes again.

Narrative Imitations of the Beatitudes

Beginning with the episode of Jesus preaching the Beatitudes, Luke's narrative arrangement of scenes represents the mind of its major character Jesus directly (6:13–8:56). In these scenes Jesus is at his best and most confident when, through allusions to time past and his visions of time future, he looks away from the present time and world.

When Jesus comes down from a hill where he has spent a night alone at prayer with God (6:13), his confidence seems unassailable. He selects twelve disciples for special attention, alluding to Jacob's twelve sons who God promised would be the foundation of a great nation. Jesus thereby daringly projects himself as another Jacob and as another God at the same time, both provider and selector. At this point, the narrator intrudes with a proleptic aside that hints of the dangers to come: "Judas Iscariot who turned traitor" (4:16) was one of the twelve. The story already knows that it is heading toward another ceremonial passover in and out of danger onto new ground. When Jesus "came down the hill with them and took his stand on level ground," his disciples hear a new teaching as succinct and gnomic and radical as the Ten Commandments Moses promulgated after coming down from Mount Sinai. Jesus projects himself here as another Moses and another Yahweh, messenger and lawgiver in one.

Jesus' new torah, or law, is concrete and direct. He blesses "you who are in need," curses "you who are rich," and advises "you who hear me" to "love your enemies." The emphasis in the Ten Commandments on how to live an orderly religious and community life changes in the Beatitudes to an emphasis on how to live an uncalculating and unconventional life, exceeding everyone's expectations: "If you love only those who love you, what credit is that to you? Even sinners love those who love them" (6:32–33).

When we consider his words while remembering the previous scenes of Jesus encountering resistance to his early preaching, we see a politics emerge from the words like a creature standing out in the midst of its camouflage. The implied author arranges these scenes to show that being surprisingly generous got Jesus into trouble time and time again. He restored a man's withered arm, "[b]ut they were beside themselves with anger, and began to discuss among themselves what they could do to Jesus" (6:11). Now in the Beatitudes, Jesus raises that behavior to a virtue, declaring that opposition to his kind of good works is inevitable and in fact a sure sign that one is succeeding: "How blest you are when men hate you, when they outlaw you and insult you, and ban your very name as infamous, because of the Son of Man" (6:22). It is a brilliant revolutionary tactic to explain away ahead of time every resistance and pain the movement will endure. At the same time, Jesus enfranchises all the have-nots as members of the movement—a group whose numbers are very great and probably consist of an uneducated and practical folk—by recommending a thinking minimal enough to cut through crusty laws like a sharp knife: "be compassionate . . . pass no judgement . . . take the plank out of your own eye." These words shape into aphorisms the idea behind Jesus' prior impromptu apologetics: "So have you not read what David did when he and his men were hungry? He went into the House of God and took the sacred bread to eat and gave it to his men, though priests alone are allowed to eat it, and no one else" (6:3–5). They promise to carry the day equally well.

A theology stands out as well when we keep the Beatitudes in mind while reading the two scenes that follow in the implied author's arrangement. The theology grapples with the potential contradiction in the teaching that suggests the only way to be satisfied is to remain unsatisfied. The sermon itself has suggested that heaven is a place where today's purposeful pains will be recompensed. Jesus says this explicitly: "Assuredly you have a rich reward in heaven" (6:23). He says it implicitly: "How blest are you who are in need; the kingdom of God is yours" (6:20); "Alas for you who are rich; you have had your time of happiness" (6:24); "Give, and gifts will be given you" (6:38).

The immediately following scene dramatizes the model life. Jesus cures the centurion's servant at a distance, embodying his own precept to give without question. He accepts the centurion's message at face value, even exclaiming, "Nowhere, even in Israel, have I found faith like this" (7:9). Next, Jesus raises the son of the widow of Nain back to life (7:11–17). He has been promising a reward in heaven which, by implication, reduces the jarring finality of death. Here his authority over death in the real world validates his teaching just as before his healing of the paralytic man validated his power to forgive sins (5:18–26).

An attendant philosophy emerges from the arrangement of the next two scenes. Jesus explores ways one could be satisfied living with want even before one came into a heavenly reward. In the first scene, John awaits his execution. Whatever his inner feelings, he shows only outward curiosity as to how the work he was engaged in is going. From prison he sends disciples to ask Jesus whether he is the one John was once preaching about. Jesus responds to John's questions with acts and words recalling Isaiah's descriptions of the servant who was to bring about a new economy: "The poor are hearing the good news." Jesus leaves the matter there, without offering any help to John in any other way, as if John did not require any more satisfaction than Jesus has already provided. After John's disciples go back to report, Jesus goes on to talk about John as a man who has done his task; he has "prepared a way." Jesus also describes John as one who was not rich, not shimmering with refracting brilliance and ideas like reeds wavering in a wilderness. Instead it was as a prophet of old whom, as the Beatitudes predict, a modern-day rich man Herod has "outlawed and insulted."

The final scene presents the philosophy straight. A Pharisee invites Jesus to his house. The scene contains a little bit of everything we have seen before. Jesus causes a stir by claiming to forgive sins. He oversteps the bounds of social and moral propriety by allowing an "immoral woman" to fuss over him in public. Jesus meets the challenge of an established person's disapproval in such a way that the person is made to look small and mean. He forces an admission out of his opponent that he uses against him. What is newly illustrated in this scene is the notion, first articulated in the sermon, that the world of the outcast and the insulted, as Jesus defines it, has everything the opposing world has, and more: "You see this woman? I came to your house: you provided no water for my feet; but this woman has made my feet wet with her tears and wiped them with her hair. You gave me no kiss; but she has been kissing my feet ever since I came in. You did not anoint my head with oil; but she has anointed my feet with myrrh" (7:44–47). Jesus sees she is giving more than a conventional, political, and genteel person would give. The woman is sincere. The Pharisee would have been only ceremonial with his kisses. Looked at this way, outcasts could sense that whatever was going on in their lives might be perfectly all right. The impoverished might be able to improvise scenarios as deserving as any.

By looking back and forth between the sermon of the Beatitudes and the episodes with which the implied author surrounds it, we see Jesus' teaching as dramatic art. He makes allusions with his gestures to older narratives; he draws concepts out of dramatic situations in his own story and orchestrates further situations to elaborate the concepts. As he looks around with an artist's eye, he can see unusual things: a contented man in prison, an exemplary woman in an immoral life, and hypocrisy in a religious leader's behavior. The arrangement can make large effects, such as affixing the sermon of the Beatitudes as a hinge between two blocks of scenes that illustrate it. It can have very delicate effects, such as including the observation that Jewish elders approach Jesus with the centurion's request. This shows ironically that even the authorities can make accommodations.

Jesus' teaching and the narrator's teaching also intertwine inextricably. In the scene at the Pharisee's house, the narrator, in an aside, tells the implied reader that the woman who anoints Jesus "was living an immoral life." With this information in hand, the reader's reaction to her washing Jesus' feet with her tears and hair might resemble for a moment the Pharisee's outraged fascination. Then both reader and character might better appreciate Jesus' own view of the matter at the same time. The reader vicariously experiences the mixture of admiration and surprise that surely must have been the Pharisee's. Both experience something like the gnostic moment of insight.

There is another marvelous image of the reciprocity of their teaching styles wedged between the scene with the Baptist's disciples and the scene with the immoral woman. The narrator interrupts Jesus' praise of John (7:24–28) to inform the reader of the crowd's reaction: "When they heard him, all the people, including the tax-gatherers, praised God, for they had accepted John's baptism; but the Pharisees and lawyers, who refused his baptism, had rejected God's purpose for themselves" (7:29–30). The final phrase has a disapproving tone. The sentences which follow, "How can I describe the people of this generation? . . .," could be heard as the narrator intensifying the critical aside into a real diatribe, or as Jesus continuing with his. The sentiments suit either voice equally well. Character and narrator are close to becoming one.

To the extent that the strategies of the implied author, Jesus, and the narrator coincide, purely narrative effects extend Jesus' teaching far beyond the small groups Jesus himself addresses. Jesus preaches episodically, the narrator discursively. For example, after Jesus preaches the Beatitudes, the narrator says in an aside that three women, Mary, Joanna, and Susanna, accompany Jesus and the twelve and provide for them out of their means. The disciples whom the Beatitudes blessed for having needs, it now appears, differ from the rich in that they have no set source of income that determines their lives or behavior. Rather, support follows from their work, as these women whom Jesus cured help provide for the furthering of his mission. People of their ilk are nomadic grazers.

Other details in this aside imitate the spare poignancy of the Beatitudes. The narrator mentions that Joanna is "the wife of Chuza a steward of Herod's." Perhaps this plays on the irony that someone close to the established government, which Jesus criticizes, can defy it by following Jesus. Perhaps it shows that Jesus welcomes an individual in his train, whatever his or her family ties. Perhaps it hints that Jesus has divided a household. It cannot be said for sure. By these tantalizing hints, the narrator draws attention to the texture of the curtain which his words draw before an enormous amount of background information. The narrator selects only pinpoints to provide a perspective. Similarly there is no setting for Jesus' parable about the sower. It is said that he recounts it "as they made their way to him from one town after another," not specifying whether he told the parable several times, at each encounter with each group, or once, as they all came together. We do not know how to envision the encounter with his mother and brothers who cannot get to him because of the crowd, or how they react to his sharp comments about who his real relatives are. We do not know why Jesus wants to cross to the other side of the lake, or what the disciples think as they readily comply. We have seen this sort of description before. The narrator erects a series of bare verbal scaffolds that hold up to the reader's view for a moment some striking remark or gesture Jesus makes. We are not intended, no doubt, to wonder much about the mass of peripheral details that cling to every remark and human gesture, whether trivial or momentous. Yet even as we accept the convention and read each story for its particular illumination, part of the effect consists of a continual readjustment of perspectives. Each bright object has a different size and shape and hangs at a different angle. In this section, this narrative technique is more than usually significant. It provides an overture to what Jesus does in the major scenes in the section when his actions extend the ramifications of the Beatitudes further.

Luke's narrative imitations of Jesus' mind as expressed in the Beatitudes convey his fascination with the difference between the time of the real world that holds mortal beings in thrall and the timeless realm of real values Jesus constantly holds in view. As Jesus masters devils and powers seething in a timeless realm beyond human ken, we see a good reason why he has claimed that amassing wealth and political control over other human beings is a waste of time. Wealth and power cannot touch the real, timeless, stranger world he is privy to. Worse, wealth and power foster the illusion that humans can control the events of the temporal world. Rules, coercion, and even common sense can nail the truth down, whereas in Jesus' mind, any human concern with the things of this world ignores the strange otherness of the real, spiritual world. Luke's Jesus on the road to Emmaus reminds his disciples that only an exercise in parataxis—juxtaposing the real events they have heard reported with the storied events they have always known—will open their minds to insight.

Conclusions: Canonicity and Closure

Right from the beginning of the gospel, the implied author of Luke is highly conscious of the "writtenness" of the new narrative being conveyed. He is also aware of the old narrative out of which the new story emerges. Luke's own phrases for this idea link his early stories with the episode on the road to Emmaus. Toward the beginning, at 3:4, just as John the Baptist is about to begin his public life, the narrator refers to a prophecy "as it is written" (*gegraptai*) in Isaiah. This is to indicate yet another precedent for his own story. Toward the end, at 24:26, on the road to Emmaus, after Luke's main character Jesus has risen from the dead, Jesus begins reviewing all the precedents in biblical narrative for his own story with the more emphatic "thus it is written" (*houtes gegraptai*). Both phrases use the present perfect. This is the Greek verb tense for an action that was done once and still stands accomplished. Both narrator and character see the established canon out of which their new story emerges as already written; but in addition, it remains for them an open book to which they can still add words. Understanding their motives as they do so requires in turn that one understand all the scriptures that were already written. We need to reread the canon of stories in the venerable scriptures or Hebrew Bible which precedes it.

Robert Alter's recent book *The Art of Biblical Narrative* provides an appropriate introduction to such a rereading. The book has sensitive discussions of many important stories in the Hebrew Bible whose characters wind up peopling New Testament allusions. More importantly, Alter's discussions include general observations about the poetics of the Hebrew Bible—basic descriptions of how the stories work. There are enough similarities between the narratives of the Hebrew Bible and the narratives of the Christian scriptures for many general observations Alter makes about the first to be extended to the second. Alter finds, for example, that the older narratives are full of allusions to past stories in their own tradition. Heroes act like heroes before them; God reiterates the same promises and the same saving actions. Frequently we find slightly different versions of what seem to be the same episodes occurring close to one another in the same narrative sequence. Alter finds the continuities significant, representing the endurance of God's "unswerving authority . . . beyond all human manipulation" as sacred time goes by (pp. 91, 107). God's contributions to human welfare remain constant. In his own way, Luke seems to be taking comfort in the same basic belief. His ultimate authority is the same God who spoke to Moses from on high. In the scene of the Succession on the Mount, this God brings together Moses and Elijah and Jesus as if they were fellow actors in the same unfolding epic drama.

On the other side of the coin, departures from the norm that we can find in every older narrative Alter discusses represent each character's freedom to fashion his or her own fate within the continuing designs of God. Characters dominate their scenes with arresting, unpredictable dialogue. The omniscient narrator serves as a stand-in for God, passing over the hidden motivations of characters in silence—as when Abraham lifts the knife or David orders Uriah into the fray—because the narrator, like God, remains unwilling or perhaps even unable to invade an individual character's inner sanctum. We have noted Luke's reticence in delving into the motives of his characters.

Alter's notion of canonicity justifies reading the Bible as literature. Authentic stories blend providence and improvisation, realism and fantasy, facts and religious ideas. We read them wrongly if we try to separate out the probable facts of the matter, e.g., the real events of the escape of an enslaved tribe from forced labor in Egypt, and divorce them from their sometimes fabulous setting. Bible narratives are true in different ways than history is true. Instead of inviting us to imagine ourselves back in time, they invite us to read on in the collection of stories in which they are contained. In their own way, the scholars or authorities who included Luke's Gospel in a canon of stories beginning with Genesis and ending with Revelation intuited a familial continuity among them all.

But to go a step further than Alter does and to read Luke's Gospel as if it belonged to the same canon of works Alter insists on calling the Hebrew Bible—to read Luke's Zechariah as another Abraham and his Jesus as another Jacob—requires our departing somewhat from Alter's sense of canonicity. Alter unambiguously forbids reading what Christians call the Old Testament in such a way as to make it appear that the older narratives and the new "comprise one continuous work" (p. ix). Echoing Tertullian, Alter rightly asserts that these two collections were written in different languages in very different historical circumstances by different people and consequently possess "different literary assumptions." He has a legitimate distaste for traditions begun with Paul in his epistles and continued by the Fathers of the church and by the dogmatism of our day that would read the older narratives as "foreshadowing" the newer. For to do so is to disregard not only the sensibilities of non-Christian believers but the intention of the original authors who could never have anticipated the literary works that would come after theirs. As Schleiermacher said, inspiration happens only one book at a time.

But while we have already seen that the Fathers were more than willing to read the older narratives as foreshadowing the newer, from what I have already remarked of Luke's opening scenes, it seems that Luke was at least ambivalent about his narrative's place in the canon that preceded it. Certainly he relies on that canon extensively. His John is an imitation of older heroes as his Jesus is an imitation of John. Certainly Luke transcribes the venerable conventions of the older narratives into a new key to demonstrate that Jesus is a character who brooks no imitation. The word "gospel," it could be said, is the term given to a literary genre that presumes to close a literary tradition down. It is intended to be the last work in a series, and so at once depends on, sums up, and renders the previous works complete. The term gospel literally means "good news—*eu-angelium, god-spel*—and could refer both to the happy fact that a literary tradition is now complete and can now make full sense, and to the relief a reader can feel that there is no need to read any further. The last return is in. The instincts of the Fathers of the church were correct when they featured the New Testament's own sense of closure.

Certainly there are literary qualities in a gospel unlike those found in the older narratives. Luke is intent upon endings whereas the older narratives are open to continuities. Luke pairs Jesus with a traditional biblical hero like John as much to give Jesus legitimacy as to suggest his superiority. The older narratives pair Cain and Abel, Ishmael and Isaac, Esau and Jacob, Joseph, David, and their older brothers to suggest the dependency of one brother on the other and the continuing familial bonds among all the pairs or groups. Luke's story is shot through with a sense of closure. Every chapter from the first points to the finale of its own story and of all the older stories it wants to take with it. As Alter points out, the older narratives are more meditative. They have been arranged in an order that suggests some historical development from the time of the Patriarchs to the time of Judges, Kings, the exile, and the return; but each narrative remains free to examine a particular aspect of the perennial bonds between providence and history, promise and fulfillment.

When Luke was done, however, when the implied author closes out the narrative with the final three episodes, the Emmaus episode among them, the question about the relationship of Jesus' story to the previous stories was still unresolved. Luke's lack of resolution, I believe, would satisfy Alter's stricture against subordinating the venerable scriptures to the new. I believe that Robert Alter, as well as any other intelligent Jew or Christian or lover of literature, can both admire and approve of Luke's achievement.

Therefore we are still left with the magic of the Emmaus episode as magic. It is still unprecedented and unexplained, even in Luke's own narrative. Until reading this episode, a reader could supply a naturalistic explanation for how a character's mind changed in every description of changing minds in both the Hebrew or Septuagint scriptures or Christian scriptures, including the earlier episodes in Luke's Gospel adjacent to the episode of the synagogue and the cliff. Even in the scene with Jesus at the cliff, the reader could account for the disappearance of Jesus from the clutches of the mob as the result of his remarkable but plausible ability to use the confusion in a crowd to save his skin. Similarly Jesus' growth from a callow preacher to an accomplished teacher appears remarkable but not extraordinary. Only in the Emmaus scene does a gospel narrator take pains to make a change of appearance inexplicable. In this way the episode breaks free of all the prior narrative constraints in the biblical tradition. It is uncanny, precisely because the implied author implies simultaneously that Jesus' story belongs with the previous scriptures, while a paratactic gap keeps them forever apart in an endlessly provocative juxtaposition.

The Fellowship of Mind

Erasmus, Luther, Schleiermacher, and Fitzmyer have pointed out, each in his own way, the importance of fellowship in the mysterious episode that takes place on the road to Emmaus. One mind cannot think alone. As the two disciples walk along at the beginning of the episode, we find them struggling to put together pieces of incongruent information. A man who taught certain things has died, but now is reported to be alive again. To put these pieces together requires making connections between ideas whose relationship has not yet been defined. In their experience or knowledge, there has never been a story that contained these particular chapters. Most stories about the death of the main character treat the death as the capstone of that life—the ultimate event that explains all the others. This particular story, the disciples seem to realize, breaks from the tradition. The death of the main character is but another episode, not the ultimate episode. Precisely because the story about Jesus appears to be continued, any meaning one would give to it would be provisional. That is what they try to determine.

Thus, as the episode begins, the two disciples have already perceived that the Jesus story is open-ended in a special and unsettling way. When Jesus asks what troubles them, they respond by describing the pieces of the puzzle that they find themselves unable to fit together. This is where Jesus begins. He tells them that the pieces they possess will only make sense when they realize that the whole puzzle includes everything written about the messiah in Moses and the prophets. The new story is not unprecedented—or at least not unanticipated—if one simply knows where and how to look. Jesus' point is that they do not have to look far. The scriptures provide pieces that have long been on the table.

In the kind of religious thinking that this episode represents, there is really never any new information. There are only new combinations to piece together. Jews and Christians alike have long been comfortable with the understanding that the canons of their respective scriptures have been closed for millenia. That is because they have understood that both their scriptures are kaleidoscopic. New configurations of familiar material continually evolve before the eyes of the viewer.

In this scene, of course, Jesus will suggest to the two disciples a new style of fitting the pieces of the picture together. Before we consider again what he teaches them, we can remark on other significant details of the way these two disciples think *before* their astonishing moment of insight.

Their thinking does not take place in isolation. First of all, they rely on others for the basic information they have learned, in this case from "some women of our company." Second of all, the two disciples sound each other out as the first step in trying to explain the extraordinary reports. Calvin understood that only a collective or a community of religious thinkers thinks rightly about the meaning of a savior. Origen, aware of how the Emmaus episode ends, evoked the conviviality of a meal to suggest the spirit in which the community should read. Whereas both critics were certain they knew what the group should think, however, the two discussants never get that far during the short time elapsing in the incident on the road to Emmaus. That incident, until its final moment, portrays the process of their groping toward insight, not taking possession of a certainty.

The two disciples try to put the pieces together on the road. They are independent thinkers, outside any official building or temple while they talk, just as Mary was the moment an angel found her by herself. They are undogmatic. Remarkably, when a stranger arrives, they allow him to join their conversation solely on the strength of the stranger's interest in what they are saying. What is more, they suffer apparently gladly his strong statement that they are dull learners, slow to believe what the prophets have said. They appear willing to listen to anyone who has something sensible to say about the difficult problem they are trying to address together. Therefore there is a special atmosphere in which their thinking takes place that becomes an important condition of what they think. The atmosphere is critical, but not polemical. All parties to the discussion are intent upon discovering the truth of what they have heard. Their common inclination shapes the way they will configure the evidence they have gathered for consideration.

What is it, finally, that they learn? In the brief glimpse the episode provides, nothing is said about the content of what they learn. Instead, the two disciples exclaim about the pleasure of the process of learning: "Did we not feel our heart on fire as he talked with us on the road and explained the scriptures to us?" (24:32). More specifically, they exclaim about the pleasure of explaining the scriptures as literature. Jesus teaches the disciples to treat the venerable scriptures as stories whose meanings are new every time they are read. The insights to be gained this way are sweet. They are expected to come, although it is never certain at which moment in reading they will come. The disciples were astonished at the moment when the lesson ended and they finally got the point. They did not seem to anticipate that it would end as it did.

Nor is anything said about what each man came to believe because of this experience. Luke, like his literary ancestors, respects the privacy of the precincts of the mind where one makes these kinds of decisions. In reading this episode, the reader gets to hear only that they came to an understanding in unison: "Did we not feel our heart on fire . . ." Similarly, I acknowledge that the insights about reading the scriptures as literature in this chapter have been instigated, if not anticipated, by all the others that preface mine. The episode on the road to Emmaus invites us all to join a fellowship of mind.

Chapter Five

An Epilogue on Method

> Their eyes midst many wrinkles,
> their eyes,
> Their ancient, glittering eyes, are gay.
>
> *W. B. Yeats, "Lapis Lazuli"*

Insiders and Outsiders

The implied reader of scripture is as ancient and as eternal as the words that make up the sacred text. As we saw in chapter 1, such a reader is written "inside," watching the scene as the implied author arranges it, listening as the narrator speaks. This is not quite what Frank Kermode has in mind when he defines an "insider" as a reader who maintains membership in some religious organization claiming a rightful interpretation of what the words mean. Because such a reader reads as part of an organization of people dedicated to living truthfully, this insider wants to get more intimately involved in the scene than even an implied reader can. He or she wants to penetrate beyond or behind its narrative arrangements, usually to prior events believed to be more real than the literature that represents it. The insider wants to become like one of the presumably once-living disciples on the road to Emmaus. The insider yearns to hear precisely what Jesus said at the historical moment he said it. Only some real historical event can support an affirmation of faith in what transpired at a real moment in time. Even the interests modern orthodox biblical scholars have in the author, the editing of the narrative, or the milieu in which the sacred text was written or edited are only various ways of getting back closer to the actual events that the author wrote about.

In contrast, an "outsider" moves away from the position of the implied reader in the opposite direction. This reader comes alive the moment a living reader averts eyes from the scene and begins to think about what he or she has read. Again, this is not quite what Frank Kermode has in mind when he uses the term. He literally refers to secular readers "looking on," considering the verbal artistry of scripture as its first condition for being sacred. They are like lovers who for a moment can coolly recognize that the beloved belongs to no one. In my broader sense of the term, they become outsiders when they move away from the text into their own minds. The meaning of the sacred text becomes compounded of what the words say and their *gnosis* understands, what the readers immediately and somewhat inexplicably "see," and then what they think about. I am using *gnosis* now as an interpreter's two-fold response to the written narrative. It refers to the overt workings of the reasoning mind before and after the moment of insight about the meaning of a narrative text that always appears, as it were, out of nowhere. In short, we could include among outsiders those intent upon what we have called the literary meanings of scripture and those fascinated with their own educated, imaginative response to those meanings.

James Barr, a biblical theologian and an insider, would welcome the collaboration of biblical scholars who are insiders and outsiders in these terms. Of the former he says:

> The Christian biblical scholar has as his God-given task the study of Scripture. He does it not as a mere secular job but in the consciousness that he is handling the Word of God and that what he is doing is of immense practical and spiritual importance for the Church. This is his motivation and his commitment. But he recognizes that perfectly valid and constructive biblical study, positively significant for theology and Church, can be carried out and is carried out by scholars who do not share this motivation, and he welcomes this as a gift of God in the interpretation of Scripture, even when the scholars concerned may be quite lacking in religious interest. The recognition of such valid non-theologically-motivated biblical scholarship is not a grudging negative aspect: rather, it is a positive recognition of the freedom of the Scripture to address us other than through the mediation of our own tradition (pp. 110–11).

I conclude this book with hopes of responding to Barr's invitation in several ways. Properly speaking, an "epilogue" reflects on the implication of the thesis of the book after it has been presented. The thesis has been that one could legitimately read Luke's Gospel as an outsider—and thus have something to offer in the scholarly exchange Barr recommends. Now the question for reflection is: Why read this way? What precisely does such a reading have to offer both insiders and outsiders? I begin with a pointed discussion of their differences. It is important in particular to address the protests of insiders less expansive than Barr who believe it is illegitimate to read sacred scripture as outsiders wish to do.

Secrets

Kermode says in his insightful book *The Genesis of Secrecy* that any outsider like himself is drawn to what he calls the "secrets" of a gospel narrative, in his case, of Mark's narrative. This is a term to which he gives two meanings. It refers to the mysteries Jesus teaches his select disciples when he conveys his teaching in parables "in order that" disbelievers will not be able to grasp the meaning and be saved. Kermode makes much of the word *hoti* in the Greek of Mark. It occurs in a speech of Jesus where he tells his disciples that he teaches with parables "in order that" they will not understand. This seems to indicate that Jesus obscures the issue for anyone who does not directly intuit the meanings he passes on. Matthew changes the word to *hina* in his version of the passage, so that Jesus says he uses parables "because" his disciples do not understand. This seems to indicate that the parable is to help their understanding by casting the teaching in a vivid form. Kermode expands on this notion of secrets when he says that the secular interpreter of narrative comes to understand all narratives, the gospel included, as *hoti* texts. They obscure truth by compounding meaning beyond all accounting. He continually points out the compounding complexities of Mark's narrative techniques:

> It is, one might add, a paradox applying to all narrative that although its function is mnemonic it always recalls different things. The mode of recall will depend in some measure on the fashion of a period—what it seems natural or reasonable to expect a text to say. This is another way of affirming that all narratives possess "hermeneutic potential," which is another way of saying that they must be obscure. The apparently perspicuous narrative yields up latent senses to interpretation; we are never inside it, and from the outside may never experience anything more than some radiant intimation of the source of all these senses (p. 45).

This idea recovers much of the gnostic notion of understanding, especially as illustrated in narratives such as the *Acts of Peter and the Apostles* and a narrative episode in Luke's Gospel such as Peter's Tragic Recognition. In each, Peter becomes aware as much about what is clear as about how little he understands. When reading critics such as Kermode and others in this chapter, we become aware of the tenacious grip gnostic ideas still have on the human imagination. What is particularly remarkable about them is that they often seem new to their advocates. That has always been the charm of gnostic thinking: to see things as new.

In this broader definition of Kermode's, Mark's "secrets" extend to every aspect of his gospel narrative that resists explanation. I think we could extend it to Luke's magic. The trick in the Emmaus episode is magic in two senses of the term. It is a literal trick in that it is not clear how it was done, or even who did it. As we saw in chapter 1, coy use is made of a passive construction as "their eyes *were held*" (*ekratounto*). There is another passive verb along with an alpha-privitive, where the text literally says "he was *made to be*" (*egeneto*) "*not visible*" (*aphantos*). The reader finds both agency and cause are veiled. At what level do these things happen? Is it Jesus who does the deeds? Or is it God, the narrator, or the mental state of the two disciples? It is also a secret trick in that it is not clear why it was done, what the implicit message of the medium was, or why Jesus needs to teach his disciples without their knowing who their teacher is. Ready explanations might come easily to hand, such as Eduard Schweizer finds when he writes: "The turning point does not come through a miracle but through scripture. In table fellowship Jesus gives them the reality of his presence; his word takes the form of a visible gift." Schweizer explains the disappearance by saying, "This is an extreme way of saying that when God enters into human life and is recognized as God, the divine is never in a position to be apprehended" (p. 373). Still, all explanations need to be supplied. Neither Jesus nor the narrator ever say a word about what the motive behind the trickery is. To the extent that any reader would continue to entertain questions about the use of magic in the scene, he or she would be postponing making an affirmation of faith indefinitely—or what is the same thing—as long as answers remain outstanding. He or she would be suspending the act of belief and reading the biblical narrative "as literature." As Roland Barthes writes of reading the New Testament narrative as literature: "Everyone feels that the work cannot be pinned down" (p. 25 in Iser).

I would now like to consider what seem to me four major differences in the way insiders and outsiders read and respond to the secrets of scripture. I indicate in passing the use each might make of the other's method.

Intention

One reason traditional biblical interpreters, or insiders, dislike the idea that scripture could be aesthetically satisfying—that it might have meanings that could never be pinned down—is that, as we have seen before in chapter 3, they are prone to believe the truth must lie someplace. This is so even if, for the moment in which the interpreter reads and thinks, the truth remains secret or obscured. James Kugel, for example, whose work on biblical parallels I cite in chapter 1, never seems to be able to decide which kind of interpreter of Hebrew biblical parallelism he wants to be. In speaking of the possible aesthetic effects biblical writers using parallelism might have had in mind when they make their verbal images "shimmer," he writes: "Whether this stylistic device made the resulting text sound more sacred, or simply more poetic, we cannot say because we cannot fully penetrate this mentality" (p. 42). Here it is interesting that he does not trust himself to choose between sacred meaning or poetic effect (between the Bible as sacred writ or the Bible as literature). A few lines later, he suggests that the reason he cannot choose is that "we have lost the biblical habit of reading B as A's completion" (p. 42). This statement implies that knowing the habit is catching the intention of the original writers, and if this is now "lost," it must at one time have been available. When it was, and only then, the intention was clear. He more than implies that this once-living intention is the only thing worth worrying about in interpretation. Kugel is an insider because he is interested in those aspects of a text that lie deeper than its words.

On this point, I consider proper Kugel's hesitancy in making presumptions about authorial intention. But I do not consider any lack of absolute certainty on this matter a barrier to reading the Bible as literature. We have already discussed the matter of intention, coming to the conclusion in chapter 1 that all that remains of it is the arrangement of the writer's words. As long as scholars work on this arrangement, as Kugel does, they get as close to that original intention as any human reader can, even if, as in the case of Kugel, they cannot be satisfied at that level of uncertainty. Anyone who has useful things to say about this arrangement, as Kugel does, says something useful to an outside reader who might come to altogether different conclusions about what the text says.

A Sense of Tradition

I think another reason for Kugel's ambiguity about the Bible's artistry is his sense that reading the Bible "as literature" is anachronistic at best, and impertinent at worst. For the same reasons, the current Lutheran bishop of Stockholm and erstwhile dean of the Harvard Divinity School Krister Stendahl does not like the practice to which the term is usually applied. Its practitioners "lack historical perspective" (p. 205). They do not realize how many of their insights have been long anticipated by biblical critics. Indeed, he says, just as biblical critics have taught literary critics how to read, the Bible taught literary writers how to write.

I agree for reasons I try to make clear in chapter 3. When we read in this tradition, we find surprising aesthetic insights of scholars who only wished to be dogmatic. We learn much from them about how to interpret scripture, including gaining a sense that after all the time and intellectual effort orthodox readers have spent on the sacred text, nothing really new is left to be said. But I have also made clear that orthodox scholars do not necessarily possess a privileged understanding of their own interpretive tradition. They would benefit from other, perhaps more critical reviews of what their own tradition sees and cannot see.

Reverence

A third reason Kugel and Stendahl dislike the idea of reading the Bible as literature has more to do with the demeanor with which it is done than the particular method in itself. If the critic is reverential, these two insiders would admire the criticism, whatever its technical clumsiness. If not, they would not, whatever its technical expertise. A case in point is that Kugel claims many rabbis have made "reasonable" interpretations of biblical parallelism even though he finds their interpretations wrong. His explanation is basically the same one Augustine wrote in a letter to Jerome. If the interpretation features charity, it cannot err (p. 43). As Kugel puts it: "Surely there is an 'Oral Law' that accompanies every reading of the Bible, one rooted in time and space, in the particulars of religion and theology and general culture, which will make a certain approach to the Bible right and wise and good and make all others wrong or irrelevant, superstitious or blasphemous" (p. 304).

I submit my own reading of Luke's Gospel in chapter 4 as evidence that a literary reading can be reverent.

Commitment

I think another, and perhaps the most important reason why scholars such as Kugel and Stendahl distrust claims for the scriptures' aesthetic worth is because these claims seem to them distinctly subordinate to the ethical demands scripture makes on the reader. Amos Wilder, perhaps the most humanistic and elegant of Christian biblical critics since Erasmus, has addressed this mistrust by saying that in all literature, the scripture included, ethics and aesthetics go together. He means that aesthetics illuminates ethics with a kind of interior light. But it is ethics—the conduct of right action—that provides any literature, whether secular or sacred, with its deepest value. The best literature is always earnest, bent on action or decision. Therefore, Wilder, like Kugel and Stendahl, could not imagine a valid interpretation of scripture to end with a description of its aesthetic play, its ambiguities, and its implications. It simply would not go far enough. In commenting on the Emmaus episode, for example, Wilder emphasizes the implicit ethics of the oral speech Jesus used with the disciples on the road to Emmaus. He echoes Erasmus's reading of this episode when he praises Jesus for confronting his hearers intimately, face to face (p. 24). Jesus, he says, does not write because speech is more direct than writing (p. 21). Jesus thus identifies with his listeners because he uses their ordinary speech (p. 27). He does not argue because his intent is to reveal, not persuade (p. 29). His teaching is always tasteful (p. 31). This teaching invites the listener to respond directly, just as many of the characters do whom Jesus engages in dialogue (p. 62). Throughout the episode Jesus uses a language that is easy to remember so that the listener can recall it and muse upon it. Wilder concludes that Jesus uses the rabbinic parable style of teaching but greatly refines it (p. 85).

Wilder ultimately says that because these stories center on the story of the miraculous resurrection of an otherwise realistic character, they require the reader to affirm the literal realistic truth of this miraculous resurrection. It is not enough to say that the resurrection "works" in terms of the story. It must have really worked out in real life this way. Like the Fathers, as we saw in chapter 3, he insists that the Christian gospel story must be mundane. It must both reflect the real world that once was *and* the real world in which the reader lives and ought to act ethically. Similarly, the Jewish scholar Kugel demands that the reader of the Hebrew scriptures recognize that history lies beyond the sacred words. In this history God confronted his people. A reader of the words now experiences the encounter and must decide how he or she is to respond.

Now we have encountered an irreconcilable difference between inside and outside readings. They are to be distinguished, as Kermode has said, precisely on the unwillingness of a secular, literary critic to curtail wondering about the narrative secrets in order to decide how to act in response to them. The question now remains, How decisive is this difference? Do the methods become irreconcilable at this point? Can they still inform each other? Yes, they can, but the insider has more to learn from the outsider than vice versa. The outsider will always press on further with an aesthetic reading than the insider is willing to do. Until that point where gnosis yields to *pistis,* or faith, they still have much to teach each other. Let us elaborate, first, on the difference.

Postponing Affirmation

We can cite no less an orthodox authority than Paul Ricoeur for reading the scripture slowly: "A theory of interpretation which at the outset runs straight to the moment of decision moves too fast. It leaps over the moment of meaning, which is the objective stage, in the nonworldly sense of 'objective.' There is no exegesis without a 'bearer (*teneur*) of meaning' which belongs to the text and not to the author of the text" (p. 68). And Ricoeur sees his own interests as part of a modern program among some modern religious thinkers to slow down the act of interpreting the gospels. They are responding to certain ideas developed by modern secular theorists of literature that even the gospel itself could be understood as a "text." By this term Ricoeur means that "it expresses a difference and a distance, however minimal, from the event that it proclaims" (p. 56).

Admittedly, this does not mean that Ricoeur would be happy allowing interpretation to become purely descriptive or lingering with the text. He believes that the act of interpretation, if sufficiently alert and expert, can slowly and painstakingly recover the essence of the "event" or world that it represents. By this he means something even beyond the mind or intention of the original author that Schleiermacher sought out. He wants to move beyond hermeneutics for meanings more impersonal and perhaps more historical: the truth of things which the text reflects.

Thus Ricoeur, like Kugel and Wilder, believes as an insider that the scriptural texts are different from ordinary narratives. They have a certain "specificity" that derives from their "aiming at God's trace in the event" (p. 80). He is not only talking about the subject matter when he says this. He is talking about his already established belief that these texts bear especially forceful traces of God: "To recognize the specificity of this form of discourse, therefore, is to guard ourselves against a certain narrowness of any theology of the Word which only attends to word events. In the encounter with what we could call the idealism of the word event, we must reaffirm the realism of the event of history . . . " (p. 80). His statement cannot be faulted as a statement of belief.

As has already been made clear, there is no denying the difference between Ricoeur and Kermode on this point. Both apply the concept of "aesthetic ideas" in Kant's *Critique of Pure Reason* in different ways. When Kant says that artistic objects "occasion much thought" (*viel zu denken*), Ricoeur takes him to mean that more meaning was poured into the vessel than it could hold. He believes that the imagination recovers that excess meaning and thus reaches behind the object. Indulging in the romantic terminology of Heidegger, he writes: "My deepest conviction is that poetic language alone restores to us that participation-in or belonging-to an order of things which precedes our capacity to oppose ourselves to things taken as objects . . ." (p. 101). The sacred text is an object. But when we encounter it properly, in an inspirational reading, it sweeps us into an understanding beyond what any words could express. This is not a narrative gnostic understanding as it has been defined here in the preface and chapters 1 and 2. It is not tailored to the reader. It is "right," it is true, it is out there, but available to any right-thinking reader who would share with any other similarly thinking reader an orthodox understanding.

Kermode, on the other hand, interprets Kant to mean that the art object gives rise to *more* speculations than the original object could ever define. The imagination develops the excess through the play the object stimulates. The imagination takes off from the object. The difference between Ricoeur's reading of scripture and Kermode's would be the direction in which interpretation tends—moving deeper into the world the words represent, or deeper into the mind the words stimulate into thinking.

The only common ground two such different approaches could share would be their insights about what the aesthetic arrangement of the biblical narrative *was.* Now the question is, How many different readers will this ground support?

Common Ground

Another orthodox theoretician of biblical reading is helpful here with a notion of an appropriate biblical response reminiscent of both Aristotle and Ricoeur. Like Wilder to some extent, but with less of an emphasis on ethical thinking and more on emotional response, William A. Beardslee believes that literary form of any kind instigates reaction. The form represents a worldview or life-style and presents it in such a way as to challenge the reader to act in a certain way. He derives this premise from his reading of Aristotle's *Poetics,* stressing Aristotle's concept of *catharsis.* The reader somehow participates in the form itself, until experiencing a strong feeling in response to the form's orchestration of emotions. This is the idea that "form is a formula for a response." Beardslee thus treats reading as a form of charismatic encounter with a force. The writer bottles the force up in words which the reader releases by reading.

Beardslee claims that this is a new kind of biblical literary criticism. Traditional scholars looked behind the text for its historical facts or compositional history. Now some modern scholars consider what its ongoing encounter with modern readers might reveal. At its best, a modern reading entails a reader abandoning his or her rigid preconceptions of what a text says or religion means and allows the text liberty to stimulate the imagination. But as we have seen, Beardslee is recovering here something that is not new at all. It is merely another version of the gnostic method of reading, in which reading stimulates personal insights and then provokes a personal reflection. As we might suspect, Beardslee does not stop here. He brings his method up to date when he articulates, as Calvin did, the basically orthodox premise that there is such a thing as a "proper" catharsis. These texts have their roots, he says, in ritual and prophecy. To respond to them, therefore, means more than "treating the New Testament books simply as words of imaginative literature" (p. 12). One has to be prepared to have a properly religious experience in reading them, however unexpected its nuances might be.

But what I find nonetheless interesting about Beardslee's method is that it contains within it the gnostic practice of insightful reading. It is simply down beneath the sediment of orthodox caution. Where this sediment is cleared away, we expose the common ground he and Frank Kermode can share.

Let us grant that the impulse behind writing scripture is religious, with roots in ritual and prophecy. We can grant too that the proper response to it would be religious in the sense that the reader who takes the texts seriously takes seriously their questions about God and human beings, their relations with each other, and together their relations to the earth and society. But the reading of the artistic articulation of these religious ideas can be slow. It can linger with what Schleiermacher called *Verstehen*, "the act of getting what the text says." This activity would be deemed sufficiently complex and pleasurable to occupy the mind a long time. Reading this way, the aesthetes among the readers of scripture would savor their catharsis. Their models are the disciples Jesus met on the road to Emmaus sitting around the table agape at the spot from which Jesus had disappeared. At this point in their story, the two disciples only possess the kind of understanding Luke learned from his gnostic narrative models. For all we can surmise from the narration of this episode, the only other thing they could have learned was what they thought about their insights. The moment these insights occur, their instigator disappears. The disciples are on their own. And again, from all that we can surmise from the narration of the episode, they were left to think about the question that has preoccupied me here: What is the relation of a new story to its venerable predecessors?

Canonicity

It is altogether in the the spirit of their inquiry that, speaking specifically of the Christian scripture's relationship to its literary predecessor, Roland Barthes says: "It is something other than its own history, or the sum of its sources, its influences, its models. It forms a solid, irreducible nucleus in the unresolved tangle of events, conditions, and collective mentality" (p.

25 in Iser). But as we have seen, Luke developed and changed the gnostic narrative notion of innovation. In his narrative, an apprehension of the new included a protracted meditation on its relationship to what went before.

In this regard, we could consider Luke's narrative account of Jesus as a "postfiguration" of previous scriptural heroes. Postfiguration is a term Theodore Ziolkowski applies to modern retellings of the Jesus story in which novelists abstract plot and character from the gospel stories of Jesus and elaborate them into fictions that reflect modern social, theological, and psychological concerns. Ziolkowski himself does not apply the term directly to the gospels, only to modern literary works that use a technique he traces to the nineteenth-century, mainly German theological interests in the myths and form of the gospel stories. But what he says about the origins of this literary technique allows us to trace its fundamental ideas back to the Fathers, and beyond them to the gospels themselves. Ziolkowski features David Friedrich Strauss's *Life of Jesus* (*Das Leben Jesu,* 1835):

> Strauss, true to his Hegelian temperament and training, attempted to reconcile the thesis of the supernaturalists with the antithesis of the rationalists by synthesizing them into what he called a *mythic* interpretation. He had noted that many of the deeds and miracles attributed to Jesus were fulfillments of expectations pronounced in the Old Testament. Rather than accepting them on faith of explaining them away by rational means, he concluded that these elements were actually literary conventions added to the accounts of the life of Jesus by the authors of the Gospels, who wanted to make of the historical Jesus a figure that corresponded in every respect to the predictions of the prophets (p. 35).

But Ziolkowski does not believe that what Strauss did was strictly new. It was another version of the interpretive method of "filling in." It simply continued the patristic comparative method using nineteenth-century interpretive techniques to make it appear more scientific. According to Ziolkowski, Strauss's importance is due to his rediscovering the figural way of thinking, whereby a literary figure is thought to establish a connection between two events or persons, the first of which signifies not only itself but also the second, while the second encompasses or fulfills the first. "For instance," he writes, drawing on the well-known essay "Figura" of Erich Auerbach, "Abraham's readiness to sacrifice his son Isaac prefigures God's willingness to let his son Jesus die on the cross. Conversely, though no causal relationship is intended in the modern sense of the word, the events surrounding Jesus' life are arranged in such a way as to verify the predictions in the Old Testament" (p. 49). According to Auerbach, figural thinking emerged in early Christian times as a response to a specific historical situation and need. After it was clear that the second coming was not imminent, there was a need to justify Jesus' teaching. This was accomplished by giving his story a "pedigree," as Luke has his Jesus do for the benefit of the disciples on the way to Emmaus. Thus, his gospel itself could be called a "postfiguration—the conscious construction of a fiction to conform to existing predictions in earlier texts" (p. 52). This would place Luke's Gospel among the first of the fictions concerned with filling in the bare details of the Jesus story. Its earliest accounts were innocent of the detail even the first audience must have been hungry for. When we project the term back onto an original gospel text, we are saying that even this text was a "reading" of a previous text, but one that deliberately added a statement to a previous statement, with no intention of cancelling it out. Figura, in other words, was the recognition of the Bible's canonical parataxis. It is the other side of the interpretive coin from allegory, or the desire for syntaxis.

What Ziolkowski is describing here is something we have been talking about throughout this book in many different terms and contexts. It could be called a "neo-gnostic" notion that slakes the gnostic thirst for the new with a particularly delectable vintage. We find it in harsh terms in Tertullian's critique of Marcion. It is the notion that the new is indeed different from the old, but it is impossible to understand how unless we also understand how the old "foreshadowed" the new. I believe that this notion finds its most satisfying articulation in the magical episode of Jesus' appearance to the two disciples on the road to Emmaus. When we attend to its implications, we must abandon the belief that the newer story absorbs and dominates the older scripture. This is a belief that Christian orthodoxy usually commends—even at times commands. Yet we must abandon it. But that does not have to mean making a nearly opposite act of faith—that the newer story does *not* absorb the older scripture. It can mean simply suspending judgment. One can privilege the moment in Christian history when Luke left off writing his narrative. At that moment, especially in the Emmaus episode, he left undecided just what the relationship between the older scripture and the newer story was. Any reader who harked back to Luke's writing could leave the question open, as open as the inference of his narrative parataxis.

This is to admit that there is a critical difference between a paratactic method of reading and those Fackre includes under the heading of narrative theology, as we saw in chapter 1. For a Christian, Fackre insists, those readings always end in the affirmation of belief in Christian dogma. But it is a significant difference in degree, I maintain, but not in kind. Literary-critical readers meditate continuously on the parataxis in the narratives.

Perhaps they describe the theological implications of that parataxis. But they leave to their betters (or their better selves) any decision whether the meaning of any religious texts reflects a reality worthy of belief. Those we could call "neo-gnostic readers" respect the gap between reading and believing. They dwell upon that ancient moment of gaity when on their way to Emmaus two disciples saw before their eyes the meaning of an ancient book and a contemporary life—and together began to think about it.

Why should one read this way? Simply because, as Jesus tells his disciples, you cannot get the religion right unless you get the literature right. To get the literature right is a humanistic endeavor in a double sense. As Schleiermacher reminds us, to understand the scripture correctly, we need to appreciate that it was a human being who arranged the passages as they appear. In the terms of Wayne Booth that we have been using, a living author at one time created an implied author who stays with the text forever, displaying its significant arrangements for all who will look. Appreciating these arrangements is a humanistic endeavor in another sense as well. One way we demonstrate that the best of what it means to be human is in the making of practical things like narratives or bowls or boats *better* than they need to be to serve their simple functions. This is what Luke did when he arranged his informative narrative for Theophilus extraordinarily well. Thus we experience from our appreciative reading of a narrative like this, as we do from our careful handling of a beautiful bowl or boat, the spirit of generosity with which it is made. It is this spirit, in turn, that should animate how things are used. We should celebrate the Christian scriptures as exquisite artifacts of human language. This is the way to measure the power of the insights Jesus instigated in his most thoughtful disciples.

Works Cited

Primary Sources

Ambrose. *"de Isaac et anima,"* Liber Unus, Caput V. *Patrologia Latina.* Edited by P. Migne. Vol. 14. Paris, 1888. Cited hereafter as *PL.*

Athanasias, Patriarch of Alexandria. Ep. 3. *PL* 13: 1037.

Aristotle. *The Rhetoric.* Translated by W. Rhys Roberts. New York: The Modern Library, 1954.

Aquinas, Thomas. *Summa Theologia,* part 3. Ottawa: Commissio Piana, 1953.

Augustine. *"Sermo 232 in diebus Paschalibus,"* part 3, b. *PL* 67.

Bede, The Venerable. *"Homilia 62, in feria secunda Paschae."* *PL* 102.

Caesarius of Arles. *"De eo quod dominus quas in vinum mutavit."PL* 67.

Epictetus. *The Discourses as Reported by Arrian, The Manual and Fragments.* Translated by W. A. Oldfather. London: Heinemann, 1927. Loeb Edition.

Ephiphanius. *Haereseologicii Panaria. PL* 32.

Fitzmyer, Joseph, ed. *The Gospel According to Luke.* Vols. 28, 28a of *The Anchor Bible.* Garden City, N. Y.: Doubleday & Company, Inc., 1985.

Godefried, The Venerable, the Abbot of Admantensis. *"Homiliae Festivalis." PL* 174.

Gregory the Great. *"Homilia 23." PL* 76.

Jerome. *"Ad Pammachium." PL* 23.

John of Damascus. *Dialectica. Patrologia Graeca.* Edited by P. Migne. Vol. 94. Paris, 1888.

The Nag Hammadi Library in English. Translated by James M. Robinson and members of the Coptic Gnostic Library Project of the Institute for Antiquity and Christianity. New York: Harper and Row, 1977.

The Facsimile Edition of the Nag Hammadi Codices. Leiden: E. J. Brill, 1972.

Novum Testamentum Graece et Latine. Edited by Augustinus Merk, S. J. Rome: Sumptibus Pontificii Instituti Biblici, 1944.

Origen. *De principiis*. In *Die griechischen christlichen Schriftsteller der ersten drei Jahrhunderte*. Edited by P. Koetschau, vol. 4: 380. Leipzig, 1897.

Schleiermacher, Fr. D. E. "*The Hermeneutics*: Outline of the 1819 Lectures." Translated by Roland Haas and Jan Wojcik. *New Literary History* 10:1 (Autumn 1978): 1–16.

Smaragdi, Abbatis. "*Sermones Feria Secunda Paschae*." *PL* 102.

Tertullian. *Adversus Marcionem*. Edited and translated by Ernest Evans. Oxford: Clarendon Press, 1976.

———.*De praescriptione haereticorum*. Edited by R. F. Refoule. Paris: Editions du Cerf, 1957.

Wernerus, Abbot. *Opera Omnia*. *PL* 157.

Secondary Sources

Aichele, George, Jr. *The Limits of Story*. Philadelphia: Fortress Press, 1985.

Alter, Robert. *The Art of Biblical Narrative*. New York: Basic Books, 1981.

Aquinas, Thomas. *Catena Aurea in Quator Evangelia*. Vol. 2. Ottawa: Augustae Taurinorum, 1889.

Auerbach, Erich. *Mimemis*. Translated by Willard Trask. Princeton, N. J.: Princeton University Press, 1974.

Barr, James. *Canon, Authority, Criticism*. Philadelphia: The Westminster Press, 1983.

Beardslee, William A. *Literary Criticism of the New Testament*. Philadelphia: Fortress Press, 1977.

Bengel, John Albert. *Gnomon of the New Testament*. Translated and edited by Andrew R. Fausset. Edinburgh: Smythe, 1873.

Betz, Hans Dieter. "The Origin and Nature of Christian Faith According to the Emmaus Legend." *Interpretation* 23 (1969): 32–46.

Black, Matthew. *An Aramaic Approach to the Gospels and Acts.* Oxford: Clarendon Press, 1946.

Blackman, E. C. *Marcion and his Influence.* London: S.P.A.K., 1948.

Bloom, Harold. "Lying Against Time: Gnosis, Poetry, Criticism." In *The Rediscovery of Gnosticism: Proceedings of the International Conference on Gnosticism at Yale: New Haven Connecticut, March 28–31, 1978,* edited by Bentley Layton, vol. 1: 57–72. Leiden: E. J. Brill, 1980.

Booth, Wayne. "Distance and Point of View: An Essay in Classification." In *The Theory of the Novel,* edited by Philip Stevick, 87–107. New York: The Free Press, 1967. This is an expanded version of chapter 6 of Booth's book, *The Rhetoric of Fiction.* Chicago: University of Chicago Press, 1961.

Brande, W. T. *A Dictionary of Science, Literature, and Art.* New York: Harper and Brothers, 1843.

Brown, Raymond E. *The Birth of the Messiah: A Commentary on the Infancy Narratives in Matthew and Luke.* New York: Doubleday, 1977.

Bultmann, Rudolf. *Die Geschichte der Synoptischen Tradition.* Göttingen: Vandenhoeck & Ruprecht, 1958.

Burke, Kenneth. *The Rhetoric of Religion: Studies in Logology.* Boston: Beacon Press, 1961.

Burton, Henry. *The Gospel According to Luke.* New York: A. C. Armstrong and Son, 1893.

Caird, C. B. *Saint Luke.* Philadelphia: The Westminster Press, 1963.

Calvin, John. *Commentary on a Harmony of the Evangelists* part 3. Translated by Rev. William Pringle. Edinburgh, 1846.

Chadwick, Henry. "The Domestication of Gnosis." In *The Rediscovery of Gnosticism: Proceedings of the International Conference on Gnosticism at Yale, New Haven Connecticut, March 28–31, 1978,* edited by Bentley Layton, vol. 1: 3–16. Leiden: E. J. Brill, 1980.

Chatman, Seymour. *Story and Discourse.* Ithaca, N.Y.: Cornell University Press, 1978.

Childs, Brevard S. *The New Testament as Canon: An Introduction.* Philadelphia: Fortress Press, 1985.

Cohen, Gillian. "The Psychology of Reading." *New Literary History* 4/1 (Autumn 1972): 74–90.

Daniélou, Jean. *Origen.* Translated by Walter Mitchell. New York: Sheed and Ward, 1955.

Danker, Frederick W. *Luke.* Philadelphia: Fortress Press, 1976.

Dawsey, James M. *The Lukan Voice: Confusion and Irony in the Gospel of Luke.* Macon, Ga.: Mercer University Press, 1986.

de Man, Paul. *Blindness and Insight.* Introduction by Wlad Godzich. Minneapolis: University of Minnesota Press, 1983.

Dibelius, Martin. *From Tradition to Gospel.* Translated by B. L. Woolf. New York: Charles Scribner's Sons, 1935.

Dodd, C. H. "The Appearances of the Risen Christ: an Essay in Form-Criticism of the Gospels." In *Studies in the Gospels,* edited by D. E. Nineham, 102–33. London: Basil Blackwell, 1967.

Drury, John. *Tradition and Design in Luke's Gospel.* Atlanta, Ga.: John Knox Press, 1977.

Easton, Burton Scott. *The Gospel According to Luke.* New York: Charles Scribner's Sons, 1926.

Eile, Stanislaw. "The Novel as an Expression of the Writer's Vision of the World." *New Literary History* 9/1 (Autumn 1977): 115–28. Translated by Teresa Halikowski-Smith.

Eliade, Mircea. *Cosmos and History.* Translated by Willard R. Trask. New York: Harper and Row, 1959.

Erasmus, Desiderius. "Paraphrases in N. Testamentum." *Opera Omnia,* vol. 7. Batavia: Peter Vander Aa, 1706.

Fackre, Gabriel. "Narrative Theology, an Overview." *Interpretation* 37/4 (October 1983): 340–52.

Fish, Stanley. "Literature in the Reader: Affective Stylistics." *New Literary History* 2/1 (Autumn 1970): 122–61.

Franklin, Eric. *Christ the Lord.* Philadelphia: Westminster Press, 1975.

Frei, Hans. *The Eclipse of Biblical Narrative.* New Haven, Conn.: Yale University Press, 1974.

Genette, Gérard. *Narrative Discourse.* Translated by Jane E. Lewin, and introduction by Jonathan Culler. Ithaca, N.Y.: Cornell University Press, 1980.

Grant, R. M. *Gnosticism and Early Christianity.* New York: Columbia University Press, 1959.

Grötius, Hugo. *Annotiones in Novem Testamentum.* Vol. 3. Groningal, 1827.

Hahn, G. L. *Das Evangelium des Lucas.* 2 vols. Breslau: Verlag von E. Morgenstern, 1894.

Harnark, Adolf von. *Marcion: Das Evangelium vom fremden Gott.* Leipzig: J. C. Heinrichs, 1921, 1924.

Hirsch, E. D. *Validity in Interpretation.* New Haven, Conn.: Yale University Press, 1967.

Iser, Wolfgang. "The Reality of Fiction: A Functionalist Approach to Literature." *New Literary History* 7/1 (Autumn 1975): 7–38. (First published in *Roland Barthes: Literatur oder Geschichte.* Translated by Helmut Scheffel. Frankfurt, 1969.)

Jonas, Hans. *The Gnostic Religion: The Message of the Alien God and the Beginnings of Christianity.* Boston: Beacon Press, 1972.

Kee, Howard Clark. *Community of the New Age: Studies in Mark's Gospel.* Macon, Ga.: Mercer University Press, 1983.

Kellogg, Robert. "Oral Literature." *New Literary History* 5/1 (Autumn 1973): 55–66.

Kermode, Frank. *The Genesis of Secrecy: On the Interpretation of Narrative.* Cambridge, Mass.: Harvard University Press, 1979.

Kugel, James. *The Idea of Biblical Poetry.* New Haven, Conn.: Yale University Press, 1981.

Lapide, Cornelius à. *Commentaria in Sacram Scriptorum,* part 8. Naples, 1857.

Lévi-Strauss, Claude. *Structural Anthropology.* Translated by Claire Jacobson and Brooke Grundfest Schoepf. Garden City, N.Y.: Anchor Books, Doubleday Company, 1967.

Lowth, Robert. *De sacra poesi Hebraeorum.* 1753, revised 1763. Cambridge: James Munroe, 1834.

Luther, Martin. "Evangelium am Oster Montage, Luke 24: 13–35." *Martin Luthers Werke,* Weimar edition, vol. 21: 221–29.

Marshall, Howard I. *The Gospel of Luke: A Commentary on the Greek Text.* Grand Rapids, Mich.: William B. Eerdmans, 1978.

Moulton, Richard G. *The Literary Study of the Bible.* Boston: D. C. Heath Company, 1906.

Origen. *The Commentary of Origen on S. John's Gospel.* Edited by A. E. Brooke. 2 vols. Cambridge: 1896.

———. *"Homiliae in Lucam,"* PG 13.

Owen, John J. *Commentary on the Gospel of Luke.* New York: Leavill and Allen, 1859.

Pagels, Elaine H. *The Gnostic Gospels.* New York: Random House, 1979.

Peel, Malcolm L. "Gnostic Eschatology and the New Testament." *Essays on the Coptic Gnostic Library.* Reprint from *Novum Testamentum* XII, 2: 141–65. Leiden: E. J. Brill, 1970.

Perkins, Pheme. *The Gnostic Dialogue.* New York: Paulist Press, 1980.

Plummer, A. *A Critical and Exegetical Commentary on the Gospel according to S. Luke.* New York: Scribners, 1964.

Ricoeur, Paul. *Essays on Biblical Interpretation.* Edited by Lewis S. Mudge. Philadelphia: Fortress Press, 1980.

Sandmel, Samuel. *A Jewish Understanding of the New Testament.* Cincinnati, Ohio: Hebrew Union College Press, 1986.

Schleiermacher, Fr. D. E. *Über die Schriften des Lukas, ein kritischer Versuch.* Berlin: bei G. Reimer, 1817.

Schmithals, Walter. "Die gnostischen Elemente im Neuen Testament als hermeneutisches Problem." In *Gnosis und Neues Testament,* edited by Karl-Wolfgang Tröger. Berlin: Gütersloher Verlaghaus, 1973.

Schneidau, Herbert N. "The Word Against the Word: Derrida on Textuality." *Semeia* 23 (1982): 5–28.

Schweizer, Eduard. *The Good News According to Luke.* Translated by David E. Green. Atlanta, Ga.: John Knox Press, 1984.

Shemoth, Rabbi. *Exodus Rabba.* Translated by H. Freedman. London: Soncino Press, 1932.

Starobinski, Jean. "The Struggle with Legion: A Literary Analysis of Mark 5:1–20." *New Literary History* 4/2 (Winter 1973): 331–56.

Stendahl, Krister. "The Bible as a Classic and the Bible as Holy Scripture." *Journal of Biblical Literature* 103/1 (1984): 3–10.

Sternberg, Meir. *The Poetics of Biblical Narrative.* Bloomington, Ind.: Indiana University Press, 1985.

Talbert, Charles H. *Luke and the Gnostics.* New York: Abingdon Press, 1966.

Tuckett, C. M. *Nag Hammadi and the Gospel Tradition.* Edinburgh: T. T. Clark, 1986.

Vallée, Gérard. *A Study in Anti-Gnostic Polemics: Irenaeus, Hippolytus and Epiphanius.* Waterloo, Ontario: Wilfrid Laurier University Press, 1981.

Verweijs, P. G. *Evangelium und neues Gesetz in der ältesten Christenheit bis auf Marcion.* Utrecht: Domplein, 1960.

Whitehead, A. N. *Science and the Modern World.* New York: MacMillian, 1925.

Wilder, Amos N. *The Language of the Gospel: Early Christian Rhetoric.* New York: Harper and Row, 1964.

Wojcik, Jan. "The Prophet in the Poem"; "The Uncertain Success of Isaiah's Prophecy: A Poetical Reading." In *Poetic Prophecy in Western*

Literature, edited by Jan Wojcik and Raymond-Jean Frontain, 13–30, 31–39. Rutherford, N.J.: Associated University Presses, 1985.

Yamauchi, Edwin. "Pre-Christian Gnosticism, The New Testament and Nag Hammadi in Recent Debate." Exerpted in *New Testament Studies* 10/4 (1985): 22–28; from *Pre-Christian Gnosticism.* Grand Rapids, Mich.: Baker Book House, 1983.

———. "Pre-Christian Gnosticism in Recent Debate." *Themelios,* 10:1 (1984): 22–27.

Ziolkowski, Theodore. *Fictional Transfigurations of Jesus.* Princeton, N.J.: Princeton University Press, 1972.

Index

Aaron, 37

Abel, 28, 34, 45, 138

Abraham, 35, 105, 107, 110, 121–23, 137, 151

Absalom, 35, 36

Acts of Peter and the Twelve Apostles (gnostic text), 62–63, 64–67, 73, 74, 110, 143; *Facsimile Edition,* 67

Acts of the Apostles, 17, 21, 58, 93, 101; not continuous with Luke, 46; gnostic passages in, 57

Aichele, George, 71; the hermeneutical dream, 52; gnostic sense of time, 56, 57, 125

Allegorical method, 39, 86

Allegory, compared to midrash and palimpsest, 10

Alter, Robert: theories of Hebrew parallelism, 34–35, 38, 40, 45, 106, 121–23; *The Art of Biblical Narrative,* 136–38

Ambrose, Bishop of Milan, 85

Amnon, 35, 36

Anachrony, 123

Anagogic method, 39

Andrew, 30; character in *Gospel of Mary,* 72

Anna: symbolic barren woman, 113

Apocalypse of Paul, 67

Aquinas, Thomas, 91; *Catera Aurea,* 89; *Summa,* 89, 90; Jesus as teacher, 89–90

Aramaic, 17, 24, 25, 52

Aristotle, 18, 41; *Rhetoric,* 23; *Poetics,* 149; *catharsis,* 149

"As it is written": meaning of phrase in Luke's Gospel, 135

Asyndeton, 34; compared to parataxis, 25

Athanasius, 85

Auerbach, Erich: "Figura," 152–53

Augustine, 85, 99, 114, 146; concept of *sermo humiles* in, 10; interprets Emmaus, 86–87

Barr, James, 142

Barthes, Roland, 144, 150

Basil: cited by Grötius, 95

Bathsheba, 122

Beardslee, William A.: concept of *catharsis,* 149

Beatitudes, 131–35

Bede, the Venerable, 85, 90

Bengel, John Albert, 94

Bethlehem, 111, 126

Betz, H. D., 99, 103

Bible as literature, 76, 136, 140, 145

Black, Matthew: studies of Jesus' spoken language, 24–25, 52

Blackman, E. C.: views on Marcion, 77

Bloom, Harold: Septuagint as "strong text," 40; Jewish Bible as "strong text," 55; "misprision," 55; cites Irenaeus, 57

Book of Thomas the Contender, 58

Booth, Wayne, 15, 16, 18, 19, 21, 153; the implied narrative dialogue, 22

Brown, Raymond S., 127

Burton, Henry, 99

Caesar Augustus, 126

Caesarius of Arles, 86

Cain, 28, 45, 138

Caird, C. B., 100

Calvin, John, 3, 95, 96, 101, 139, 150; "Harmony," 93–94; follows Luther, 93

Canaanites, 123

Canonicity: concepts of, 135–37, 150–53

Cantonnage, 47, 50–51, 73

Capernaum, 117, 118, 120

Centurion, 133

Chadwick, Henry, 5, 59

Chatman, Seymour, 16

Childs, Brevard S.: Luke's use of the Septuagint, 103

Chrysostom, John, 90

Cleopas: character in Luke, 13, 96, 103

Coleridge, S. T., 14, 53

Commentary: limits of, 102–4

Coptic language, 52

Council of Alexandria: condemns Origen, 84

Daniel, 91, 100

Daniélou, Jean: modern critic of Origen, 84